The Cleanroom Approach
to Quality Software Development

WILEY SERIES IN
SOFTWARE ENGINEERING PRACTICE

SERIES EDITORS:

Patrick A.V. Hall, The Open University, UK
Martyn A. Ould, Praxis Systems plc, UK
William E. Riddle, Software Design & Analysis, Inc., USA

Fletcher J. Buckley • Implementing Software Engineering Practices

John J. Marciniak and Donald J. Reifer • Software Acquisition Management

John S. Hares • SSADM for the Advanced Practitioner

Martyn A. Ould • Strategies for Software Engineering: The Management of Risk and Quality

David P. Youll • Making Software Development Visible: Effective Project Control

Charles P. Hollocker • Software Reviews and Audits Handbook

David Whitgift • Software Configuration Management: Methods & Tools

John S. Hares • Information Engineering for the Advanced Practitioner

Robert L. Baber • Error Free Programming

H. Ronald Berlack • Software Configuration Management

Ken Shumate and Marilyn Keller • Software Specification & Design

L. Jay Arthur • Rapid Evolutionary Development: Requirements, Prototyping, & Software Creation

Michael Dyer • The Cleanroom Approach to Quality Software Development

The Cleanroom Approach to Quality Software Development

MICHAEL DYER

John Wiley & Sons, Inc.
New York • Chichester • Brisbane • Toronto • Singapore

To
Carol
Edward and Agnes

In recognition of the importance of preserving what has been written,
it is a policy of John Wiley & Sons, Inc. to have books of enduring
value published in the United States printed on acid-free paper, and
we exert our best efforts to that end.

Library of Congress Cataloging-in-Publication Data

Dyer, Michael, 1933–
    The Cleanroom approach to quality software development / Michael
Dyer.
        p. cm. — (Wiley series in software engineering practice)
    Includes bibliographical reference and index.
    ISBN 0–471–54823–5 (cloth)
    1. Computer software—Development. I. Title. II. Series.
QA76.76.D47D94   1992
005.1—dc20   91–37245
                                                            CIP

Printed in the United States of America
10 9 8 7 6 5 4 3 2 1

Printed and bound by Malloy Lithographing, Inc..

Contents

Foreword   **xi**

Preface   **xv**

1   What Is the Cleanroom Method?   **1**

    1.1   Cleanroom Background   1
    1.2   Cleanroom Process   3
        1.2.1   Cleanroom Process Organization   4
            1.2.1.1   Software Specification   5
            1.2.1.2   Software Development   6
            1.2.1.3   Software Correctness Verification   6
            1.2.1.4   Independent Software Product Testing   6
            1.2.1.5   Software Reliability Measurement   7
            1.2.1.6   Statistical Process Control   7
        1.2.2   Cleanroom Impacts on Software Development   7
            1.2.2.1   What Each Component Technique Can Buy   8
            1.2.2.2   Process Impacts   11
            1.2.2.3   People Impacts   12
            1.2.2.4   Cleanroom Process Potentials   12
    1.3   Motivation for Using the Cleanroom Process   13

1.3.1   Software with Known Mean Time to Failure   13
1.3.2   Software with Near Zero Defects   15
1.3.3   Quality Software which Is Cheaper to Produce   16
1.4   Cleanroom's Impact on the Software Process   16
1.4.1   Impacts on Software Specification   17
1.4.2   Impacts on Software Design   18
1.4.3   Impacts on Software Implementation   19
1.4.4   Impacts on Software Developer Testing   19
1.4.5   Impacts on Independent Testing   20
1.4.6   Impacts on Software Development Organization   20
1.5   Cleanroom's Impact on the Software Product   21
1.5.1   Impact on Software Defect Rates   21
1.5.2   Impact on Software Design Simplicity   24
1.5.3   Impact on Software Development Productivity   24
References   25

2   What Has Been the Experience with Cleanroom?   27

2.1   Early Cleanroom Experiments   29
2.1.1   Statistical Testing Feasibility Experiment   30
2.1.2   Statistical Testing Effectiveness Experiment   31
2.1.3   Cleanroom Experiment Conducted by the University
        of Maryland   32
2.2   Software Development Experience   33
2.3   What Lessons Were Learned?   35
2.3.1   About the Cleanroom Method   35
2.3.2   About Software Specification and Design   37
2.3.3   About Software Implementation   38
2.3.4   About Software Test and MTTF   39
2.3.5   About Staff Organizational Structure   39
2.4   Were the Underlying Concerns Addressed?   40
References   42

3   How to Get Started with Cleanroom   43

3.1   Cleanroom Introduction Strategy   44
3.1.1   Baseline Development Capability   44
3.2   Cleanroom Project Planning   46
3.2.1   Training in the Cleanroom Method   47
3.2.2   Selecting the Cleanroom Components for a Project   49
3.2.3   Planning the Introduction of Cleanroom   49
3.2.3.1   Milestones for Formal Specification Methods   51
3.2.3.2   Milestones for the Functional Correctness Model   51
3.2.3.3   Milestones for Eliminating Developer Testing   52

3.2.3.4 Milestones for Verification Based Inspections   52
3.2.3.5 Milestones for Statistical Testing   53
3.2.3.6 Milestones for Software MTTF Prediction   53
3.3 Cleanroom Project Management   54
3.4 Technology Insertion   55
3.5 Educational Considerations   56
   3.5.1 Requirements Specification Workshop   57
   3.5.2 Correctness Verification Workshop   58
   3.5.3 Statistical Testing Workshop   58
References   60

4 The How To's of Cleanroom Software Development   61

4.1 Benefits of Striving for Design Simplicity   62
4.2 Specification/Design/Implementation Overview   63
4.3 Software Specification   67
4.4 Software Design   69
   4.4.1 Theoretical Basis for Formal Software Development   70
      4.4.1.1 Liberties Taken with Structured Programming Theory   71
4.5 Software Implementation   71
   4.5.1 Stepwise Design Refinement   72
      4.5.1.1 Elaborating Subfunction Specification   73
   4.5.2 Elements of Structured Design   75
      4.5.2.1 Structured Data Design   77
   4.5.3 Software Design Expression   78
   4.5.4 Example of Software Design Elaboration   79
      4.5.4.1 Specification of the Software Component   79
      4.5.4.2 Top Level Design of the Software Component   80
References   84

5 The How To's of Correctness Verification   85

5.1 Correctness Verification Overview   86
5.2 Functional Correctness Verification   87
   5.2.1 Software Verification Practice   90
      5.2.1.1 Software Verification Example   91
5.3 Verification Based Inspections   94
   5.3.1 Importance of Formal Inspections to the Baseline Capability   96
      5.3.1.1 Formal Inspections for Software   97
      5.3.1.2 Formal Inspection Process   98
      5.3.1.3 Benefits of Formal Inspections   99
   5.3.2 Merger of Functional Correctness and Formal Inspection Models   100

5.3.3   Verification Based Inspection Practice   101
5.3.4   Verification Based Inspection Example   102
5.3.5   An Example of a Larger Application   105
References   110

6   The How To's of Cleanroom Testing 111

6.1   Traditional Testing Focus   111
   6.1.1   Software Structural Testing   112
      6.1.1.1   Coverage versus Cost Dilemma   113
   6.1.2   Software Functional Testing   117
      6.1.2.1   Coverage versus Cost Dilemma   117
      6.1.2.2   Comparison of Sampling Strategies   118
6.2   Why Testing with Verification?   120
6.3   Cleanroom Statistical Approach   123
   6.3.1   Upfront Data Analysis   124
   6.3.2   Generators for Statistical Testing   125
   6.3.3   Statistical Testing of a COBOL Language Processor   126
   6.3.4   Statistical Testing of an Avionics Application   130
   6.3.5   Application Experience   136
   6.3.6   Requirements Coverage with Statistical Test   131
   6.3.7   Test Process Impacts   137
   6.3.8   Impacts on Test Personnel   138
References   138

7   Software Reliability 141

7.1   Industry Focus on Product Quality and Reliability   142
   7.1.1   Application of Existing Reliability Theory   143
7.2   What Is Software Reliability?   145
   7.2.1   Is the Current Focus Correct?   146
7.3   Cleanroom Definition of Reliability   147
   7.3.1   Cleanroom Reliability Model Derivation   149
   7.3.2   Cleanroom Reliability Model Operation   151
7.4   Cleanroom Reliability Model Experience   152
   7.4.1   An Example of Cleanroom Reliability Model Use   155
   7.4.2   Examples of Quality Analyses Using Software MTTF Data   160
      7.4.2.1   MTTF Analysis of Software Subfunctions   160
      7.4.2.2   MTTF Analysis of Software Failures   161
7.5   Reliability Model Considerations   162
   7.5.1   Shanthikumar Model   164
   7.5.2   Littlewood Model   164
   7.5.3   Littlewood-Verrall Model   164

7.5.4 Deciding Model Effectiveness   165
7.6 Merging Software Reliability with Traditional Theory   166
References   167

8   Where Can Cleanroom Lead?   **169**

8.1 Quality Software with No Productivity Impact   170
     8.1.1 Requirements Specification Productivity   170
     8.1.2 Software Design and Development Productivity   171
     8.1.3 Software Test Productivity   172
8.2 Statistical Process Control   173
     8.2.1 Why the Cleanroom Method Allows Statistical Process
            Control   174
8.3 Product Certification with Reliability Warranty   175
     8.3.1 What Are the Future Prospects?   176
     8.3.2 The Cleanroom Role in Software Warranties   177

Appendix A   Cleanroom Test Case Generator   **179**

Appendix B   Cleanroom Reliability Analysis Package   **187**

**Appendix C   Cleanroom Verification Based Inspection
               Syntax Analyzer**   **191**

Index   **193**

About the Author

Foreword

It is a pleasure to introduce Michael Dyer who is introducing the Clean-room method for software development in this text. Mike and I worked on this idea from the very beginning in the early 1980s, along with Richard Linger whose work Mike describes in the text.

Mike and I go back considerably further to the early 1960s and Clean-room is based on our work together in structured programming, modular design, formal specifications, chief programmer teams, and top down software development. Creating software under statistical quality control and incremental development were added to the previous methods as part of Cleanroom in the 1980s.

Mike and I are both very concerned with how to be practical in introducing new methods in the software field. With each introduction, some experienced programmers decide not to follow. If the benefits of the new methods are small, those who decide not to follow may well be justified and not be hurt. But if the benefits are large, those who do not follow may lose out.

Mike was deeply involved with developing a curriculum of pass/fail courses in software engineering in IBM's Federal Systems Division in the 1970s in which management was also required to participate with or before their programmers. The management team became much stronger with results to show for it in the process.

A HISTORICAL LESSON IN TYPEWRITING

A hundred years ago people faced problems in using the new typewriters. How to type text and tabular material without errors at reasonable rates? Executives had written their own letters. Typing was error prone. One had to look at the keys, of course, while typing, so a reasonable way was to memorize the text, a sentence at a time. But in going back and forth between the text and the typewriter, small mistakes or lapses were very possible from time to time. Correcting a character, even a word, might not be so bad. Correcting a missed sentence, early on the typed page, was better fixed by starting the page over.

With this background for almost a human generation of using typewriters, the new idea of **touch typing**, typing without looking at the keys, was a very strange one. ''That's silly. Who could possibly do that?'' In teaching typing, people who look at the keys can get useful work done in the very first day. In fact they learn practically all there is to know about a typewriter in the very first day, and just need to get more practice and skill by typing. In teaching touch typing, people get no useful work done in the fist day or the first week. ''Why would anyone spend time in such a useless activity?''

Of course, we know how touch typing turned out as an internationally useful method that put typewriters into business offices on a mass basis. Typewriter makers improved their products in many ways, but the reason typewriters were made in such quantities was due to people knowing how to use them well rather than companies knowing how to make them well. But we also know that very few key looking typists learned how to touch type. It was the young generation coming into the field.

There is a lesson in touch typing for software development. In software, teaching a programming language and how to compile and execute programs allows people to write programs immediately. Very likely, such programs will require considerable debugging, and many text books say just that. And with more and more experience in programming alone or in teams, errors and unit debugging are just an expected and integral part of programming.

However, people with the right education and training need not unit debug their software any more than people need to look at the keys when they type. Yet, just as in touch typing, serious programming begins only with formal methods, more explicit design, and verification from specifications. Even so, not all of today's programmers will move into programming without debugging. Many of today's programmers as opposed to the key looking typists will make the move, perhaps half, but certainly not all.

ZERO DEFECT SOFTWARE IS REALLY POSSIBLE

In spite of the experiences of this first human generation in software development, **zero defect** software is really possible. However, there is no fool proof logical way to know that software is zero defect. The proof is in the using without finding any failures. Mathematics is very helpful in creating software that executes zero defect. But it is insufficient to guarantee it. Statistics is also very helpful in creating software that executes zero defect, but is also insufficient. As noted, the proof is in the using.

Three illustrations of zero defect software follow, all real time applications. First, the **U.S. 1980 Census** was acquired by a nationwide network system of 20 miniprocessors, controlled by a 25 Kloc program, which operated its entire ten months in production with no failures observed. It was developed by Paul Friday, of the U.S. Census Bureau, using functional verification in Pascal. Friday was given the highest technical award of the U.S. Department of Commerce for the achievement.

Second, the **IBM wheelwriter typewriter** products released in 1984 are controlled by three microprocessors with a 65 Kloc program. It has had millions of users ever since, with no failures ever detected. The IBM team creating this software also used functional verification and extensive usage testing in a well-managed environment to achieve this result.

Finally, the **U.S. space shuttle software** of some 500 Kloc, while not completely zero defect, has been zero defect in flight. The IBM team also used functional verification and extensive usage testing to achieve that result. The space shuttle software is such a large, complex, and visible product that there are real lessons in it. All programmers were required to complete the curriculum of six pass/fail courses in understanding programs as rules for mathematical functions and functional verification of programs and modules.

Harlan D. Mills

Preface

The Cleanroom method is the first practical attempt to place software development under statistical quality control and to deliver software with a known and certified mean time to failure (MTFF). The significance of a process under statistical quality control to the software industry is that it affords software management with objective visibility into the software development process and with the ability to change the process to achieve quality objectives. It provides management with some assurance that a status of 90% complete does, in fact, mean that there is only 10% more work to be accomplished. This is a far cry from conventional software methods, where 90% complete usually implies 90% or more still to go.

Cleanroom requires the use of mathematics based software design and verification methods to create original software of sufficient quality to **forego programmer testing (debugging) of code** and to **require statistical based testing for evaluating software reliability**. Unit debugging by the programmer compromises the correctness hypothesis of an original design and gives rise to complex software errors, resulting from the tunnel vision of unit debugging. With the prospect of unit testing, the programmer focuses on getting a program's mainline code working, first, and addressing the other parts of the solution (e.g., exception handling logic), as time and effort permit. Treating the nonmainline logic as an afterthought in the design generally leads to its awkward solution, delivered with little or no testing. The Cleanroom alternative is the top-down stepwise refinement of a total design, with correctness verification of that design required at each refinement step. The entire design must be thought through, rather than brought together with a trial and error process that typically leaves in the design errors of omission and incompleteness.

It is a software industry fact that software of any complexity can not be exhaustively tested and that a sample of the possible inputs must be relied on for the testing which is performed. The conventional method of asking the tester to select these inputs may find lots of errors but may not provide lots of improvement in product quality. It is also accepted that errors can have significantly different effects on the failure rate of software and that the greater payoff comes from discovering and removing the errors with high failure rates during testing. Statistically based testing with random sampling driven from input probability distributions is uniquely effective at finding the errors with high failure rates.

At first glance, the top-down random testing strategy may seem unfair or impossible to satisfy, since programmers must be prepared to deal with a growing set of eventualities in test, beyond their own choosing or control. This turns out not to be the case with the Cleanroom method since its mathematically based design and verification methods provide the increased levels of precision and correctness needed to have the process work.

SIGNIFICANCE OF THE SUBJECT MATTER

Software products have been notoriously difficult to develop with reliable operating characteristics. One reason for this is that these products handle logical complexities which surpass anything imaginable just a few years ago. Another reason is that the logical complexities have lead to more process development problems that can be handled by the available software development processes.

The present state of the art in software development is based on specifying and designing products in response to a requirements analysis and then selectively testing the product against inputs which are thought to be typical for those requirements. Often the result is a product which works well for inputs similar to those used in the testing but which can be unreliable in other circumstances.

This perceived unreliability calls into question the underlying quality of the process used for software development. In current development practice, the focus of quality improvement seems to be limited to more and longer testing and to be seriously considered only for software with life-threatening characteristics (e.g., flight control). Ten to 15 years ago, 50 to

60 defects for every thousand source lines were accepted as the industry standard and, sadly, that number has not dropped to any great extent over the years. Added reliance on early product delivery for trial use by selected users extends the testing, but adds too little, too late to influence the quality of the shipped product.

Compounding the quality concern is the increasing demand for more development productivity, as the application opportunities grow while the developer resource shrinks. Today software pervades every aspect of daily life and is no longer the luxury for scientific research. This ever expanding volume of software necessarily draws off valuable resources for maintenance and enhancement of existing products, while denying resources for the development of desired new capabilities.

RATIONALE FOR WRITING THIS BOOK

In the past several years, the use of the Cleanroom method has been discussed in the software engineering technical literature. No definitive text is available which defines the method, the motivation for its development, or the experiences and lessons learned from its use. This has led to misconceptions and miscommunication regarding the Cleanroom method and its many novel components.

The purpose of this text is to define the Cleanroom method as conceived by its originators and the roles intended to be played by its component parts. Experience with the Cleanroom method in software product development has provided additional insight which is shared on the introduction of Cleanroom into an existing software development environment. Where feasible, the adoption of the total Cleanroom method is the preferred strategy for maximum effectiveness. This is not the only way to gain from the Cleanroom ideas and a suggested sequence is discussed for introducing the Cleanroom components and realizing the incremental benefits of the method. Where existing techniques are established in a development environment, trade-offs are discussed which should be considered in the decision for staying with the existing method rather than adopting the Cleanroom equivalent.

ABOUT THIS BOOK

The book is intended for an audience of software engineering professionals and their technical management, who are looking for new methods for

xviii PREFACE

quality software development. In addition, it would also be useful as a graduate level text, since it integrates the activities of various engineering disciplines into a total software development process.

The book is organized into eight chapters. Chapters 1 through 3 give an overview of the Cleanroom method providing a summary of experience with its use and insight into introducing Cleanroom into an existing work environment. These chapters should be read by everyone. Chapter 1 provides an overview of the Cleanroom methodology and its component parts, a historical perspective on the Cleanroom work, and discusses the rationale and goals for Cleanroom. Chapter 2 discusses where and how Cleanroom methodology has been used, the quality and productivity results of each use, and the lessons learned on the technical effectiveness of the component parts. Chapter 3 focuses on the procedural and personnel aspects of Cleanroom's introduction into an existing software development organization, with emphasis on the process changes and the technical training that must be implemented for successful technology transfer.

Chapters 4 through 7 give a more detailed discussion of the major technical aspects of the Cleanroom method; namely, mathematics based design, correctness verification, statistical testing, and software reliability estimation. These subjects are essentially independent topics that can be read separately, depending on the reader's interests. There are some logical connections in the sense that correctness verification is most effective with a mathematics based design method and reliability prediction is only effective using data from some form of statistical testing environment. Chapter 4 provides definition for the formal methods that are basic to Cleanroom software design and for the systematic process which is identified for developing Cleanroom software. Chapter 5 provides definition for the functional approach to software correctness proving, describes the application of functional verification in software design, and introduces the notion of a verification based inspection process. Chapter 6 introduces the idea of basing the validation of requirements on a testing approach which uses a statistical sampling of representative inputs. Chapter 7 introduces the concept of software reliability and describes an approach to certifying reliability for delivered products based on a statistically driven test process.

Chapter 8 deals with future roles for the Cleanroom method, once Cleanroom is established within a business enterprise. This chapter introduces the concept of software warranties based on reliability certification and the benefits of a development process under statistical quality control, which can feedback process corrections to ensure achievement of product quality objectives.

Acknowledgments

First, I must thank my friend and mentor, Dr. Harlan Mills, for his inspiration and guidance in my endeavors to define and evaluate the different technologies that comprise the Cleanroom method. Without his support, the ideas might not have reached their current level of maturity. Next, I am particularly grateful to Vincent N. Cook, President of IBM's Federal Systems Division during the formative stages of Cleanroom research, who sponsored this work and promoted its adoption within IBM. Without dedicated management backing, technology innovation to address the challenges of software development could not be possible in the competitive industrial environment.

In defining the Cleanroom method described in this book, I was ably assisted by many colleagues. Al Currit (IBM Rochester laboratory) and Bev Littlewood (City University of London, England) are thanked for their assistance in formulating the statistical methods, which are part of Cleanroom. Two IBM colleagues, Jerry Gerber and Duvan Luong must be noted for their respective work on the Cleanroom support tools and test procedures. Finally, I owe a debt of appreciation to countless numbers of summer interns who contributed to different parts of the Cleanroom method during the early 1980s.

Another kind of appreciation goes to the early users of the Cleanroom method, who were not deterred by the seemingly impractical ideas on Software development—no programmer testing, verifying correctness, statistical test sampling, and defining software MTTF. They helped evaluate Cleanroom's effectiveness as a practical development approach and mature the ideas into practice. Terry Baker, Vic Basili, and Rick Selby were very early supporters with their experiments at the University of Maryland. Particular thanks go to Rick Linger, Pat McKay, Frank McGarry, Scott Green, and their teams, who proved the ideas in the real working environment of customers, costs, and schedules.

Finally a special thanks goes to Ara Kouchakdjian who helped crystalize many of the Cleanroom ideas over the years and who along with Tom Kraly and Fred Luppino contributed to the quality of this book through their thoughtful and thorough review of its draft.

CHAPTER 1

What Is the Cleanroom Method?

Cleanroom is the name of a software development method which was organized to support the measurement and certification of software mean time to failure (MTTF), prior to the release of software to its user. Cleanroom is also the label for a collection of software engineering techniques that are the components of the Cleanroom software development method and which can be used singularly or in various combinations. The net benefits realized from the Cleanroom method and its components are the release of software with significantly higher quality and with predictable field reliability (MTTF). The costs experienced in developing this higher quality software are, themselves, significantly less than those reported with current software development practice.

This chapter provides some historical perspective on the research conducted within IBM's Federal Sector Division to define the method, to identify and interface the component software engineering techniques, and to experiment with the application of the method on real-world problems. An overview of the method is discussed which explains the role intended for each component and the rationale for selected techniques. The impact of the Cleanroom experience on the software product and its development process are reviewed and future potentials of the Cleanroom method are identified.

1.1 CLEANROOM BACKGROUND

Cleanroom is a method for developing software with known and predictable reliability. It addresses the question of the quality and the reliability of software products, as experienced by their users. The term Cleanroom was selected to draw attention to a development process that strives to prevent the introduction of errors during software development.

The kernel idea was originated in 1980 by Dr. Harlan D. Mills, who was then an IBM Fellow at IBM's Federal System Division. It defined an extension of the software engineering program that he had authored in 1975. The premise of the kernel idea, as identified in his note entitled Software of Certifiable Reliability [1], was that:

> By conducting software development under closely managed and controlled conditions, that track the entire history of software from creation to incorporation in a product, a certified reliability in MTBF (Mean Time Between Failures) of the product can be developed concurrently with the product.

He labeled ''the closely controlled development operation'' as the ''Clean Room'' and formulated a novel basis for predicting the MTBF of software. Development would be performed with modern software engineering methods [2], which defined a top-down strategy for software development, the use of structured programming techniques, and the introduction of software verification based on functional correctness ideas. The same methods had been the underpinning of the previously introduced software engineering program.

Mills noted that software reliability required a different theory than what had been formulated for hardware reliability. Unlike hardware, the basis for software failures was logical rather than physical and these failures were due to design errors rather than software aging. He suggested that, as a basis for a software MTBF, we might ''consider a universe of possible executions'' with software execution controlled ''by a probability distribution over this universe.''

From this kernel idea, the Cleanroom method for software development has evolved, which organized a set of software engineering techniques and tools to support the routine development of software with certifiable reliability. In this process, the consideration of software reliability and its certification was the driving force. The formulation of mathematical models for estimating software reliability and validating the accuracy of these models was an initial concentration. A more difficult aspect of this reliability focus was defining a testing environment that would support statistical inference, such as reliability prediction, and, at the same time, perform the critical validation role of functionally testing software applications of any complexity.

The certification approach demanded a complete and public record of all software executions to ensure accurate inputs for the reliability prediction. This required the delivery of software from the development to test organizations with significantly higher quality than achieved with available methods. The introduction of function-based correctness verification offered the best potential for achieving the higher quality. A Cleanroom design procedure was organized that started with more precise specification methods, carried over the formal design techniques, introduced verification-based inspection procedures, and also required formal configuration control of software, prior to its first execution. Note that MTTF is used rather than Mills' original MTBF to conform with current research in software reliability. The terms are essentially equivalent.

The early work on the Cleanroom method was spent evolving these various ideas and techniques, experimenting with their use in real development opportunities, creating tool prototypes to support their use, and identifying the technical training that was required to achieve routine use of the method. The resulting Cleanroom process, its component technical engineering techniques, and the experiences realized from its use are the subjects of this book, which is written to gain further use and acceptance of the Cleanroom method within the software development community.

1.2 CLEANROOM PROCESS

Cleanroom represents the first practical attempt at putting the software development process under statistical quality control with a well-defined strategy for continuous process improvement. To reach this goal, a Cleanroom unique life cycle was defined which focused on mathematics-based software engineering for correct software designs and on statistics-based software testing for certification of software reliability.

The Cleanroom focus on error prevention during the development life cycle is a refreshing departure from current development practice where software errors are accepted as inevitable and the focus is placed on error detection. Cleanroom also recognizes that it is impractical to place trial-and-error development processes under statistical control. Meaningful control data can not be obtained from the attempted execution of software which has a high error content and unpredictable execution characteristics. For these reasons, the Cleanroom software development strategy relies on formal software engineering methods [2] and rigorous correctness verification for creating correct designs. The added care and formality, by both the software designer and the independent inspectors, results in higher levels of software quality and helps to ensure the readiness for release from development.

For statistical quality control of software development, some basis for monitoring the software quality level must be defined. Unlike manufacturing, the basis can not be found in the large numbers of similar products which are produced, since software is a logical one of a kind product. Nor can it be found in the physical aging of the software statements, since the execution of these software statements is deterministic and always gives the same result for the same input. Rather the basis must be found in the testing of the software product, where another departure from current development practice is required. Testing in the Cleanroom process has a statistical rather than selective basis and is always focused on the total product rather than its parts. In hardware, physical dimensions and the statistical tolerances

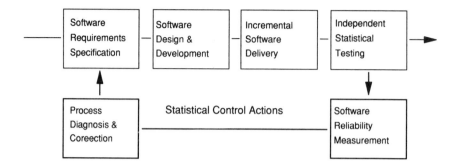

Figure 1.1 Development Process Flow

on physical parts are additive components and can be combined for considering the statistical quality of a product. The combination of software parts is more complicated, with no practical rules for collecting part failures because of the deep and complex logical interactions between parts.

Statistical control of software development should exhibit many of the same control features found in modern manufacturing processes—process outputs are sampled, measurements are computed, quality trends are diagnosed, and, as needed, corrections are fed back into the process. Software reliability in terms of MTTF can be the measurement taken from test execution results and used to drive process changes. These changes (e.g., tighter specifications) would be introduced to ensure achieving the software's reliability targets. The Cleanroom defined version of a statistical control process for software development is shown in Figure 1.1, where the measurement, diagnosis, and correction actions are superimposed on the normal flow of control in the development process.

1.2.1 Cleanroom Process Organization

In defining the Cleanroom software development process, competing software engineering and functional testing techniques were examined and traded-off, with significant weight given to the insertion of new techniques into existing business environments. The Cleanroom process that resulted is organized as a set of component techniques, which can be applied individually and can also provide significant development benefits. If the total Cleanroom process is adopted for software development, it represents a radical departure from current software development practice. The process extends beyond the boundaries of what is normally interpreted as software development and deals with software specification at one extreme and with functional software testing at the other extreme. The process introduces new controls for software development, imposes new roles and responsibilities on the various engineering disciplines, eliminates some seemingly core methods from the development process, and raises the level of training and proficiency required in the engineering disciplines.

Where possible, the total Cleanroom process should be used for software development to realize its full potential for enhancing product quality and process productivity. However, transitioning to a totally different development process is not always practical within an ongoing software development environment, where an incremental introduction of the Cleanroom components has proven to be a more effective strategy for technology transfer. Each of the half dozen components addresses a specific aspect of the software development process, makes a separate contribution to the development, and has a unique set of considerations for process insertion. The components have been used individually and in combination with demonstrable positive results. This incremental realization of positive results generally leads to the gradual introduction of the total process, which can now be accomplished without the trauma of switching to a radically new development process.

The Cleanroom components are organized along the six technical lines of software specification, software development, software correctness verification, independent software product testing, software reliability measurement, and statistical process control.

1.2.1.1 Software Specification   With the Cleanroom process, there is an implied requirement for correctness, completeness, and stability in the software specifications, so that the correctness of the software design can be verified as it is elaborated. In practice, software requirements are typically neither fully known nor verifiable during the early stages of software development and it might appear that the Cleanroom process has little or no application for the typical software development project. To the contrary, the ideas of forcing requirement deficiencies into the open and of establishing early control of the requirements process, as espoused by the Cleanroom method, should be required practice for all software development.

If software development is treated as a trial-and-error process, incomplete requirements can be accommodated as just another source of trial and error, with a blurring of accountability between specifiers and developers. Cleanroom is different in that it forces software design against the early specification of requirements and, in that process, forces stability and completeness in these specifications. The result is stricter accountability between specifiers and developers and the early introduction of a controlled approach to stabilizing the product requirements.

Software specifications are typically documented in natural language, with which it is difficult to accurately provide perspective and guidance on the total function and performance. In the Cleanroom method, more formal notation is introduced for accuracy and to resolve many of the issues that would be subsequently raised by the software designer attempting to verify the correctness of a design. The specification content is broadened to identify the packaging of software requirements into incremental releases and to establish the reliability (MTTF) targets for the product. Cleanroom centralizes project focus on the software specifications as the single source document on which to base all software design and all subsequent validation of requirements implementation.

1.2.1.2 Software Development

In the Cleanroom process, a rigorous and formal design method is identified as a necessary element for generating software whose correctness can be verified. A design method **[2]** based on structured programming theory is recommended for Cleanroom use. This method defines a limited set of primitives for capturing design logic, defining software structure, and organizing the software's data. The primitives are used in a systematic and stepwise refinement of the software requirements and in the construction of a software design whose correctness can be assessed and confirmed at each step.

1.2.1.3 Software Correctness Verification

In this design method, correctness is defined as the equivalence between a requirement and the design, documented with the design primitives, which supposedly implements the requirement. Designs are verified using the functional technique for correctness verification **[3],** first by the designer when constructing a design and subsequently by independent inspectors when reviewing the design. Correctness proofs in the functional approach work off the design structure rather than the embedded application logic, which allows the same proofs to be used across all design levels. With some algebraic manipulation, the question of correctness for a total software product can be reduced to the summation of the correctness proofs for the component parts.

1.2.1.4 Independent Software Product Testing

Software products are tested for two reasons: first, to ensure that the software correctly implements its design (structural testing) and, second, to ensure that the software satisfies its specified requirements (functional testing). Structural testing is primarily the responsibility of the software developer, while functional testing is generally performed by an independent organization.

In the Cleanroom method, only functional testing is performed since the correctness verification techniques, woven into the formal design method, satisfy all goals defined for structural testing. The one consistent element in all current Cleanroom experience is that high-quality software was developed without any structural testing (i.e., unit and string tests). Functional testing is still required in the Cleanroom method for validating the implementation of the original requirements. In the Cleanroom method, a statistical approach **[4]** to functional testing has been defined and proven effective in validating requirements satisfaction. In this approach, functional testing is driven by probability distributions that are defined against the requirements and generally track requirements usage in the software's operating environment.

1.2.1.5 Software Reliability Measurement The most commonly used measure of software quality is a count of the number of errors per thousand lines of product source code (ksloc). The numbers are easy to gather and can give some notion of relative quality when comparing development projects. Industry averages of the errors per ksloc generated during typical software development projects are available and can be used as benchmarks against which to compare quality results. The difficulty with this measure is that it is useful to the software developer but has marginal value for the software user. At delivery, software with a high error count may have been well tested and delivered with most errors found and repaired. However, products with low counts may have been poorly tested and delivered with significant numbers of yet to be discovered problems. The errors per ksloc metric gives the software user no visibility into what quality will be exhibited in use.

Software reliability, in terms of MTTF, is a more meaningful measure for the user, which gives a positive quality indicator (longer MTTF is better) and which can be estimated prior to software delivery. When tied to a statistical testing approach, as in the Cleanroom method, MTTF predictions during software development can accurately reflect subsequent operational experience.

1.2.1.6 Statistical Process Control Cleanroom allows for continuous process improvement through the effective use of reliability measurements taken during incremental releases of the software. Typically, incremental releases of software are staggered across a development schedule, so that MTTF readings from early releases can have dramatic impact on any combination of the specification, development, and test phases. To gauge where corrective action is required in the process, the variance between the recorded and the target MTTF's can help identify what and how much correction is needed. When the total Cleanroom process is used, software development under formal statistical control is achievable.

1.2.2 Cleanroom Impacts on Software Development

The Cleanroom software development method is different enough that its total adoption could represent a radical departure from existing development practice. Several of the component techniques are used selectively by development organizations or are the subjects of ongoing research and experimentation, but the composite set of techniques packaged into a single development method is a dramatically different approach. The underlying premise of a software development process with built-in statistical control for process improvement is novel. It may suggest one practical approach to achieving the level five plateau, defined in the Software Engineering Institute's (SEI) process assessment strategy [5].

In addition to the Cleanroom method, several other software development ideas which are embodied in the component techniques might seem equally radical. Notable in this list are stabilizing software specifications to support software verification, applying functional verification across the spectrum of software ap-

TABLE 1.1   Cleanroom Component Techniques

	Technology Focus	Cleanroom Perspective
Baseline Capability	Defined process	Starting point
Design and inspection	Early quality visibility	
Software Specification	Software quality	Focal point
Formal description	Software correctness	Drive verification
Usage/build data	Customer acceptance	Drive validation
Software Verification	Software quality	Software quality
In construction	Error prevention	Correct designs
In inspection	Confirmed correctness	Zero defect quality
No Developer Test	Software quality	Software productivity
Statistical Testing	Customer acceptance	Requirements validation
MTTF Prediction	Software reliability	Certified MTTF
Statistical Process	Process improvement	Software warranty

plications, replacing software structural testing with software verification, configuration managing software prior to its execution, using statistical samples for functional testing, and introducing reliability as a software metric. There has been a good deal of study on requirements specification and software verification techniques, but little acceptance by software practitioners. Statistical testing with random sample generation and predicting software MTTF are ideas that have been ridiculed in the technical literature. Eliminating the unit and string testing performed by software developers is viewed as an absurd idea. However, the Cleanroom experience shows that these counterintuitive ideas can play valuable roles and contribute to a software development process for building software with quality approaching zero defect levels.

1.2.2.1   *What Each Component Technique Can Buy*   If adoption of the complete Cleanroom method is not possible, the component techniques used singularly or in combination can significantly improve an organization's software development practice. The component techniques within the Cleanroom software development process are summarized in Table 1.1, together with their technology focus and contribution with an incremental introduction of the Cleanroom method. Most of the component techniques can be introduced by themselves but some require the simultaneous introduction of other component techniques to work and produce effective results. A road map for introducing the Cleanroom component techniques into a development organization is shown in Figure 1.2.

For this discussion, a reasonable baseline practice for software development

B
A
S
E
L
I
N
E

P
R
O
C
E
S
S

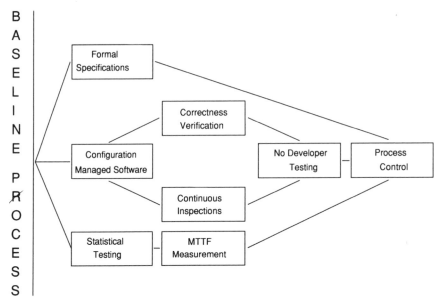

Figure 1.2 Roadmap for Introducing Cleanroom Component Techniques

must be assumed to which the Cleanroom component techniques can be added. As a minimum, the baseline practice should embody a software design method based on structured programming principles [2] and also include a software inspection technique for early error detection. The design method should support a top-down and systematic refinement of software requirements, an incremental software release strategy, a minimal set of constructs for design logic, and some facility for data abstraction and encapsulation.

The Fagan formal inspection method [6], if no inspection practice exists, can be easily introduced into an existing development process, which is why inspections are assumed for the baseline capability. When introduced, formal inspections should provide an early error detection capability that removes 50% of the software's design and implementation errors, based on industry experience across a wide span of applications. When applied with additional rigor and frequency, the formal inspection contribution to the error discovery picture should grow to the 70 to 80% error removal range, as reported by various sources [7,8].

The baseline assumes only a systematic design method and formal inspection procedures, which should reflect the basic set of techniques used by most software development organizations. The baseline further assumes that requirements specifications are documented in natural language, that developers perform some form of unit and string testing, that software is configuration-managed after release to the independent test organization, and that functional testing is performed in some ad hoc manner. Ideas such as formal specifications, correctness verification, statistical-based testing, software reliability, and statistical process control are definitely not considered in the baseline capability.

The first technique that can be introduced into any development practice is to place all software under formal configuration control prior to its first execution. This has an immediate psychological effect on the developers, which translates into a quality improvement for their software. Knowing that all execution errors will be given public scrutiny leads to more conservative designs which exactly match the requirements, use solutions with high confidence of working, and are prepared with more care.

Limiting or eliminating the testing performed by software developers is the next technique which can be introduced. While this seems to be the most radical proposal within the Cleanroom method, it turns out that, as confidence builds in the error discovery capability of the formal inspection, the need and role of developer testing diminishes. Developing software on other than the host computer system (personal computers rather than mainframes) tends to speed up the demise of developer testing. This technique gives a similar quality impetus as noted for configuration control prior to test, while also having a positive impact on software development productivity [9,10].

Correctness verification incorporated into the existing software design method is the next technique to be considered but requires both technical training and developer commitment. This step is the first toward introducing defect prevention into the software development process with correctness verification interwoven into the software design method. The software developer should see defect ranges well below the 50 to 60 defects per ksloc industry averages and even the 20 to 40 defect rate reported with the baseline process [11]. Verification-based inspections [10] should improve the formal inspection results with early error detection rates in the 90% range.

Statistical testing techniques can be used in concert with the above development techniques or independently with an existing test operation. In either case, the technique gives an immediate improvement in the objectivity, the precision, and the completeness of test samples used for software functional testing. The focus on software usage inherent in the statistical approach can only improve customer acceptance of software, after functional test completion. As an aside, it should be obvious that this testing idea is not a radical departure from current practice which relies on early customer ship programs [12] and the like, to get a usage perspective on the product to be delivered.

Techniques for the prediction of software reliability during development require the previous introduction of all of the above component techniques. Statistical testing provides the representative failure data for model input. Software design with correctness verification provides to the independent test organization mature software against which statistical test samples can be effectively run. Software under early configuration control provides the assurance of a public record on all software execution, as required for MTTF certification.

Evolving a statistical control process for software development (the real Cleanroom objective) requires the complete Cleanroom method starting with the formalization of the software requirements specification. Precision and correctness in the specification is key to the development effort and the target reliabilities define

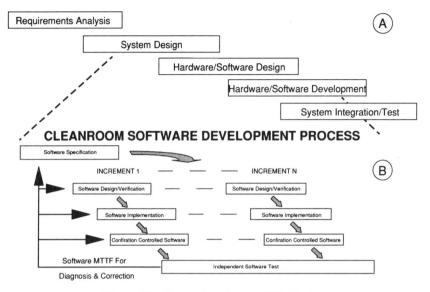

Figure 1.3 System Development Life Cycle

the rationale for process measurement and improvement. Introducing the total Cleanroom method is no easy task and the typical software development organization will grow into the method after building confidence in the Cleanroom's component techniques.

1.2.2.2 Process Impacts The most commonly used life cycle model for software development is shown in Figure 1.3.A and is defined as a set of activities with controlled movement from one activity to the next but with some overlap to allow rework between activities. This model, commonly called the ''waterfall'' model [13], establishes the necessary discipline for control of software development and has been scaled to address applications of every size. For large software developments where a single software release is not practical, the incremental development of multiple releases can be accommodated within the model, by executing the software design, implementation, and test steps, repetitively. For software developments where software requirements are immature or sketchy, the ''spiral'' adaptation of this model [14] can be accommodated by executing all of the steps, repetitively.

The Cleanroom method assumes the incremental development version of this model and superimposes a feedback loop, which is driven by the continuous measurement of software MTTF. As shown in Figure 1.3.B, MTTF measurements are made at each release of a software increment and evaluated to decide whether changes are required in the software development to improve MTTF. The evaluation compares the MTTF prediction at a current release against the software's target MTTF. Corrections are fed back to one or more steps, depending on the size of the MTTF discrepancy and the recommended remedial actions.

1.2.2.3 People Impacts   Software correctness verification and statistical testing are the two areas of most concern to people developing software with the Cleanroom method. Software verification forces increased levels of completeness and accuracy in the software specifications and the software designs. This requires understanding and reasonable fluency in formal design methods and in functional correctness methods, topics that are not in the repertoire of most software engineers. Education and supervised use in real problem situations are generally needed to develop the required levels of expertise. As confidence in the use of these methods is gained, the reluctance to deliver software without developer testing diminishes and is replaced by a developer challenge to deliver zero defect code to the test organization.

Statistical techniques present a formidable challenge to the test community. They demand a requirements validation rather than an error discovery focus in functional testing, force a reliance on distribution-driven test sampling, introduce randomness into test selection, and establish software MTTF as a reliability metric. Incorporating these ideas and techniques into software testing and test management practice requires significant education for anyone without a technical background and may dramatically change the qualifications for software testers.

1.2.2.4 Cleanroom Process Potentials   Adopting the total Cleanroom method as standard software development practice would significantly change a development organization. First, though statistical control is directed at development process improvement, it can play a risk analysis role for determining the software's readiness for delivery. As Mills suggested in his original note [1], the economics of continued testing versus software delivery can be judged from the incremental rates of change in software MTTF and the costs associated with testing additional software increments. Sequential sampling techniques [15] have further potential for making the trade-off between confidence in MTTF projections and readiness for software delivery. These latter techniques also show potential for making quantifiable trade-offs between MTTF confidence levels and the optimum size of test samples, to reduce overall testing costs, and permit more competitive software development performance.

Second, Cleanroom has many different component techniques addressing software quality and should result in software of distinctly higher quality being routinely delivered. This enhanced quality focus starts with the accuracy and completeness of the software requirements specification. In software development, it continues with the verification of designs as constructed and the independent verification-based inspection of those designs. In requirements validation, statistical testing is performed with representative usage data, with software execution in representative usage environments, and with continuous monitoring of the software reliability. Moreover, the software development is performed under strict statistical quality control with continuous process improvement to guarantee achievement of quality objectives.

A potential end product from this intense quality focus is the issuance of software warranties based on levels of software MTTF. The Cleanroom insistence on a complete public history of software executions and failures allows a certification of the software MTTF at delivery. The quantification of confidence levels and testing sufficiency provide a technical basis for the business risk analysis to back-up a warranty offering. The Cleanroom software development method is the only published development approach that even allows the consideration of warranties by the software industry.

Significant productivity gain over the software life cycle is also a real potential from the use of the Cleanroom software development method. Current experience identifies improvement in software development productivity from the Cleanroom method which are due to several factors. These include more accurate and complete specifications, simpler software designs, less rework due to software errors, and no developer effort spent in testing, to mention a few. In addition to productivity savings during software development, the more significant payoff is in development life cycle productivity. The near zero defect quality levels in delivered software essentially eliminate a requirement for postdelivery software maintenance. While the idea of growth in both quality and productivity may seem counterintuitive, all indications from projects using the Cleanroom software development method are that this is a definite trend and that the growth can only get better over time.

1.3 MOTIVATION FOR USING THE CLEANROOM PROCESS

Since the Cleanroom method is acknowledged as a radical departure from current methods for developing software, what would attract software engineers in trying and subsequently embracing the Cleanroom method?

1.3.1 Software with Known Mean Time to Failure

The principal attraction to the Cleanroom method is the capability for creating software with significantly higher quality and demonstrated reliability when executing in the planned usage environment. In the software methodology marketplace, there are a variety of design and implementation techniques that are advertised and can be used to define predictable software development processes. Any number of these methods can be used to develop software which is seemingly complete and which can pass through various levels of validation and acceptance testing. However, only the Cleanroom method can give an assurance in the form of a software MTTF that the software will perform correctly with minimum failure in its intended usage environments. To the intended software user, this is the crux of his interest in introducing the software into the operating business environment, namely, how long will the software (and his business operations) run without failing. The Cleanroom method addresses this concern and is set up to provide a software MTTF value that has been certified through a rigorous validation process.

The reason for postdelivery surprises with other software development methods is that they tend to not focus on the planned use of the software and to track software quality with measures that give no software usage insight. The methods focus more on satisfying the requirements specification and tracking how this software development compares with previous developments. While these relative quality measures should be of interest to the developer to ensure that the development process and the resultant software are getting better and not deteriorating, they should not be tracked to the exclusion of metrics which give insight into the software's operating environment.

During software development, it is critical to focus on the software use. This is rarely done, however, because of the demands for getting the software implemented, tested, and accepted. Rather than look at modifying the development process, as in the Cleanroom case, most development organizations extend their development process with some form of early customer ship program. The idea is to deliver nearly completed (through most levels of testing) software to selected customers who will be likely users and ask them to shake down the software before its official release. This is a worthwhile strategy since it gets real users running the software in their environments but tends to be too little and too late. Since the software is essentially completed and through design, implementation, and most of test, there is little opportunity for considering any major revisions or extensions. Another strategy is to include an operational demonstration as some final form of testing, where the software is run for some extended period of time in a real or simulated form of the intended operating environment. This strategy is typically adopted when the software is developed for a single customer and provides a more controlled version of the early customer ship strategy, since the developer has the opportunity to fix duration, environment, scope, and other demonstration parameters.

Both of these strategies have the same drawback in that they are performed after the bulk of the software development has been completed and after the point where usage-directed changes can be effectively handled. What is needed is a way to introduce the usage or customer focus very early in the software development and have it permeate the total design and development effort.

The Cleanroom method tackles this question head-on by insisting that the entire testing program be organized for using representative samples of the intended usage environment and that the software development be structured to permit early and continuous software exposure to these representative samples. The incremental development strategy within the Cleanroom method satisfies the early and continuous exposure objective. The statistical testing technique forces the analysis of software usage and the definition of probability distributions to control the generation of representative test samples.

This statistical testing focus provides other benefits to the software development. First, it forces the definition of a test program directed to the user's or customer's needs and plans for using the software—not the developer's interpretation of how it might be used if the customer thought exactly like the developer. This is a critical distinction about how the test material is created for software testing. If the generation of test material is left to a developer or an independent tester, their sampling of possible test data will be based on their view of how the system should be used, on their opinion of what functions are important, and on their interpretation of how the software functions can be combined. If statistical-based sampling is used, then, by definition, the test data will be selected randomly, based on the probability distributions that reflect the planned software use from the customer's perspective.

Another benefit from statistical testing is the objectivity and realism that can be built into the test material. Objectivity comes from the random sampling of the complete domain of possible test data, which is superior to the arbitrary partitioning of data by testers who must mentally grope with generally large data domains. Realism comes from the probability distributions that describe the expected scenarios for operating with the software, the characterization of how the functions within the software will be exercised, and the identification of the more likely ranges of data with operating interest.

There are additional long-term benefits of a testing strategy based on statistical sampling, in that the sample size might be dramatically reduced without impacting the effectiveness of the test process. This would be analogous to polling strategies which use the responses from small numbers of people to predict election campaigns, television rankings, and all numbers of things. For software testing, this sampling approach could reduce the total test effort without impacting confidence (now measurable) in the quality of the delivered software.

1.3.2   Software with Near Zero Defects

A second equally likely reason for using the Cleanroom method is the potential for creating software that experiences near zero defects after delivery to its users. The Cleanroom method employs functional correctness verification during the design and implementation steps to prevent the introduction of errors into the software. Reported industry data [16,17,18] indicates that these errors are in the range of 50 to 60 per ksloc, requiring significant error detection effort for their removal prior to delivery. Cleanroom experience indicates that the number of inserted errors can be reduced to the 0 to 20 errors per ksloc range, thus dramatically reducing the error detection effort and giving the software engineer a shot at achieving near zero defect software.

The Cleanroom method does not assume that software verification is perfect and, therefore, that there is no role for software testing in the development process. Quite to the contrary, the statistical testing strategy is directed at rooting out those errors that are most likely to cause failures in the software's operating environment. A test strategy based on random sampling from usage distributions should by definition select software inputs with the highest potential for causing failures in the software's operating environment. Software inputs are selected for a test sample based on their likelihood of occurring in the operating environment. Any failures that they trigger are caused by the high failure rate errors and the removal of these errors should build high confidence that no failures should occur during the useful life of the software. *While zero defect software in an absolute sense is unattainable, software with an extremely high probability of not experiencing failures is attainable.*

1.3.3 Quality Software Which Is Cheaper to Produce

Increased productivity across the software life cycle is a third reason for selecting the Cleanroom method. The requirements for postdelivery maintenance to correct errors and design deficiencies should drop dramatically. With maintenance being 40 to 60% of the life cycle cost and error/deficiency repair accounting for half of the maintenance, minimizing error/deficiency repair has dramatic cost impacts. Staff is now available for addressing the new application needs rather than patching failure-prone software.

The unexpected productivity gain with the Cleanroom method is the savings realized during software development. These savings are unexpected because of the added effort required for more accurate software specification, verifying correctness as each design step is constructed, and inspecting software to confirm correctness. While some of this added effort could be recovered by the minimal or nonexistent developer testing effort, a net gain in productivity was never anticipated but seems to be the case in all Cleanroom experience.

The productivity gain is probably larger when other cost items, such as computer time, documentation, and so forth are factored into the calculation. Where these were tracked in Cleanroom experience, the trend has been reduced costs for all of the nonlabor related items.

1.4 CLEANROOM'S IMPACT ON THE SOFTWARE PROCESS

The life cycle model for software development within which the Cleanroom method is defined was shown in Figure 1.3.A, where the necessary engineering activities for the development of a typical system are identified. At the start, the requirements for a system must be analyzed, the design of a solution to those requirements must be formulated, and an architecture defined for the component hardware and software parts. Specifications for the component parts are then developed to allocate subsets of the requirements to each component. These specifications are the basis for the component design which defines the component implementation. As the component implementations are completed, they are released for integration into the evolving system and tested to ensure their correct interfacing with the rest of the system. Testing is continued to validate that the allocated requirements are satisfied and to gain system acceptance for customer delivery. Figure 1.3.A doesn't show the typical postdelivery activities of ongoing user support and system maintenance as problems, changes, and upgrades are identified.

The software development steps in this life cycle model can be extracted from the life cycle model, as shown in Figure 1.3.B for the Cleanroom method. Any implied sequentiality in the figure should not be construed as constraining the

REQUIREMENTS SPECIFICATION
Function and Performance
but with
Usage and Build Statistics

SOFTWARE DESIGN/IMPLEMENTATION
Incremental Software Development
but with
Correctness Verification not Unit Test

INDEPENDENT SOFTWARE TEST
Integration & Test of Released Increments
but with
Representative Statistical Usage Samples

SOFTWARE ACCEPTANCE
Demonstrated Function and Performance
but with
Certified Software MTTF

Figure 1.4   Summary of Cleanroom Impacts on a Development Life Cycle Model

Cleanroom development method to a strictly sequential development strategy. Within the ''waterfall'' life cycle model, incremental development is shown as a cornerstone for Cleanroom development and accommodation for the recently identified ''spiral'' life cycle model **[14]** is also definable. *The key point is that the Cleanroom process is **not** restricted or limited to a sequential life cycle development model.*

The introduction of the Cleanroom method would impact most steps in the life cycle model, as summarized in this section and discussed in further detail in subsequent parts of this book. The net effect of these impacts is summarized in Figure 1.4 which gives the role of each step and the change resulting from the Cleanroom method.

1.4.1   Impacts on Software Specification

Software specification covers the work of sorting out, from a total set of requirements, those which are allocated to the software to be developed. The software specification defines the functional requirements that must be implemented in the software. It also describes any performance budgets that constrain the execution time, size, and so forth of that software and any environmental constraints within which the software must operate (e.g., interfaces, modularity, documentation, packaging, and standards considerations).

With the Cleanroom method, an additional requirement is levied on the software specification, namely, that it be written with more formal notation to support correctness verification during design. In current practice, software specifications are written in natural language and, possibly, augmented with tables, charts, drawings, and so on to provide more concise description. For Cleanroom design, greater accuracy is implied in the software specification content. As described in Chapter 4, the use of formal methods in the generation of the software specifications is the preferred approach and several acceptable methods are enumerated (e.g., box structuring techniques, formal specification languages [Z, VDM, etc.], and problem specific grammars). These formal methods force a more exacting analysis of the requirements and tend to minimize ambiguity, inconsistency, and incompleteness in the resultant software specification. The methods support the verification of developed specifications so that specification correctness can be demonstrated at the start of software design.

An alternative approach is to continue with natural language description and rely on subsequent interaction between the designer and specifier to force the closer analysis and to resolve ambiguity, inconsistency, and so forth. This approach to specifications is much less efficient than spending the effort for accuracy and completeness during generation but it is the common practice in most software organizations. As discussed in Section 1.5, use of the Cleanroom method generally results in an early and more accurate form of software specification. This is achieved directly through the use of formal methods in the specification generation or indirectly through the perseverance of the Cleanroom designer attempting to verify design correctness.

In addition to more formal specifications, the Cleanroom method forces the consideration and inclusion of data on software usage and construction plans during specification generation to drive the subsequent statistical testing. This includes the identification of software inputs and their expected usage probabilities to structure the test data bases. Any incremental release strategy for the software development must be elaborated to factor the planned availability of the software function into the test planning. This supports the Cleanroom test philosophy of concentrating the test of software function at its release to test and relying on regression testing of that software function in all subsequent incremental releases.

1.4.2 Impacts on Software Design

A baseline assumption in the Cleanroom method is that software design is performed with a technique based on structured programming theory. If that is not the case, then introducing a design technique based on structured programming theory would be an impact. Several techniques are available through the technical literature which can satisfy this baseline requirement.

Assuming a baseline capability, the major design impact is the introduction of functional correctness verification into the design process. The Cleanroom design ethic is one of requirements specification, followed by design of a solution to the specification, followed by verification of the equivalence between the design and requirements. This ethic is applied in small design steps that give a decomposition of a specification into appropriate logic tying together a breakdown of the original specification into more detailed level specifications. These in turn need subsequent design and verification. Verification is integral to the design construction and imposes a control on the designer which gates the refinement of the software specification.

A second impact in the design step is the introduction of verification-based inspections to provide an independent confirmation of the design correctness. The verification-based inspection, which is discussed in Chapter 5, builds on the formal inspection practice [6] but reorients the inspection to correctness confirmation rather than error detection. The reorientation is achieved through the use of design language analyzers that can determine the structure of the design and formulate the sequence and content of the questions to be addressed in inspections. The questions and their flow reflect the thought process which would be followed in performing a correctness proof based on the functional verification approach. Again formal inspections are assumed in the baseline capability, so the move to verification-based inspections should be simplified. If that baseline assumption is not the case, then verification-based inspections should be directly introduced.

1.4.3 Impacts on Software Implementation

The impact to software implementation from the Cleanroom method will depend on the approach to software design. If design and verification are performed to full detail in the design step, then implementation becomes a transliteration of design notation into programing language notation. This is a very straightforward process requiring little effort and probably lending itself to mechanical translation, assuming tool availability. This approach of elaborating a design to full detail with a design language has been successfully used in several of the Cleanroom projects, as discussed in Chapter 2.

An equally acceptable approach is to split the design refinement between the use of design notation and the use of the implementation programming language. This requires the continuation of design and verification in the implementation step. The implementation impact is that the software coding would now be performed stepwise, with each step verified for correctness and with verification-based code inspections performed to confirm correctness. This approach assumes sufficient structured programming features in the selected programming language and an enforcement procedure to prevent a regression to old coding practice.

1.4.4 Impacts on Software Developer Testing

The impact to this step is that it is no longer performed in the Cleanroom method. Close adherence to functional correctness verification ensures that all of the error detection situations addressed by developer testing are addressed in verification as shown in Table 1.2. With the Cleanroom method, the only reasons for software engineers to execute their software would be to check the feasibility or performance of newly defined algorithms, to exercise support software facilities, and to confirm operating system services. In each case, a software design is not being tested but rather the capabilities of support facilities are trying to be understood.

TABLE 1.2   Comparison of Structural Testing and Correctness Verification Goals

Testing Focus	Equivalent Verification Focus
Each coded statement	Design verified to full detail
Each coded branch	Loop termination and predicate checks
All steps in math algorithms	Design verified to full detail
Program unit interfaces	Parameters specified for all units
Data domains/ranges	Domain/range specified in definition
Error conditions	Full detail includes error conditions

1.4.5   Impacts on Independent Testing

The Cleanroom method does not preclude testing because of software correctness verification, but rather relies on independent testing to validate that the software requirements were correctly implemented. To ensure that the testing focuses on software usage, the Cleanroom method impacts traditional testing approaches by introducing statistical techniques. This impact on the tester has proven to be one of the harder obstacles to overcome in obtaining acceptance of the Cleanroom method. At the same time, statistical test techniques have the greatest potential for significant savings in the single most expensive part of software development.

1.4.6   Impacts on Software Development Organization

The Cleanroom method separates software design and implementation from software test, as usually performed by the same people up through unit test. It has been traditional for software engineers to unit test and debug their own designs but the Cleanroom method expects experienced professionals to design software without the immediate feedback of execution. Design languages attempt to decouple the software design and its execution. The Cleanroom method takes that separation of source code design and unit test a step further by eliminating the need for unit test of designs whose correctness has been verified.

This separation provides new opportunities for concentrating on the quality of software designs. Designers who must turn over software before its execution face a new kind of external scrutiny of software quality. Designs will be expected to be ''right the first time'' and exhibit greater integrity than designs created with cut-and-try methods, where the design tends to deteriorate into the patchwork of the resulting code. Designers will be expected to work only with ''half compilers,'' which give some syntax checking and data cross-referencing support but do not support the execution of the designs.

The definition of an independent test organization which plays an active role from the start of the software development through its delivery introduces a new level of software quality control. Problems with the quality of the software design

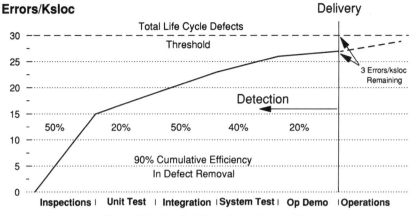

Figure 1.5   Typical Error Detection Profile

and with its eventual field reliability are exposed through the testing of the very early software increments. Putting the test organization on equal footing with the design organization, holding it responsible for the realistic validation of software capabilities, and requiring it to certify the software MTTF should result in a better check and balance on the reliability of the developed software.

1.5   CLEANROOM'S IMPACT ON THE SOFTWARE PRODUCT

Work on the Cleanroom method was originally started to improve the quality of delivered software and initial experience indicates that this purpose has been met. The quality improvement can be observed in quantitative terms from measures of software defects and in qualitative terms from improved software specifications, simpler software designs, faster error isolation and repair, and fewer reported postdelivery problems.

1.5.1   Impact on Software Defect Rates

During the past decade, software engineering practice has been introduced to improve defect prevention and detection during software development. Top-down design, structured programming, incremental release strategies, and so forth have all contributed on the defect prevention side. Formal inspections have contributed on the defect detection side and significantly reduced the testing responsibility for defect detection.

Figure 1.5 gives a typical profile [19] of how the various defect detention techniques could work together to ensure the delivery of software with reasonable quality. The profile assumes software development using the baseline capability, discussed earlier in Table 1.1, where an average of 30 errors per thousand lines of

TABLE 1.3   Trends in Software Quality

	Total Defect Rate	Postdelivery Rate

Traditional Development
  Unstructured design
  Only testing for detection
	50 to 60	5 to 10

Baseline Development
  Structured programming
  Formal inspections
	20 to 40	1 to 4

Advanced Development
  Correctness verification
  Formal specification
  Statistical testing
	0 to 20	0 to 1

software are typically introduced during the design and implementation of the software. The profile identifies the percentage of errors which, on average, could be removed by each of the defect detection techniques. In this case, inspections account for the removal of half of the 30 total and leave an average of 15 errors to be handled by the various forms of testing. The developer's unit testing would remove 20% of the remaining 15 errors and leave an average of 12 errors for the independent or nondeveloper testing (integration, system, and operational demonstration) performed prior to delivery. The total defect detection process is 90% effective, with about three errors per thousand lines of code leaking through the process, to be found by the user during software operations. The illustrated profile should be viewed as representative though different levels of effectiveness could be achieved from individual defect detection techniques and from the total detection process.

The same published data [19] also identify trends in software quality with the introduction of software engineering techniques with defect prevention and detection capability, as shown in Table 1.3. Unfortunately, the averages depicted in this table have not changed dramatically, based on more recent reports [17] on error rates realized during software development.

To get some feel for the levels of quality improvement being realized with the use of the Cleanroom method, two snapshots of reported data are provided. The second version of the COBOL S/F Structuring Facility [9] was developed in five software increments, as shown in Table 1.4, without any unit testing by the developers. Error rates were measured from the start (first software execution) through the completion of independent statistical testing and, as indicated, ranged from 1.4 to 5.7 errors/ksloc, with an average of 3.4 errors/ksloc. Table 1.4 might suggest a possible correlation between the size of the software increment and the recorded error rate, but the correlation was not seen in other versions of the software where the larger increments often exhibited the lower error rates.

TABLE 1.4   Error Rates for COBOL/SF Version 2

	Lines of Code	Errors Found	Errors/ Kloc	Errors in Field
Increment 1	4,150	6	1.4	1
Increment 2	11,125	24	2.2	2
Increment 3	10,080	23	2.3	2
Increment 4	19,543	111	5.7	4
Increment 5	7,117	15	2.1	1
Totals	52,015	179		10

179 Errors / 52,015 Loc = 3.4 errors/kloc

A similar picture of quality improvement was seen in the application of the Cleanroom method in the Software Engineering Laboratory (SEL) at NASA Goddard **[10]**. Error rates were measured from the start (again first software execution) through the completion of independent statistical testing and averaged 3.3 errors per ksloc. This compared very favorably to the six errors per ksloc which was the average experience of similar software developments in the SEL environment. To understand the basis for this dramatic improvement, the errors found during the different development steps were collected and it was discovered that some 90% were found and corrected before software execution. Table 1.5 gives this breakdown of error type by detection mechanism within the development process and provides a rationale for the high quality of the software seen in test.

In both the COBOL and SEL cases, the reported postdelivery errors were extremely small and measured in fractions of one error per ksloc.

TABLE 1.5   Effectiveness of Error Detection Mechanisms (Given in Percentages)

Mechanism	Design Reviews	Code Reading	Compilation	Testing	Total Percent by Fault
Syntax	0	4	100	0	7
Control flow	20	8	0	12	12
Interface	24	17	0	34	20
Initialization	1	5	0	12	4
Declaration	45	19	0	5	25
Data use	0	32	0	23	19
Computation	10	9	0	11	9
Displays	0	6	0	3	4
Total Percent by Mechanism	32	53	5	10	

1.5.2 Impact on Software Design Simplicity

One result experienced in all uses of the Cleanroom method was a demonstrated simplicity in the designs which were produced. This simplicity exhibited itself in many ways during the course of the software development. Designers, being faced with some combination of correctness demonstration and confirmation, releasing software prior to its first execution and having the software exposed to statistically representative test samples, tended to be conservative in their designs. The result was a software design which satisfied the requirements (no less but no more) and used only known and easy to verify design ideas (nothing complicated nor exotic). This was seen repeatedly in the verification-based inspections where 90% or more of a design could be confirmed in a straightforward manner and where design pieces whose correctness could not be proved simply were generally returned for further simplification.

The same simplicity was evident during the independent testing of the software where it could have been expected that the developer would need to execute the software to re-create error conditions and diagnose the source of failures. This turned out not to be the case [9,10] and developers were able to diagnose problems directly from their listings of software statements. This was possible because the designs were well structured and straightforward, so that diagnosing for errors turned out to be a simple analysis. This finding confirmed some of the earlier reported results from a Cleanroom experiment conducted at the University of Maryland [20]. In projects [10] where the development organization had historical data on the time spent in finding and fixing errors, the reduction in effort was like an order of magnitude with repair cycles going from weeks and months to hours and days. This reduction is particularly remarkable since the software was always under formal configuration management, which imposed procedures and regulations on the fix and repair cycle.

1.5.3 Impact on Software Development Productivity

Software quality was the underlying objective of the work in developing the Cleanroom method and some negative impact on software productivity was expected. The added care in developing correct designs and the verification emphasis on inspections were new and different kinds of work, which were originally thought to add an additional 50% to the software design. The reduction (possible elimination) in developer test effort would compensate for some but not all of the additional effort. Similarly, in the area of independent software testing, the added analysis in defining probability distributions and building statistical data bases for test sampling was originally thought to add some delta to the test effort. Since this area of statistical testing was relatively unknown, a calibration on the size of the delta effort was difficult, with an original expectation that the delta would be less than an additional 50% of testing effort.

A surprising result of the Cleanroom work is that software productivity did not go down and, in fact, increased in several cases. From the development side, design simplicity and the complete elimination of developer testing resulted in reduced effort that more than compensated for the work to integrate correctness into the software designs. In the case of the COBOL S/F and NASA SEL projects **[9,10]** the reported productivities were in the range of 750 lines of source code per labor month, which is three to four times higher than the average productivities reported in the software literature. From the testing perspective, the structure that statistical techniques provided to the sampling process and the exceptional quality of the software to be tested resulted in either the same or better productivity for performing independent software validation.

References

1. H.D. Mills, "Software of Certifiable Reliability." Unpublished correspondence. January 1980.
2. R.C. Linger, H.D. Mills, and B.I. Witt, *Structured Programming: Theory and Practice,* Addison-Wesley, 1979.
3. H.D. Mills, "Mathematical Foundations for Structured Programming," IBM TR FSC72-6012, 1972.
4. M. Dyer, "Statistical Testing: Theory and Practice." Tutorial at the 7th International Software Testing Conference, 1990.
5. W. Humphreys, *Managing the Software Process,* Addison-Wesley.
6. M.E. Fagan, "Design and Code Inspections to Reduce Errors in Program Development," *IBM Systems Journal,* Vol. 15, No. 3, 1976.
7. B. Kolkhorst, "Space Shuttle Testing and Validation," Software Real-Time Testing and Validation Conference, 1990.
8. M.W. Bush, "Formal Inspections," Proceedings of Achieving Quality Software Tutorials, 1991.
9. R.C. Linger and H.D. Mills, "Case Study in Cleanroom Software Engineering," COMPSAC'88 Proceedings, 1988.
10. S. Green, et al., "The Cleanroom Case Study in the SEL," NASA Goddard SEL Series SEL-90-002, 1990.
11. A.J. Jordano, "DSM Software Architecture and Development," IBM Technical Directions, Vol. 10, No. 3, 1984.
12. B.J. Pine II, "Design, Test and Validation of the Application System/400 Through Early User Involvement," *IBM Systems Journal,* Vol. 28, No. 3, 1989.
13. W.W. Royce, "Managing the Development of Large Software Systems," Proceedings of WESCON, 1970.
14. B.W. Boehm and P.N. Papaccio, "Understanding and Controlling Software Costs," *IEEE TSE,* Vol. 14, No. 10, 1988.
15. A. Wald, *Sequential Analysis,* Wiley, 1947.
16. R.B. Grady, "Role of Software Metrics in Managing Quality and Testing," Proceedings of the Sixth International Software Testing Conference, 1989.
17. R.G. Mays, et al., "Experiences with Defect Prevention," *IBM Systems Journal,* Vol. 29, No. 1, 1990.

18. J. McCall, "Introducing Software Metrics into Your Company," Proceedings of Achieving Quality Software Tutorials, 1991.
19. B.M. Knight, "On Software Quality and Productivity," IBM Technical Directions, No. 2, 1978.
20. R.W. Selby, V.R. Basili, and F.T. Baker, "Cleanroom Software Development: An Empirical Evaluation," University of Maryland, TR 1415, 1985.

CHAPTER 2

What Has Been the Experience with Cleanroom?

The Cleanroom method has been and continues to be used for software development in a wide variety of application areas. Generally, software development organizations start by using selected capabilities in the Cleanroom method and try additional capabilities as confidence is built. A number of projects now use 90% of the Cleanroom capabilities with statistical process control being the capability receiving the least attention.

Table 2.1 shows a profile of the use of the Cleanroom method within completed and ongoing development projects. The table reports only on projects which use the Cleanroom method, in some fashion or other, and not on all the software development projects within an organization. Since statistical quality control has not been used within any projects, a separate column was not used for reporting this point. Table 2.1 highlights that two universal characteristics of all the recorded projects are that they have a baseline design capability (i.e., mathematics-based design method and formal inspections) and that software is developed without developer testing (i.e., placed under configuration control prior to any execution).

The other components of the Cleanroom method are used to varying degrees within projects. On the development side, the functional correctness model for software verification is used to a significant degree and forces an early recognition for improved formality in specifications. The completed projects essentially used natural language specifications but most ongoing projects have introduced a formal specification method (i.e., 80% of the IBM efforts and all of the external efforts). On the independent testing side, most of the completed projects used statistical techniques and we would expect that to carry over into the ongoing projects. While projects may use statistical methods for test, they do not necessari-

TABLE 2.1 Profile of Cleanroom Method Experience (Percent Projects Using Cleanroom Component Technique)

	Formal Specification	Baseline Design	Correctness Verification	No Unit Test	Statistical Testing	MTTF Prediction	Average Total Usage
Completed IBM projects	33	100	66	100	66	50	69
Completed external projects	0	100	0	100	100	0	50
Current IBM projects	80	100	100	100	40	40	76
Current external projects	100	100	50	100	50	0	66

ly use the testing results for MTTF estimation, so lower percentages are usually seen for this Cleanroom component.

The usual project strategy is to start with the development-related features of the Cleanroom method (i.e., correctness-proving and verification-based inspections). Since the Cleanroom method is viewed as a software engineering process, using the software development components is the likely starting point. These ideas have been introduced both as a package, all at one time, and incrementally, usually starting with the more rigorous inspection process. As the benefits from the correctness ideas are realized, attention is turned to the formality of the software requirements specification, which was recognized as key to maximizing the correctness benefits. The difficulty with taking this next step is generally related to organizational considerations, since the specifiers are typically not in the software engineering organization. Rather, an engineering or analysis organization is responsible for creating specifications for hardware, software, and other aspects of systems (e.g., communications). Transferring what are regarded as software methods into these nonsoftware groups requires commitment and diplomacy.

As a parallel or a subsequent step, the statistical testing techniques are also introduced for the independent validation of the software requirements. Again this may be a difficult step, since the functional testing performed by independent test groups is viewed as a nonsoftware activity. Introducing this change in focus and sampling strategy also requires initiative, commitment, and diplomacy. Reshaping the testing strategy has generally been more difficult than introducing formality into specifications, since it requires a fundamental change in test philosophy and not just the introduction of new methods. Introducing reliability measurement is generally a subsequent step which is seen as an easy extension once the statistical test commitment has been made.

None of the above steps will be taken just for technology enrichment but need to be driven by the development organization's management which has in mind a real business objective. Since reliable software was the motivation for starting the Cleanroom research, quality and reliability should be the principal business motivators but that is seldom the case and only when customer-driven. If software reliability is accepted as the rationale, then the productivity, schedule, and cost benefits tend to accrue but this is generally a hard sell to management if their focus is on near-term profit and loss.

2.1 EARLY CLEANROOM EXPERIMENTS

Before attempting the use of the Cleanroom method in an actual project environment, experimentation was required to fully define the component techniques, to organize procedures for their use, and, where necessary, to develop support tools. Most of the experimentation was concerned with the testing and reliability prediction aspects of the method, since these were the most novel ideas which needed to be expanded into usable practice.

Correctness verification, while not part of the baseline process, was well defined in the technical literature and procedures for its use had been formulated as part of the introduction of the earlier software engineering program [1]. In this case, there was more need to try these techniques on real problems than to continue experimentation and research. At the time work was getting started on Cleanroom (early 1980s), formal specifications were still a research subject and no particular approach was surfacing as a preferred technique. Again no experimentation was conducted and natural language specifications were accepted as the norm for the early Cleanroom work.

Three experiments were performed which addressed the feasibility of the statistical test concept, the effectiveness of the statistical method in terms of software failure discovery, and the integration of the component techniques into a software development method. While the idea of driving functional testing from probability distributions sounded plausible, the mechanics of how this would work for problems of reasonable and high complexity needed further elaboration and substantiation. Similarly, while we might show its feasibility, there was still a concern on the error detection effectiveness of the statistical test techniques. Finally, since the Cleanroom method involved many component parts (techniques) which had never been integrated, there was also the question of how things tied together and what glue was needed to have a development method with integrity.

2.1.1 Statistical Testing Feasibility Experiment

To demonstrate feasibility, the testing of the software for the operator command function in a Sonar processing system under development within IBM was selected. The testing, which had been planned to be performed by an independent verification and validation (IVV) group within the software organization, was viewed as sufficiently complex to provide a convincing checkout of the statistical techniques. The objectives of the experiment were to demonstrate that meaningful test procedures (cases) could be generated from probability distributions, that software IVV testing could be performed with the generated test samples, and that the software IVV test goals for error detection and requirements validation could be achieved.

The software was to be tested over a four-month period and was scheduled for delivery from the development organization in three increments during that period. Based on the complexity of the software, the allocated test time, and number of test personnel, a sample of 200 test cases was identified as necessary to drive the testing and was split approximately into $\frac{1}{4}$, $\frac{1}{4}$, and $\frac{1}{2}$ to address the three increments.

To create the test cases, a support tool was written that addressed the definition of the statistics on the inputs which drove the software processing of the Sonar operator commands and which would generate test cases in the proper input formats for the Sonar software. The tool permitted the definition of input formats, input contents, and probabilities defining the likelihoods of input appearances during the software execution in the actual Sonar environment. The tool was a list processor that traversed the hierarchy of input descriptions within a data base and

TABLE 2.2 Comparison of Error Detection Effectiveness

	Errors Seeded	Conventional		Statistical	
		Seeded Found	New Errors	Seeded Found	New Errors
Interfail time estimator	9	7	6	7	5
Panel driven data set selection	27	15	18	14	16
Parse table generator	24	16	0	19	0

that relied on a random number generator to control the selection of a particular input with particular data content.

The results from this experiment were that probability distributions could be developed to describe the Sonar operator command application, that realistic and representative test cases could be automatically generated from the distributional information, and that the tests could be effectively used in validating the requirements. While the testers were not particularly comfortable with relying solely on the statistically generated test cases, these represented 70% (200 of 285 cases) of the total tests which were run. The remaining 30% were a combination of tests for a regression test bucket which contained a majority of statistically generated cases for handling various illegal input conditions that were tester-defined but questionable from an operational perspective and for validating requirements which had not been addressed in the statistical samples.

2.1.2 Statistical Testing Effectiveness Experiment

To demonstrate the effectiveness of the statistical approach as a testing method, a parallel testing experiment was conducted. Three distinct software programs were selected which were each about 2,000 lines of code and which had been previously released as well-tested programs. For each program, one tester was asked to perform functional testing using conventional test approaches and a second was asked to do the same using the statistical approach.

To establish some control over this experiment, each program was seeded [2] with a set of errors, which were not disclosed to the testers. When all or most of the seeded errors within a program were found, the testing for that program was terminated. This approach helped to ensure that sufficient but not excessive testing would be conducted in each case. Generally, some 50 cases were executed for each of the test approaches in testing each program, which was considered to provide reasonable functional coverage of the 2,000 lines of code in each case.

The results as seen in Table 2.2 indicate that the statistical and conventional techniques were comparable in their error detection capabilities. In two of the cases, the testing from the experiment uncovered new real errors in the software which had been released as well-tested. The same errors in a program (both real and seeded) were generally found by each technique though several errors were uniquely found by one but not the other technique. This difference in error detection was attributed to the particular validation focus taken by the tester using the conventional approach or to operational focus defined into the probability distributions for the statistical approach.

2.1.3 Cleanroom Experiment Conducted by the University of Maryland

The first attempt at using the Cleanroom method for software development was an experiment [3] conducted by the Computer Science Department at the University of Maryland. The software development was a class exercise defined for a senior level elective course on formal methods for software design and addressed the development of a hypothetical Electronic Message System for the University's computer science department. Fifteen three-person teams separately developed versions of the software with final products ranging from 800 to 2,300 source lines of code. Ten of the teams used the Cleanroom method and the other five teams used more traditional development methods. The Cleanroom teams used a syntax checker without automated type checking across module boundaries but did not execute their programs. All testing was performed by a third party and used statistical techniques. The other five non-Cleanroom teams used a variety of programming techniques (e.g., modular design, program design languages, functional testing, and design reviews) and did execute their programs.

The teams were given six weeks to develop the application with four delivery dates scheduled for completion of high level design, low level design, code, and documentation. The class was composed mostly of part-time graduate students who were working as software developers with various industrial organizations and had an average of 1.5 years of professional experience. They were therefore accustomed to working in nonacademic development environments and could provide useful results on the applicability of the Cleanroom method for software development.

This experiment demonstrated that the Cleanroom method could be used to develop the application with 60% of the teams able to deliver more than 90% of the specified requirements. The Cleanroom teams were able to satisfy the specified requirement more completely than the non-Cleanroom teams and were more successful in executing the statistically generated test cases. All of the Cleanroom teams met the scheduled product deliveries, whereas only 40% of the non-Cleanroom teams were able to achieve on-schedule deliveries. The code developed by the Cleanroom teams generally had more commentary, was less complex (based on a control flow metric), had more procedure calls and IF statements but less CASE and loop statements, and used a smaller number of data variable references.

The experiment also demonstrated that the apparent psychological obstacles to Cleanroom could be overcome. These obstacles had been thought to include the elimination of developer testing, the insistence on correctness verification, and the third-party testing with statistically generated samples. An analysis of the results indicated that the quality of the Cleanroom-developed code came from a combination of added design care, reliance on simple (conservative) design ideas, and the effective use of correctness verification. Though close to 90% of the Cleanroom developers indicated that they missed the satisfaction of executing and testing their own code, this did not impact the overall software quality and completeness. More than 80% of these Cleanroom developers stated that they would use the Cleanroom method in their subsequent work. The results from this University experiment tended to substantiate the Cleanroom method as a viable software development approach and to confirm the position that conventional developer testing could be replaced with software verification practice.

2.2 SOFTWARE DEVELOPMENT EXPERIENCE

Once the experimentation was completed, use of the Cleanroom method for software application development was initiated and results from two of these efforts have been discussed in the technical literature. A number of other application developments have been completed and/or are in process. These unpublished developments address applications areas such as the run-time services for operating systems, data base management applications, environments for controlling software testing, and various avionics applications.

The first published results on the use of the Cleanroom method was for the COBOL Structuring Facility (COBOL/SF) [4] which is an IBM Program Product that automatically translates unstructured COBOL programs into a structured form. It is comparable in function and complexity to a COBOL compiler and uses function theoretic technology to perform the structuring analysis. The objective of this program product is to assist data processing organizations in the maintenance of COBOL programs by reducing the complexity of the existing COBOL code and by increasing its readability for understanding the encoded program logic.

This product was developed over several years, starting with a prototype capability and moving through two initial product versions to the current version #2 of the program product. The prototype and earlier versions provided structuring capability exclusively for the COBOL II language, defined for the IBM VS operating system. The current version #2 system provides the structuring capability for the earlier OS/VS COBOL language which doesn't contain the structured programming features of the COBOL II language but is more widely used across application areas. The current product fully automates the structuring analysis, generates structure charts to map the translated program hierarchy, and provides software complexity [5] and modularity analyses. The version #2 product is composed of some 52,000 lines of new PL/I source code and an additional 28,000 lines of PL/I code which was reused from the earlier versions.

The current version #2 of COBOL/SF was developed top-down in five increments, using the formal specification, functional verification, and statistical test components of the Cleanroom method. The development team performed no unit testing of the software but was able to achieve significant product quality without impacting the project's productivity and schedule goals. The product's initial field test involved the structuring of some half million lines of COBOL code packaged in some 300 application programs and was completed with only ten errors discovered within the program product. These were all trivial errors for which diagnosis and repair could be accomplished in a matter of hours, which further attests to the effectiveness of the Cleanroom method in creating straightforward software designs.

The second published results on the use of the Cleanroom method were for an application development [6] in the Software Engineering Laboratory SEL, at the NASA Goddard Space Flight Center. This laboratory, in addition to supporting the Goddard space missions, is chartered to study and manage the introduction into NASA of new software engineering technologies. The Cleanroom method was selected for study, based on its potential for enhancing the quality of the software used in space applications and for reducing the time and effort spent in software test and rework. The study objective was to quantify the impact on software quality when the Cleanroom method was applied to problems in the SEL environment.

The software selected for development within this Cleanroom study was the Coarse/Fine Attitude Determination Subsystem (CFADS) of the Attitude Ground Support System (AGSS) for the Upper Atmosphere Research Satellite. The CFADS software represented about 12% of the software within the AGSS support system and was estimated at some 22,000 lines of FORTRAN source statements. The final product size was 34,000 lines of FORTRAN and graphics interface code where the latter graphics code (some 3,000 lines) was not developed with the Cleanroom method.

The 31,000 lines of the CFADS software was developed top-down with the Cleanroom method and was organized into six functional increments. The product was defined by a rigorous but not formal software specification. The software specification was prepared in natural language by a systems engineering group within the Goddard organization but the software developers spent a significant amount of time rigorously analyzing these requirements and resolving ambiguities, inconsistencies, and errors. The development team did not perform any unit test of the software and was also able to deliver software with significantly higher quality than seen in comparable SEL projects. The key quality indicators were that 90% of the software errors were detected prior to any software execution and that the detected error rate during statistical testing was 3.3 errors per ksloc. The early detection of most errors surpassed previous results with the use of inspection methods within the SEL and the error rate during test was half the SEL average of six errors per ksloc. These results satisfied the original intent of the study and motivated the SEL management to conduct additional and expanded development with the Cleanroom method which is currently ongoing.

Other software developments which have not published their results are, in fact, experiencing the same type of benefits from using the Cleanroom method. Product quality is measurably higher at delivery and the products are experiencing few, if any, failures in the field. The software specifications are generally more accurate and complete, either by design or through a rigorous analysis and resolution of deficiencies. Software designs are simple, which results in easier diagnosis and repair of errors detected during inspections and validation tests. Though counter-intuitive, this is usually accomplished with greater productivity and shorter schedule than would be expected using conventional development methods.

2.3 WHAT LESSONS WERE LEARNED?

Based on the early experiments and the subsequent use of the Cleanroom method for software development, many things were learned about the method, as it was defined, about its use in different development environments and about the support (training, consultation, and tools) needed to ensure its successful introduction into a development environment. *The most important thing learned was that the Cleanroom method works, results in software with significantly higher quality, and increases the productivity of the people using the method.*

Other important questions about the different components in the Cleanroom method were also answered. The functional correctness model for software verification was introduced and effectively used within the software development process. The effectiveness of verification-based inspections demonstrated that developer testing at the unit and module levels was no longer a necessary step in the software development process. In all Cleanroom cases, developer testing was eliminated and the absence of developer testing is the one universal characteristic of these projects. Statistical-based testing was defined for performing requirements validation within the Cleanroom method and was also shown to be practical across all application areas. Software reliability projections, in terms of an estimate of the software's MTTF, were defined and used data on the times between successive software failures as recorded during the statistical testing.

2.3.1 About the Cleanroom Method

The most important lesson was that the Cleanroom method is a viable method for software development. The notion that the concept was too theoretical for practical application was overcome by defining a process and supporting methods for achieving the Cleanroom objectives. The mathematical ideas for correctness verification, statistical testing, and software reliability projection were packaged into processes that were usable by a broad cross section of the software engineering population. The introduction of these processes required work on the part of the software developers and testers, to learn the concepts and modify their existing (and reasonably successful) approaches to development and test. This added work has turned out to be worth the effort, based on the successes in the initial developments and the continued use of the Cleanroom method by these projects for follow-on software developments.

A key point about the Cleanroom method is that it does not have to be used in total but is rich enough to allow choices in the use or nonuse of components. To simplify the Cleanroom introduction, methods that are familiar to a development organization and satisfy the intent of a particular Cleanroom component are acceptable for use. As shown in the Cleanroom experience profile (Table 2.1), there has been considerable variation in which component techniques are used within a particular development project. The reluctance to try the total Cleanroom method in the first development reflects a reasonable but conservative approach to technology transfer. In the initial use, the software engineering methods for design and implementation are readily adopted, since it is software that is to be developed. The demands of correctness verification highlight the need for formal software specifications, which tends to be the next logical choice as seen in its reoccurring use within the current Cleanroom projects.

Movement into statistical testing and reliability measurement needs motivation and promotion from outside of software engineering within a development project. This usually comes from a need to execute smaller numbers of tests to reduce project costs while maintaining the required levels of confidence in the thoroughness of requirements validation. Working with statistically generated test samples is the preferred solution to these two conflicting project goals. Software reliability has not received enough industry attention to stimulate its use within the Cleanroom method but that could be changing in the 1990s as software quality becomes the overriding customer demand.

In the Cleanroom experience, several different methods have been employed for software design, implementation, and inspection, which have not detracted from the Cleanroom method nor the quality and productivity results that were achieved. The point is that the selected methods provided an acceptable baseline capability and/or satisfied the Cleanroom requirements for structured programming-based and correctness-focused methods. Which design or programming language is used, what schedule and procedure for formal inspections is used, or which library system and procedures are used for configuration management are not the critical discriminators in the effective use of the Cleanroom method. There are many candidate methods, and if the basis for selection is mathematical underpinning and rigor, then many methods may be acceptable. The quality results for the PL/I-developed COBOL/SF product [4] were significant but so were the quality results for the FORTRAN-developed CFADS software [6].

The use of the Cleanroom method does not occur without some investment in terms of people training and expert consultation during start-up. The underlying Cleanroom technical ideas (e.g., formal specification, functional verification, statistical testing, and software reliability) are not trivial concepts that can be picked up by use. Formal instruction in the theory and practice of these ideas is required and technical assistance in the application of these ideas to a particular real-world problem is also required. The extent of this investment is dependent on what parts of the Cleanroom method are to be employed, which is another reason for an incremental introduction of the method. There is limited educational and consultation support available at this time but that should grow as Cleanroom exposure and use expand.

2.3.2   About Software Specification and Design

Formality in the software specification is universally identified as critical to the development of quality software with the Cleanroom method. This is either addressed head-on by the use of formal methods in developing the specifications, which is the direction within current developments, or achieved after the fact by the constant nagging of the specifier by the designer for clarification and elaboration of specification contents. From completed projects [6] which used natural language specifications, there is recognition that the completeness and accuracy of these specifications after the Cleanroom design effort were far superior than seen in the specifications for similar projects within non-cleanroom development environments.

The Cleanroom design method with a stepwise specification-design-verification regimen can be learned and used by the typical software engineer to develop quality software. The prevalent misapprehension about the usability of correctness verification by the average software engineer did not present an obstacle to its use in Cleanroom design. Based on current experience, verification was accomplished either through the use of informal proofs based on the functional correctness method [7] or through the rigorous and frequent application of formal inspection practice [8]. The constant result was that prior to any software execution some 90% of the total errors had been detected and removed, which by itself dramatically improves software quality. In those cases where functional correctness methods were used extensively, the number of total errors was also dramatically reduced further enhancing the software quality.

Designs developed with the Cleanroom method exhibit characteristics that account for their software quality. The most significant is the logical simplicity seen in the designs and directly attributable to the verification step in the design refinement. Logically complex and convoluted designs tax the human ability to perform correctness proofs and are forced into redesign to pass the verification step. This design simplicity is reported in all uses of the Cleanroom method and shows itself in the easy diagnosis and repair of errors that are detected during the subsequent testing step.

An analysis of problem closure rates was conducted at one IBM facility where the Cleanroom method was used to determine if design simplicity was reflected in faster closure rates. Closure rate is defined as the average number of days that elapse between finding an error and validating the correctness of a fix to the problem. The time accounts for diagnosing the problem symptoms, designing a fix, testing the fix, and verifying that the fix can be accepted. Since Cleanroom software is placed under formal configuration-control before any execution, its closure rates could be compared with other configuration-controlled software. As can be seen from Table 2.3, the closure rates for projects which used the Cleanroom method for some part of the software development were somewhere between 50% and 80% smaller than the average rates for similar projects using conventional development methods. To ensure that Cleanroom was a major contributor to this drop in closure rate, the rates for the Cleanroom-specific software, as opposed to

TABLE 2.3 Problem Closure Rate Analysis

Project	Project Averages	Cleanroom-Specific Averages
Non-Cleanroom		
Project 1	39.2	
Project 2	62.7	
Cleanroom		
Project 1	11.6	4.7
Project 2	19.6	10.9

the total project software, were also examined. This showed that the closure rates for the Cleanroom-specific software were 55% and 60% smaller than the average rates for all of the project's software. The conclusion from this study was that the Cleanroom methods tended to improve problem closure rates significantly and that the improvement tended to result primarily from the simplicity of Cleanroom designs.

The other significant change in the design content is the attention paid to the explicit specification of the requirements or functions to be addressed and of the problem data to be manipulated in each step of the design. The statement of function is carried throughout the whole design and documented in the form of commentary for groups of design statements. The attention to data requirements [9] is seen through the use of abstraction and encapsulation, which raise the consideration of data to levels appropriate for the problem statement and localize the manipulation of that data into self-contained parts of the design. This is a far cry from the current reliance on programming language descriptions of the problem data and introducing these descriptions into the program logic as afterthoughts.

2.3.3 About Software Implementation

The key point about the implementation step in the Cleanroom method is that developer testing of the software is not a necessary nor desirable step in the development. The absence of developer testing to perform structural tests [4,6] on the software was another constant characteristic of the Cleanroom experience. Since the same concerns addressed in correctness verification are also the focus of structural test, it became obvious to the Cleanroom developers that verified software did not require unit and string testing. The 90% error detection levels prior to software execution were the keys to making that point obvious.

The other change in the implementation step that was adopted in every case was the placing of software under formal configuration management prior to any execution. The apprehension on this point went away when the effectiveness of the design and development process was recognized for minimizing the total number of errors and for removing most errors prior to this step. Even the unwanted publicity from the formal control about trivial developer mistakes was endured and inspired greater care in development.

2.3.4 About Software Test and MTTF

Even though some form of sampling is required in the functional testing of software with any reasonable complexity, random sampling is not an immediately appealing technique. When the same random sampling is embodied in a statistically defined testing approach, it has more appeal and can be accepted as a viable validation technique. This is the case in the Cleanroom testing strategy where probability had to be introduced into the test process so that a sound basis could be formulated for making statistical inference about the software MTTF. Defining the probability distributions for the selection of the software functions in the user environment and for the selection of the data values which would be input to the software is the foundation. Randomly selecting test samples provides to the validation process a representative picture of how the software functions will be executed in the user environment and with what input data.

The basis in statistics introduces more objectivity, realism, and usage focus into sampling needed for the functional testing. The reliance on probability distributions ensures the validation of a requirement with the same vigor (coverage) as that requirement's role in the software execution. The insistence on random sampling ensures the selection of those software inputs that are most likely to trigger the more probable software failures, which gives a testing focus not found in other sampling approaches.

2.3.5 About Staff Organizational Structure

The Cleanroom experience made it clear that software development must be a team effort with each team member committed to perform a role in the team. The test and the development groups though performing distinct functions must be in frequent communication on subjects such as specification changes and required diagnostic data for requirements validation. Organizing formal configuration control and the procedures for software transfer between the groups requires a particularly well-coordinated effort.

The Cleanroom approach did force one shift in configuration management responsibilities. Generally, configuration control is handled by maintaining controlled libraries of the source code for a product on the host machine in which the product executes. Since developers are not permitted to execute the software in the Cleanroom method, separate controlled libraries are needed for the developers, which are typically not housed on the host machine. This presented the test organization with a new configuration management role which, while requiring minimal extra work, did require careful procedures to ensure consistency between the two libraries.

Since the test organization is the first group to execute the software, most Cleanroom projects used a preliminary or build-up test approach to ease the transfer of code from the developers to the testers. These tests were run primarily to ensure that all the parts of a release were transferred, that the appropriate run-time libraries (usually supplied with the language compiler) were available, and that the released code would, at least, cycle. These tests have been invaluable for getting the released software ready for functional testing and have, typically, required only a day or two of the developer's and tester's time.

In terms of the development organization, a real benefit was shown from adopting strict software design and coding standards and from enforcing the use of the standards by all project personnel. Ideally, the standards should be defined before starting a project to reduce debate over personal preferences; it seems that the actual standards are not as important as their consistent application by all project participants.

2.4   WERE THE UNDERLYING CONCERNS ADDRESSED?

There have been concerns expressed on the feasibility of using the Cleanroom method for software development. A fairly typical first reaction is that the Cleanroom method is *too theoretical and too radical* for use in real software development. This may have resulted from a misconception of what the Cleanroom method is and resolving the misconception is the principal motivation for this book. Some people think that Cleanroom simply means that no unit testing is required or allowed by software developers because of an increased focus on software inspection. Others think that Cleanroom centers on structured specifications, statistical testing, testing based on software MTTF, or some combination of these. Few understand that the scope of the Cleanroom method addresses the full range of system development, impacts the engineering, software, and test disciplines, and is not just another software development technique.

The practical results obtained by different development groups working on a variety of applications tend to discount the theoretical charge, since most of the Cleanroom experience has been with software which is sold commercially or embedded in operational application systems. The people involved in these developments were a cross section of the software engineering population and were able to apply the Cleanroom method, totally or in part, after a brief but intensive training program.

There are several seemingly radical ideas with the Cleanroom method, such as routine correctness verification, eliminating developer unit testing, and using a statistical approach to functional testing. Again there are practical results which indicate that these ideas can be effectively used but do reshape the software development process. Since the reported trend in Cleanroom experience is toward increased product quality and developer productivity, the reshaped process may be the correct direction for future software development.

Whenever a negative assessment of the overall method is given, there are also other concerns expressed about each of the new ideas embodied in the Cleanroom method. The first is the typical claim that correctness verification is *too mathematical and not usable in an environment of changing requirements.* The initial requirements specifications for most software applications are rarely correct or stable and generally subject to continuous change during the development life cycle. Attempting the verification of software designs with a shifting specification base does not seem workable or effective.

The experience on requirements stability is that, faced with the verification objective, a more complete requirements analysis is performed and this early emphasis increases both the developer's and tester's understanding of the problem domain. Ideally, the software specification should be constructed with a formal method that ensures completeness and accuracy. If this approach can not be taken, then the method used in the NASA SEL development [6] should be adopted. In this case, the potential for an unstable requirements specification was avoided through a team review process, which forced detailed design documentation. Maintaining accurate requirements elaboration with embedded code commentary in the later development steps resulted in a development which was less prone to the effect of specification changes.

The functional approach to verification, particularly in its definition of informal proofs, is aimed at introducing mathematical reasoning and not mathematical notation into the verification process. The verification-based inspection is likewise organized to hide the mathematics of a proof construction and to only involve the designer and inspector in focusing on correctness assertions about specific parts of the design. Existing Cleanroom experience indicates that formal proofs resplendent with mathematical notation, if used, involve well less than 1% of a design and are typically limited to a specific aspect of the design kernel (e.g., funds transfer in a banking application).

The second claim about the new ideas is that *developer unit testing is an essential step in software development and can not be eliminated.* Unit testing is seen as an effective method for verifying functionality, particularly for computationally intensive software, in a closed environment. The isolation of errors when the software has been integrated with the other parts of the product is viewed as difficult and error prone.

The one universal idea adopted by all projects using the Cleanroom method was to drop developer testing and rely on correctness verification or rigorous formal inspections. This approach works because of the similarity in the technical focus between developer testing and software inspections or verifications [10], as discussed in Chapter 6. The reported results [6] were that more than 90% of the software errors were detected and removed through this approach, which resulted in better quality software than generally available with the use of developer testing. With this significant detection capability, an additional concern also did not materialize on the number of problem reports which would be reported for the configuration-managed software, impacting the effectiveness of the control procedures.

The third claim that *randomized testing was neither a cost effective method nor could it provide adequate requirements coverage* did not materialize nor was it a technically accurate assessment of the test strategy. The statistical test strategy, while it uses random sampling, is controlled through probability distributions depicting representative usage and is a very systematic approach to requirements validation. If anything, the statistical approach introduces objectivity and rigor into the creation of test material for requirements validation. In the long run, this sampling technique should provide software testing with the same data reductions experienced by polling strategies—small samples can be used for inferences on large populations. This could result in a testing strategy in which a minimum sized test sample would offer the optimum approach to requirements coverage. This potential for reducing the amount of testing without diminishing the confidence in the quality of the requirements validation is the financial benefit from a statistical approach.

The fourth concern is a *distrust in the concept of a software MTTF and in its role in the software development process.* The need for a software reliability measure that addresses the software user's interest is becoming apparent as software plays a more dominant role in systems. The approach based on input variability and failure due to design flaws is technically defendable and leads to realistic results. The importance of a software MTTF statistic to software development has been demonstrated **[11]** and should increase as more experience is gathered.

References

1. M. Dyer, et al., "The Management of Software Engineering," *IBM Systems Journal,* Vol. 19, 1980.
2. H.D. Mills, "On the Statistical Validation of Computer Programs," IBM FSD Unpublished Report, 1970.
3. R.W. Selby, V.R. Basili, and F.T. Baker, "Cleanroom Software Development: An Empirical Evaluation," University of Maryland, TR 1415, 1985.
4. R.C. Linger and H.D. Mills, "Case Study in Cleanroom Software Engineering," COMPSAC'88 Proceedings, 1988.
5. T.J. McCabe, "A Complexity Measure," *IEEE TSE,* Vol. 2, 1976.
6. S. Green, et al., "The Cleanroom Case Study in the SEL," NASA Goddard SEL Series SEL-90-002.
7. M. Dyer and A. Kouchakdjian, "Correctness Verification," *Information and Software Technology,* Vol. 32, 1990.
8. M.E. Fagan, "Design and Code Inspections," *IBM Systems Journal,* Vol. 17, 1978.
9. H.D. Mills and R.C. Linger, "Data Structured Programming," *IEEE TSE,* Vol. 12, No. 2, 1986.
10. M. Dyer, "A Formal Approach to Software Error Removal," *Journal of Systems and Software,* No. 7, 1987.
11. J.D. Musa, A. Iannino, and K. Okumoto, *Software Reliability: Measurement, Prediction, Application,* McGraw-Hill, 1987.

CHAPTER 3

How to Get Started with Cleanroom

Introducing a software development method into an existing development environment is not easy and, in the case of the Cleanroom method, is further complicated because it also encroaches on the software specifier's and software tester's areas of responsibility. As a start, a clearly stated set of objectives must be defined which identify where and how much of the Cleanroom method is to be tried and which project and/or organization goals are to be addressed. A commitment must be made to these objectives by the project management, the project staff, and, where appropriate, the organization management. Without these commitments, successful use of the Cleanroom method and realization of its quality and productivity benefits would be in doubt.

When the objectives have been defined, the planning for a particular software development can be started. This entails completing Cleanroom training requirements, identifying a tailored version of the Cleanroom method to fit the particular development environment, and organizing checkpoints for re-evaluating decisions on technology selections. The training ensures that the project team has a consistent level of understanding to plan the integration of the Cleanroom ideas into their existing development environment and to implement the problem solution accordingly. The successful Cleanroom project integrates the ideas into its environment and does not try to revolutionize its development process. The successful Cleanroom project also gives itself ample opportunity to change its process, as it gains experience, rather than stick with ideas which are failing for any number of reasons within the particular project environment.

3.1 CLEANROOM INTRODUCTION STRATEGY

Since the Cleanroom method touches on the total life cycle for software develop-ment and identifies separate techniques to address each step in the life cycle, the introduction of Cleanroom requires careful planning. The organizational goals or objectives to be achieved with the use of the Cleanroom method must be clearly spelled out, since they will bound the effort. The underlying goal of the Cleanroom method is the development of high-quality software which can be delivered with a certified reliability.

The organizational goals can be quite different. They can span from simple experimentation from which to generate recommendations on the component software and testing techniques, to the mandated use of the total Cleanroom method to ensure software development under statistical quality control. These extreme positions reflect significantly different roles for the Cleanroom method within a development organization. They require significantly different levels of management, people, and support commitment; different levels of organizational investment in training and consultation with Cleanroom experts; and different ex-pectations from the organization on product quality and developer productivity gains. The following guidelines are offered for developing an organizational strategy and for identifying the steps necessary for the successful implementation of that strategy.

3.1.1 Baseline Development Capability

The starting position for introducing the Cleanroom method into an organization is that the organization currently use systematic techniques for software design and development. At a minimum, the techniques should support a top-down and in-cremental development approach, should permit a stepwise elaboration of the software design, and should embody a design method and notation that takes ad-vantage of ideas and constructs from structured programming theory. If this baseline practice is not in place, then an appropriate software design and develop-ment practice must be defined and introduced as part of the Cleanroom introduc-tion. Without the baseline practice, the use of the component techniques within the Cleanroom method should not be attempted.

Top-down development is a strategy for organizing and ordering the software development to allow for a continuous integration of the software parts, as developed, and to control the integration by early definition of the interfaces between the software parts. A software development characterized as top down infers a knowledge of how the software should look and operate not only in its final form but also at each stage of its development. Top down demands a well thought-out construction strategy, requiring significant analysis to determine the proper starting points (tops) for development, to organize the software parts and their interfacing into a software architecture, and to structure the flow of the software parts from design through implementation to integration into the evolving software product.

Incremental development defines a stepwise approach to constructing software, which supports the top-down development strategy. It involves the definition of the connected software parts, their staggered implementation on a well-defined schedule, and their orderly inclusion with other parts to build up the software product. In theory, incremental development could be accomplished through the continuous delivery and integration of small code fragments, but a more managed approach is normally adopted. The content of the software parts and the timing of their release in a software increment are carefully planned to deliver significant increases in software capability with each increment. With small- to medium-sized software (10 to 50 Kslocs), six or less increments are typically planned, which allows for adding reasonably sized packets of code and offers enough structure for an orderly buildup in software capability. For larger-sized products (greater than 50 Kslocs), the planned number of incremental steps is still kept reasonably small (in the order of a dozen) with more code delivered in each increment and a generally longer integration period planned for each increment.

To fit within the top-down incremental development strategy, software design and implementation should also be performed as a stepwise refinement of the software requirements. The refinement procedure must allow a consideration of the total set of requirements at each step, while permitting a designer to concentrate on the details of some specific requirement. This helps to ensure that a designer does not lose sight of the total requirements picture and can understand if and how all requirements are satisfied at the current design step (i.e., as some composite of design and unrefined requirements). Structured programming theory supports this stepwise refinement approach, so that any implementation method rooted in this theory is acceptable for Cleanroom development.

To characterize an acceptable design method, it should support the specification of the software requirement, provide a language for describing the design and its operating behavior, and allow for the introduction of a formal mechanism for demonstrating design correctness against the specification. To guard against the complexity of software details overwhelming the demonstration of design correctness, the concept of abstraction must be demanded and supported. This allows the separation of design details and the deferral of their consideration until the essential problem data and its kernel processing is understood and organized into the design structure.

The specification methods should be based in mathematics to allow precise reasoning about the structure and interaction of the software architecture and its component parts. Appropriate mathematical structures which have been used in the specification of software systems and software parts include formal grammars, propositional logic, predicate calculus, and so forth. Generally, different parts of a software system require different specification techniques and the exclusive use of a given technique may not be appropriate. A technique such as the box structures of data abstractions [1] would be a natural approach to specifying behavior at the software system and subsystem levels. Within the box structure specifications, formal grammars, set theoretic techniques, and the like could then be applied to precisely elaborate the detailed specifications on functional logic and data manipulation.

The design method should have a foundation in mathematics (i.e., structured programming theory), which allows the equating of software constructs (e.g., programs) to mathematical objects (e.g., functions) and which provides rules and language for reasoning about these software constructs. Software designs are developed through a systematic decomposition of a specification into the appropriate set of constructs, applying the mathematics-based rules rather than heuristic invention. Though the two processes might result in a design, the design from a systematic approach would be the only one of the two whose correctness could be verified.

3.2   CLEANROOM PROJECT PLANNING

With the decision to use the Cleanroom method comes a requirement for significant upfront planning to ensure a successful software development and a realization of the tangible Cleanroom benefits. This planning must address the three areas of establishing a consistent level of understanding within the project team on the Cleanroom method, of deciding the use(s) of the method on the project, and of establishing schedule checkpoints for assessing the Cleanroom transfer. Careful attention to this planning helps ensure successful introduction of the method and, more important, successful development of quality software.

Like any project with software development, the Cleanroom planning requires the elaboration of an incremental approach to the software development and the estimation of the resources to implement the approach. As a basis for resource estimation, the number, size, and complexity of the functional increments required in the problem solution must be characterized. The definition and organization of the functional increments should be driven by a strategy for delivering functional capability to the customer in a timely and usage-effective way. This strategy may not always be optimum for implementation but is generally optimum for customer acceptance and satisfaction. In addition to the design and implementation effort required for each increment, the planning must also address the verification-based inspection and test preparation efforts, which are activities unique to the Cleanroom method.

Resource estimation for the Cleanroom method is different than estimation for traditional development methods. The most pronounced change is the preponderance of effort required at the front end of the development, due to the preparation of formal requirements specifications, the more careful and intense design effort, and the novel preparation of a test data base. The specification effort must account for the additional effort in elaborating and validating requirements with some formal method. This type of activity is generally not typical for specifications that are usually prepared with natural language and to an acceptable level of completeness, which is finalized as part of the design process. The level of specification completeness at initial delivery is generally a function of schedule and developer's familiarity with the application. As a rule, less specification is generally tolerated for more familiar applications.

The design effort must allow for the software verification performed by the designer during construction of the design and for the extensive verification-based inspections to confirm the design correctness. These are Cleanroom activities that are not found in conventional development efforts, and require more designer and inspector time and effort. To compensate for this front-end effort, the estimate for developer testing effort, usually fairly substantial, can be minimized in the Cleanroom case. Generally, Cleanroom developer testing would be limited to exercising support software for capability understanding, to prototyping novel solution algorithms for feasibility analysis, and to "bring-up" execution for operability demonstration at delivery to independent test.

The independent test effort must accommodate earlier and more sustained test involvement in the software development process. The use of the statistical test strategy requires significant analysis of the planned operational usage of the software to define representative probability distributions and the definition and creation of a data base to support test sample generation. The certification of software reliability requires the definition of a measurement procedure for software MTTF, the acquisition of the necessary statistical models, and the implementation of a control procedure for using software MTTF for process correction. These are all Cleanroom-unique activities that require effort that is commonly not considered with conventional development techniques. A partial compensation for this additional effort can be realized in the elimination of the tester's definition of tests, which are automatically generated from the statistical test data base in the Cleanroom method.

As with conventional development methods, the schedule, staffing, and support (i.e., computer, test facility, and so on) resources must be defined for the software increments and the total project. The resource profile for a Cleanroom project is significantly different from a project using conventional methods with substantial skewing toward the front end of the project. The historical records maintained by a development organization on projects which used conventional methods would be of limited use in this estimation process. The productivity data discussed in this book and the cited references on completed Cleanroom projects would be more helpful, until a comparable set of historical records on Cleanroom projects was organized by an organization.

3.2.1 Training in the Cleanroom Method

Training in the Cleanroom method is critical so that the project team understands and appreciates the total Cleanroom method (i.e., the specifics on each component techniques and the role(s) of each technique in developing software with certified reliability). This is necessary, primarily, so that the team has the depth of technical knowledge to apply the techniques with conviction and effectiveness. The training is also prerequisite for the team's assessment and decision on using some but not all of the Cleanroom method, because of the problem characteristics or development environment. This training is best conducted in two steps: formal instruction on the technical ideas followed by hands-on experience in applying those ideas to the project's particular problem.

The Cleanroom techniques to be covered in this training should include formal methods for software requirements specification, structured programming practice, the functional correctness model, statistical test methods, software reliability measurement, and statistical process control. This is a reasonably broad spectrum of technical topics and might address methods that are currently practiced within a development organization. In that case, understanding their Cleanroom-specific definition and role(s) would be easier to grasp and making the decision on their project role would be greatly simplified.

For each of the selected techniques, additional in-depth training on the theory and practice should be given. The point of this in-depth training is to ensure that the selected technique is understood and can be applied by the entire project team. In this process, aspects of a particular technique might have to be modified to fit the particular environment (e.g., changes in design constructs to fit a particular programming language). Accommodations might also be required to conform to organizational or contractual constraints (e.g., standards on specification contents). In general, the details, on which aspects of a given technique should become practice (assuming no loss of the kernel idea), tend to be less significant than the early establishment and consistent application of the practice. This should eliminate the endless debate on personal preferences within the team and should ensure a more effective use of the technique.

However, some of the Cleanroom techniques might be viewed as beyond the scope of the project definition or the abilities of the project team. In that case, serious consideration should be given to deferring the introduction of those techniques until a later project or phase of the current development. This examination should consider the impacts on the existing business and organizational practice and the benefits or drawbacks with the use of the particular technique. To make a sensible judgment on the exclusion of a particular Cleanroom technique, the contribution of the technique and the substitution of alternative methods to perform similar roles need to be clearly understood. Relating the capabilities of the Cleanroom technique to the existing technical practice within a development environment is particularly helpful in providing a reference for judging the pros and cons of a particular technique.

In this training, formal instruction should be augmented with the attempted use of a particular technique in solving the problem at hand. Each project member should have the opportunity to apply the technique, to decide its effectiveness within the project, and to make suggestions on project practice. For the requirements specifiers and software developers, the hands-on experience should cover the specification, design, and verification of some part of the top-level design for the problem solution. For the software testers, the hands-on experience should include the attempted definition of a top-level structure for the statistical data base to be used for the project's test sample generation. The objective of the hands-on experience is to confirm that the particular techniques can be used for the application and by the project personnel. This experience is necessary for organizing a tailored version of the Cleanroom method to be used on a project.

3.2.2   Selecting the Cleanroom Components for a Project

As discussed in Chapter 1, Cleanroom is not an all-or-nothing method to software development but rather a collection of integrated components, which are intended to be used as a unit but can also be used effectively on an individual basis. The original goal of Cleanroom was to measure software reliability, which required the definition of a statistical test approach with random sampling. To support statistical testing, software with high quality was required from the software development process which required the introduction of correctness verification. With correctness verification and a requirement for a public record of all software execution for reliability certification, the role for developer testing within the process went away. To establish a foundation for correctness verification, a formal approach to requirements specification was a necessary starting point. This explains the rationale for the different Cleanroom components and their integration into a total process.

In starting a new project, a decision should be made on where the project should enter that process. For example, if measuring and using software MTTF is a critical requirement, then implementing the complete Cleanroom method should be seriously considered. If the measurement of software MTTF is not critical, then a statistical testing technique should be viewed on its own merits as a functional test candidate for adequately validating the specified requirements. Statistical testing techniques can and have been used for software products to perform functional testing without recourse to the other Cleanroom components. Verification-based inspections can be introduced into most software development processes as long as software design is based on a structured programming design method. As discussed in Chapter 2, current Cleanroom experience reflects positive results with different approaches to introducing the Cleanroom method into a development organization evolving into the acceptance and use of the total method.

Because of its breadth, the Cleanroom method lends itself to an incremental introduction into a software development environment, where, in any given instance, only the techniques appropriate to a particular problem and a particular project team are selected and used. Force fitting a technique into a development situation is usually detrimental both to the success of the project and to the acceptance of the Cleanroom method within the development environment.

3.2.3   Planning the Introduction of Cleanroom

Adequate planning for the introduction of the Cleanroom method is critical to ensure against the potential for a project disaster, caused by the unwise or unsuccessful adoption of a particular Cleanroom technique. Project managers are encouraged to establish milestones within the project schedules at which the progress of the Cleanroom technology transfer can be statused and assessed.

The number of milestones and their placement within a schedule will vary from project to project but, as a general rule, should appear frequently in the early part of the project schedule. A general rule of thumb is to schedule the initial milestones for each decision in the first two to three months of a project, since these decisions shape the development process and need early resolution (i.e., whether or not to integrate the functional correctness model into the design process). The subsequent milestones, which are intended to work out the particulars of the various decisions and to organize the support (e.g., training, tools, and consulting) required by those decisions, should be scheduled in the first three to six months. Thus the specifics of the development process for the project are settled before the start of the main development activity.

A specific goal should be defined for each milestone by the identification of a quantification of an aspect of the technology transfer of the Cleanroom method to the particular project (e.g., completion of the verified high-level design of the software solution). The intent would be to assess at each milestone whether the expected technology transfer had occurred and, therefore, whether the technology transfer should be allowed to continue as planned. The assessment allows project management to judge the progress being made in transferring the technology and using it to achieve defined project results. Project management can then decide whether changes are needed in the approach to technology transfer (e.g., more training on specific technical topics, the building of support tools, acquiring support staff, and so on) or whether the technology transfer should be stopped. In this extreme case, the plan for reverting back to established techniques should have been worked out as part of the original milestone definition, so that the recovery can proceed as effortlessly as possible. Since a recovery action is required, the planned schedule should have sufficient flexibility to ensure that there is the time and resources to implement the recovery.

The milestones should be placed in the project schedule so that sufficient schedule is always available for reversing decisions about technology insertion without jeopardizing successful project completion. The evaluations at each milestone should be focused on whether committed deliveries are on track and whether the project team is accepting the selected techniques.

From a development perspective, the technology transfers of interest would include, at least, developing the requirements specification with some formal method (e.g., box structure technique [1]), integrating the functional correctness model into the baseline formal design method, eliminating development testing from the software process, and implementing verification-based inspections. From a test and reliability perspective, the technology transfers of interest would include, at least, some form of software testing with statistically representative user inputs and the prediction of the software MTTF on a continuous basis during development. For each of these planned items, appropriate milestones should be defined that identify what was to have occurred, how success would be measured, what forward plan was to be activated, what tolerances on successful completion were acceptable, and what recovery plan would be implemented in the unsuccessful case. While this seems like excessive work, it is necessary if a judgment must be made about what technology was transferred, how successful was the transfer to the project, how should the project proceed, and what happens when the technology cannot be used by the project.

3.2.3.1 *Milestones for Formal Specification Methods* In the case of introducing formal methods for the documentation of requirements specifications, an initial milestone might be the completion of a top-level software product specification. Assuming the box structure method is the formal method, this might mean a description of a single black box that defines all product inputs, functions, and outputs; a single state machine description that maps the black box functions and identifies the required internal product states; and a single clear box description that maps the functions and states into an internal software architecture. These descriptions would be prepared by the lead engineer(s), responsible for the software requirements specification. A subsequent milestone might address the elaboration of the next level(s) of black box description for the components of the software architecture defined in the top-level clear box description. The intent of these additional milestones would be to involve all project software specifiers in the use of the formal specification method, to ensure that the specifier team can use the formal method, and that the software developers and testers can understand their workproducts.

The milestones would provide project management with the opportunity to assess whether the formal specification method would be usable for the particular problem and by the particular staff. If the defined workproducts were not completed or were unintelligible to the developers, testers, and customers, then the effectiveness of the technology transfer would be suspect and some change in specification method would be required. Before reverting back to natural language specifications, the adequacy of the initial training, the availability of expert consultation and support tools, and the levels of actual accomplishment should be reviewed. Since the specification is key to the project start-up, problems with applying the formal methods for specifications must be resolved early in the schedule and can not be allowed to linger into development. Either corrective steps are taken to get formal specifications on the project or the project reverts to established (i.e., natural language) specification practice.

3.2.3.2 *Milestones for the Functional Correctness Model* In the case of integrating the functional correctness model with the existing design practice, an initial milestone might be the completion of a verified top-level software design, which would give the first-level decomposition of the specifications for the software architecture. The description might be a few pages of design language description, prepared by the project's lead designer(s). A subsequent checkpoint might be the completion of verified designs for the next one or two levels of

decomposition. The objective for this milestone would be to give all the software designers on the project an opportunity to apply the functional model in constructing a verified design.

The milestones would provide project management with the opportunity to assess whether the design and correctness ideas could be applied by the lead and other software designers in developing a solution to the particular problem. If the designs can not be successfully completed and verified to everyone's satisfaction by the planned milestones, then the effectiveness of the initial training in the functional correctness model, the completeness of the requirements specification, and the commitment of the staff should be re-evaluated before proceeding. Any early problems with applying the correctness ideas need to be resolved with corrective steps (e.g., additional consulting support, the use of analyzers to guide verification, and so on). The alternative would be to stay with the established design practice, which probably means planning for more formal inspection and development testing at the completion of design.

3.2.3.3 Milestones for Eliminating Developer Testing
In the case of eliminating developer testing as a step in the software development process, an initial milestone might be the completion of the definition and planning of the library and configuration management procedures to support the delivery of code prior to its execution. A preliminary plan would be acceptable documentation for this milestone which would be prepared jointly by the lead software developer(s) and tester(s). A subsequent milestone might be the definition of inspection plans and milestones to ensure quality code delivery and of development procedures and tools to ensure that the design and code can be created in a nonexecution environment.

The milestones would provide project management with the opportunity to assess whether the project is serious about developing software without development testing and has put in place the tools and disciplines to facilitate this developer approach. If satisfactory definition and planning is not completed by these milestones, then the commitment of the project to this objective should be reviewed. Testing by developers is a tradition which will not go away by decree but needs effective planning for it to happen (e.g., separating the design and development from the target computer, limiting target computer access to testers, allocating a percentage [25 to 35%] of developer time to inspections, defining hand-over tests for acceptance of software into test, and so on). Unless this early planning and setup is accomplished, the development will start on the wrong foot and the project commitment to this objective will probably evaporate. Either the appropriate development environment is organized to support development without developer testing, or the project should revert to its established development practice making the necessary adjustments to accommodate developer testing.

3.2.3.4 Milestones for Verification-Based Inspections
In the case of introducing verification-based inspections, an initial milestone might be the definition of the inspection schedules, the analysis tool, and the inspection formats. The

completion of a preliminary plan, which was prepared by the lead software developer(s), would be acceptable for this milestone. Subsequent milestones might be the completion of the requirements specification for the analysis tool, of the verified top-level design for the tool, and of the preliminary plan for testing the tool. This would be another opportunity to involve a cross section of the project in applying the selected Cleanroom methods.

The milestones would provide project management with the opportunity to assess whether adequate preparation is being made for introducing the verification-based inspection into the development process (e.g., ensuring the allocation of sufficient personnel time, having the analysis tool available when needed, working out the formats of the inspection meetings, and so on). If there is project difficulty in completing these milestones, then the interest and commitment to introducing this new method should be re-examined and resolved (e.g., subcontracting the analysis tool development). Without the early definition and planning, there will not be a smooth or problem-free introduction of the verification-based inspection. Either the necessary time is taken early in the project or the project should stay with its established formal inspection practice.

3.2.3.5 Milestones for Statistical Testing
In the case of introducing statistical methods for validating requirements, an initial milestone might be the definition of a data base organization for generating the test samples. A preliminary description would be acceptable that defines a strategy for grouping the software inputs (e.g., time, syntax, safety, and so on) and for organizing a selection hierarchy (e.g., time periods, severity levels, and so on). The description would be prepared by the lead test engineer(s). Subsequent milestones might be the definition of the top few levels of probability distributions for the selection hierarchy, the selection (or definition) of a test sample generator, and the encoding of an initial set of data base entries. These latter milestones would involve a larger segment of the software testers and ensure acceptance of the statistical approach by the software testers.

The milestones would provide project management with the opportunity to assess whether a statistical approach to test sampling can be defined by the test organization and whether the mechanics of sample generation have been worked out. If there is project difficulty in meeting these milestones, then the applicability of statistical test to the particular problem needs to be re-examined and modified forms of statistical testing introduced (e.g., multiple user environments defined, existing traffic samples used in lieu of data base definition, and so on). Either the effort is spent on defining a statistical approach or the project reverts to its established practice for requirements validation.

3.2.3.6 Milestones for Software MTTF Prediction
In the case of integrating software MTTF prediction into the development process, an initial milestone might be the selection of appropriate statistical models and the definition of a prediction procedure. A preliminary plan prepared by the lead software tester(s)

would be acceptable but would have to be integrated with a statistical testing plan. Predicting MTTF would not make sense unless the input test times reflected a random sampling of representative usage inputs. Subsequent milestones might include the installation and checkout of models, the definition of model validation procedures, and the definition of MTTF prediction and assessment reports.

The milestones would provide project management with the opportunity to assess whether the project was set up for MTTF calculations (i.e., test interface, tools, and procedures) and had defined a project role for software MTTF (e.g., basic quality measure, control in a feedback process, and so on). If there is difficulty in completing the milestones, there should be a re-evaluation of the project's ability to do statistical prediction (i.e., statistics background of staff, availability of models, and so on), of bottlenecks from the testing side (i.e., statistical test plans, timing units, interfacing, and so on), and of the project's interest and commitment to doing something with the MTTF data. The fallback position would be to use more traditional quality measures and not bother with statistical modeling.

3.3   CLEANROOM PROJECT MANAGEMENT

Project management with the Cleanroom method is not measurably different from management when more conventional methods are used. One difference would be the tracking of project milestones which were included to track the effectiveness of the Cleanroom technology transfer within the project. These milestones are intended to provide project management with the opportunity to assess the introduction of the Cleanroom component techniques, to judge their acceptance by project staff, and to measure their contribution to project productivity and quality goals. Their use and role is no different from the use of checks to evaluate the effect of any new change to an organization's development process.

A second difference is the public visibility given to software quality by the early placement of software under formal configuration control and the continuous estimation of the software MTTF during development. Typically, software goes through various levels of review and inspection and various steps of developer testing, before it goes under configuration management. The theory is that enough effort (people and methods) has been given to removing errors, that the software is reasonably stable (small percent of remaining errors), and that the software can be given public (outside the project and possibly outside the company) scrutiny without embarrassment. In the Cleanroom process, software is placed under configuration management prior to its first execution, which requires higher confidence and commitment from management in the Cleanroom's zero defect design strategy.

A third difference is the leadership and conviction that must be shown by project management in challenging accepted development practices and/or myths (e.g., unit testing by developers, the ineffectiveness of randomized testing, the absurdity of software MTTF, the advanced mathematical background required for software verification, and the futility of formal methods with changing requirements). Cleanroom offers counterintuitive ideas and methods that can and have been demonstrated to be practical and usable within the typical software development environment. Project management must ensure that staff skepticism in adopting these methods is overcome by providing the training, tools, and consultation support to facilitate their effective use.

A fourth difference is to manage process improvement into the development effort. This requires observation and measurement of the process through the MTTF statistic, recognizing problems with the process through a constant or decreasing MTTF statistic, and monitoring process corrections through an increasing MTTF statistic. The incremental development strategy affords the measurement opportunities from which process corrections (e.g., increased specification formality, broader participation in verification-based inspections, and so on) can be defined for subsequent increment development and tracked for improvement effectiveness. The Cleanroom method provides a unique capability to project management for placing their software development under statistical quality control.

3.4 TECHNOLOGY INSERTION

Assuming the existence of a baseline practice (design method based on structured programming theory and formal design and code inspections), there are five separate technology topics that must be introduced into a development organization to use the full capability of the Cleanroom method. The five topics are formal software specification, functional correctness verification, statistical testing, software reliability prediction, and statistical quality control. In each case, an exact definition must be made of the technology, as it will be tailored to the needs of the particular development organization; training in the specifics of the tailored technology must be organized; and an experimental plan must be constructed to assess the effectiveness of the technology use within the organization. This three-step approach ensures the best chance for successful technology insertion and supports a strategy for technology extension as experience is gained.

Formal methods for software specification attempt to describe what should be designed and implemented in a software product in a formal, mathematical structure. They attempt to anchor software development in formal mathematics (e.g., formal logic) and offer the only real possibility for proving the correctness of an implementation (i.e., with respect to the specification). There are several candidate methods for formal specification which have been or could be used in the Cleanroom method. The box structured method [1] has been used most extensively and could be viewed as a logical extension to the structured programming theory. Other methods, notably VDM [2] and Z [3], attempt to represent in the software specification the data structures and the operations on these structures which must be implemented. The definition of problem-specific grammars to describe the desired functions and relevant data have also been used successfully.

The functional correctness model for software verification [4] attempts to demonstrate equivalence between the specification and the software design derived from the specification. The thrust is to prove that the problem function implemented in the software is the same as the corresponding function defined in the specification. Formal specifications provide crisper, more accurate function definitions and facilitate correctness verification. Other models for correctness verification have been defined [5] but the functional model seems to offer the best potential for widespread industrial use.

Statistics is the mathematical underpinning for software test, which is introduced with the Cleanroom method [6]. The test cases used for validating the requirements defined in the software specification are based on probability distributions, describing expected usage of functions and data. Statistical techniques are also used in assessing test completeness and confidence levels for wrapping-up test activities. These techniques change the current ad hoc approach to software testing and introduce objectivity, realism, and user influence into the testing.

The reliability model for software [7] is fundamentally different than the reliability model for hardware, which has a rich mathematical basis from the research performed during the past half century. The research on the software model is ongoing and will need several years to develop. The notion of failure caused by design errors and not physical aging has been accepted and the cause of failure being in the probabilistic nature of the software inputs [8] is a notion gaining acceptance.

Statistical quality control in the manufacturing world is a readily accepted idea that speaks to part sampling, quality diagnosis, and process correction. These are identically the ideas that should be worked into the software development process even though it does not have manufacturing characteristics. The Cleanroom method [9] equates incremental software MTTF estimation to part sampling, the assessing of current MTTF against a target MTTF to quality diagnosis, and the upgrading of steps in the software life cycle to process correction. Process improvement is becoming an area of industry concern that should stimulate more research and practice in the Cleanroom direction of statistical quality control for software development.

3.5 EDUCATIONAL CONSIDERATIONS

For the introduction of the Cleanroom method into a software development organization, a set of three workshops should be considered which should provide a combination of theory in a particular technology (e.g., functional correctness verification) and application of that theory to the problem at hand. For the software specifiers, a workshop on the selected formal specification method should be conducted. For the software designer/developer, a workshop should be conducted on the functional model for verifying design correctness and for delivering quality software to the test function without the need for software execution and debugging. For the software testers, a combined workshop on statistical methods and software reliability measurement should be conducted.

TABLE 3.1 Software Specification Workshop: Typical Curriculum

Problem Analysis
  Function decomposition
  Function allocation
  Requirements traceability

Box Structure Analysis
  Design principles
  Black, clear, and state boxes

Specification Preparation
  Inspections and reviews
  Incremental development plans
  Usage distributions

3.5.1 Requirements Specification Workshop

A specification workshop would establish a uniform starting point for the Cleanroom project via a formal specification document generated with the selected formal method. The methods to be considered for inclusion in this workshop should be selected from the set of technologies described in Chapter 4. The documentation formats should be tailored to the particular needs of the development organization and deal with information content, accepted notation, and so on. The training should address the resolution of an initial but complete statement of requirements, the problem decomposition into desired functional capabilities, the allocation of product function to appropriate software components, and the correlation of requirements with the allocated functions. The selected formal specification method should be reviewed in depth and applied to the preparation of the particular problem-related specification. A suggested curriculum for this workshop based on the box structure method is shown in Table 3.1.

The specification workshop should be attended by the specifiers, developers, and testers who would perform on the project, and should be one week in length. The specifiers will be trained in uniform analysis methods and standard formats, so that they can document the requirements for their particular problem. The developers and testers will be familiarized with the same techniques so that they can understand the rationale for the requirements that drive their activities.

The two major themes of this workshop are the translation of an application problem into a system design and the specification of requirements for software products. Methods for performing problem analysis, functional decomposition, and functional allocation to establish a system design should be addressed in the first half of the workshop. The second half should be devoted to methods for documenting requirements in specifications. Workshop attendees will be expected to have analysis experience and a working knowledge of set theory and algebra.

Problem analysis deals with methods for isolating the problem to be solved and for detailing a complete set of requirements to bound the problem solution.

TABLE 3.2   Software Verification Workshop: Typical Curriculum

Functional Correctness Model
Prime programs and their verification
Correctness proofs (formal and
informal)
Verification in Design Construction
Verification-Based Inspections
Design statement analysis
Design confirmation procedures

Methods should be stressed that address software life cycle considerations, requirements growth, the so-called *ility* requirements (reliability, serviceability, and maintainability), and the planned system operation. Methods and tools for examining alternative solutions (e.g., trade studies, simulations, and so on) should be discussed.

Functional decomposition deals with collecting requirements into functional groupings that are suitable for implementing as software packages. Methods for function trade-offs between hardware and software, defining functional interfaces, and establishing requirements traceability should be considered. Function allocation addresses the distribution of requirements to discrete hardware and software units, the definition of performance budgets for the allocated functions, and the completeness and consistency analysis of the allocations.

3.5.2   Correctness Verification Workshop

A correctness verification workshop would discuss the functional correctness model for software verification, as discussed in Chapter 5, and its application during the construction and inspection of software designs. The workshop would reinforce the strategy for removing developer testing of software as a development step. In addition, the workshop would discuss other correctness models and compare their capabilities with the functional model. A suggested curriculum for this workshop is shown in Table 3.2.

The functional and axiomatic models for correctness verifications should be reviewed and their similarities and differences discussed as an overview to the subject. The workshop should concentrate on the functional model, its proof rules (both formal and informal), and how these rules are used in the software design and inspection process. Methods and tools for automating the analysis of software designs to support correctness verification should be discussed.

3.5.3   Statistical Testing Workshop

A testing workshop would discuss both statistical testing and software reliability and would include a review of basic probability and statistical theory to ensure

TABLE 3.3   Statistical Software Test Workshop: Typical Curriculum

---

Statistical Theory
  Probability distributions
  Random sampling approaches
  Sequential sampling techniques

Statistical Requirements Validation
  Randomly generated test samples

Software Reliability Theory
  Logical vs. physical failure
  Probabilistic input failure
  MTTF prediction and growth
  models

Statistical Process Control

---

consistent understanding of the ideas. This workshop would be a minimum of 40 hours and depending on the mathematical background might require additional concentration on basic statistics. The workshop would be tailored specifically toward the interests of the software testers, who are most involved with the statistical ideas, but would also be open to attendance by the specifiers and developers. The developers might particularly benefit from an appreciation of the potential diversity in the test inputs, with which their code will be expected to deal.

Sampling theory would be a key topic, since it is the foundation for the test sampling approach discussed in Chapter 6, which organizes the software inputs in terms of the probability distributions that reflect the software's operational usage and from which representative samples of test inputs can be randomly generated. A separate but equally important topic would be the theory behind the software MTTF statistic and its usage in the Cleanroom method for certifying a software product's reliability. The workshop would review the key ideas behind the statistical control of a process (manufacturing, software, and so on) and the application of the software MTTF statistic for controlling the software development process. A suggested curriculum for this workshop is shown in Table 3.3.

The statistical methods covered in the workshop are limited to those which play a direct role in Cleanroom test and reliability measurement. The sampling theory discussion would focus on the definition and organization of probability distributions for an application and the structuring of hierarchies of probability distributions to represent the complex relationships in a typical application problem. The sequential sampling technique would be given special attention, since it has the potential for becoming an effective method for deciding when adequate or sufficient testing has been performed and when the predicted software MTTF indicates that a software product is ready for delivery. The software reliability discussions should deal with the theory behind the Cleanroom software reliability concept and the statistical models that are used to estimate software reliability growth during development. Statistical methods for validating models and the control processes for tracking reliability growth against a reliability target are also topics to be covered in this workshop.

References

1. H.D. Mills, R.C. Linger, and A.R. Hevner, *Principles of Information Systems Analysis and Design,* Academic Press, 1986.
2. C.B. Jones, *Software Development: A Rigorous Approach,* Prentice Hall, 1980.
3. M. Spivey, ''The Z Notation: A Reference Manual,'' Oxford University Programming Research Group, 1987.
4. H.D. Mills, ''The New Math of Computer Programming,'' *Comm. ACM,* Vol. 18, No. 1, 1975.
5. V.R. Basili, ''A Comparison of the Axiomatic and Functional Models of Structured Programming,'' *IEEE TSE,* Vol. SE-6, 1980.
6. M. Dyer, ''Distribution Based Statistical Sampling: An Approach to Software Functional Test,'' Symposium on Testing, Analysis and Verification, 1991.
7. B. Littlewood, ''How to Measure Software Reliability,'' Proceeding of the Third International Conference on Software Engineering, 1978.
8. H.D. Mills, ''Software of Certifiable Reliability,'' Unpublished correspondence, 1980.
9. M. Dyer, ''Software Development Under Statistical Quality Control,'' *Springer-Verlag NATO ASI Series F,* Vol. 22, 1987.

CHAPTER 4

The How To's of Cleanroom Software Development

Structured programming practice [1] provides the basis for constructing software designs with conviction about their correctness and strong confidence about their solution of specified requirements. The Cleanroom method introduces mathematics-based design methods [2] which improve the precision and completeness of design recording and support the routine verification of design correctness. The Cleanroom method [3] differs from traditional design practice because correctness verification is woven into each step of a design elaboration and not restricted to a small number of inspection and review opportunities.

Since design is a creative process that requires proficiency in the subject matter and intuition about solution strategies, methodology can not substitute for designer experience but can be the catalyst for getting the maximum payoff from the designer's knowledge. The designer must start by understanding the total set of requirements and organizing them into some manageable number of subdivisions—the divide and conquer principle at work. Background in the technical problem and understanding of the needs of the user are essential to this initial analysis, since all requirements (not restricted to functional requirements only) must be factored into the solution. Consideration of software packaging is equally important and introduces the software engineering perspective on software product form, software interactions, and planned release of software function. Another important consideration is the operating environment for the software—the hardware on which it runs, the interfaces with hardware and other software, and the allocated budgets for performance, reliability, availability, and so on.

When the requirements are organized to a point where the significance of each requirement and its priority in the solution strategy is appreciated, software design can start. At this point, design methodology does play a significant role by providing the models and techniques for elaborating the design. Good design practice defines the systematic and stepwise decomposition of requirements into successive levels of design logic that tie together the decomposed subrequirements. The process is repeated as many times as needed until all requirements are designed. The practice must implement a strategy of separate and decompose the requirements, connect the decomposed requirements with design logic, verify that the proposed logic at each step satisfies the specified requirement and ensure that the integrity and consistency of the initial requirements are maintained. None of the initial requirements gets dropped and no new requirements get added as the design evolves.

A key to successful design is the practice of rethinking and reworking a design continually, since the first attempted design seldom survives as the final design. The rule rather than the exception should be to review and rework a design several times (typically three to six), before being satisfied with its clarity. Design alternatives should be considered and evaluated, with no reluctance to redoing parts or the total design at any point. Probably the best debugging technique available to the software designer is to redesign a design into simpler and simpler forms before the design is finalized, let alone executed.

Another key to successful design is the correctness verification of a design at each step of its refinement, from highest to lowest, as the design is constructed. Checking correctness is not practical if design refinements are not rigorously expressed nor if refinement occurs in giant leaps from high-level functions to a maze of coding details. Rigor at all levels of description, whether using formal design methods or natural language, is critical for the completeness and thoroughness of design. Confidence in the goodness of a total design is gained from checking and being confident about a few lines of design at a time. This is true whether the few lines summarize the top-level functions of the software or some low-level details about one of its components.

The focus should be on developing a design in concert with its correctness proof. The proof can be the mental conviction derived from a discussion of correctness arguments or an extended analysis based on mathematical proofs. Designs that are easily verified should be favored and sought, whereas designs that are difficult to verify should be considered suspect and redone for greater simplicity. A reasonable rule of thumb is that when reading a design becomes difficult and proof arguments are not obvious, it is probably time to think harder about the design and come up with a simpler, more valuable design.

4.1 BENEFITS OF STRIVING FOR DESIGN SIMPLICITY

Substantial quality and productivity benefits can accrue with the suggested more careful approach to software design elaboration and with a design objective for organizing simple designs whose correctness can be demonstrated. To illustrate the benefits on a small scale, the possible designs for a program to solve a problem that has received a good deal of attention in the technical literature, particularly the software testing literature, should be considered. The problem is to design a program that inputs a set of three positive numbers and, then, determines whether these values can be the sides of a triangle and, if so, what type of triangle (equilateral, isosceles, or scalene) is formed.

Two particular variants of a program design for this problem have been well covered in the technical literature. Both exhibit the same idea for a classification algorithm; namely, attempting to classify the type of triangle by determining the number of equal values in a triplet. As can be seen from the design flows in Figures 4.1 and 4.2, significantly different designs, in terms of processing complexity, result from the decision on where in the process the classification algorithm is applied.

Figure 4.1 shows a design where the classification is attempted before deciding whether the three values can be used to form any type of triangle. Figure 4.2 illustrates a design where the decision on the validity of the values is made before attempting a classification of the type of triangle. If complexity is measured in terms of the number of logic paths in a program design, the placement of this simple check on the validity of the input values can cause a threefold difference in design complexity. In the first design (Figure 4.1) there are some 89 paths, whereas in the second design (Figure 4.2) there are some 26 paths.

A different variant of a program design for this problem, which is also discussed in the technical literature, uses a slightly different classification approach. For this variant, the classification algorithm is based on first deciding that the values can form a triangle and, then, checking whether all values in a triplet are equal or if any pair of values is equal, which define the equilateral and isosceles cases. This leaves the scalene case for all other situations. Figure 4.3 shows a design for this variant for which the number of logic paths is five. Clearly, this is a simpler design for the same problem, with a 5 to 1 or 19 to 1 reduction in design complexity when compared to the two earlier design approaches. This more optimum design should be preferred for software implementation and is used in Chapter 5 to demonstrate the simplicities of software correctness verification.

4.2 SPECIFICATION/DESIGN/IMPLEMENTATION OVERVIEW

To develop software with the Cleanroom method, there is an implied requirement for stability in the software requirements specification. Software requirements are typically neither fully known nor verified during the early part of software development so that it might appear that the Cleanroom method has no or, at best, limited application to most software development. To the contrary, the Cleanroom insistence on forcing deficiencies in the software requirements into the open and of instigating management resolution of the deficiencies should be mandatory practice within any software development method. As long as software development is treated as a trial-and-error process, incomplete requirements can be accommodated as just another source of trial and error. The preferred alternate practice would be based on the recognition that the early requirements specification is typically deficient. The resolution of the deficiencies is handled by some number of analysis iterations for stabilizing requirements, prior to their considerations in

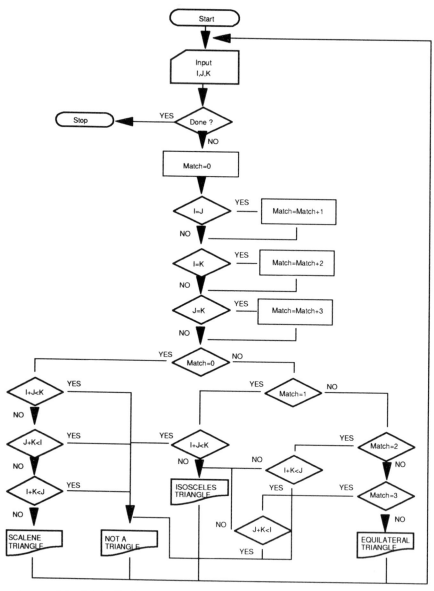

Figure 4.1   A First Variant of the Program Design for the Triangle Solver Problem

for the design of a particular software increment. This does not force the completion of all requirements analysis before any design is started but, rather, allows for
an incremental resolution of the open requirements. When poorly formulated requirements are specified and delivered to the software designer, there tends to be
an extended period of interaction to establish a starting baseline on which the
specifiers and the designers can agree. The preferred approach, as used in the

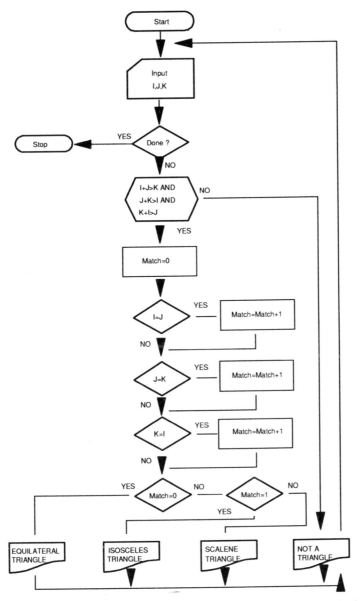

Figure 4.2 A Second Variant of the Program Design for the Triangle Solver Problem

Cleanroom method, strives for more structured requirements specifications and remedies this situation by forcing the interactions to be concluded before the specifications can be delivered.

A systematic refinement of design obviously can not be started until a reasonable design outline is prepared which includes basic details on the software

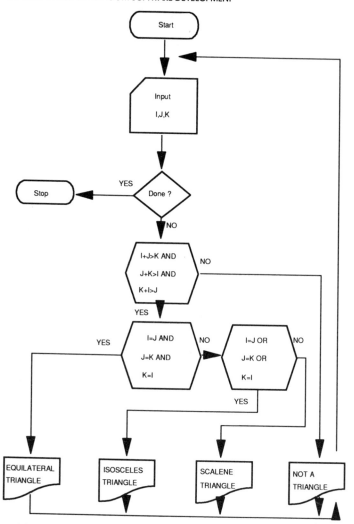

Figure 4.3   A Third Variant of the Program Design for the Triangle Solver Problem

architecture, data representations, and the underlying processing algorithms. When considering a design, many control, data, and flow alternatives rumble through the designer's mind. These must be sorted out with the important ideas recorded first and the less important points left for subsequent steps in the design refinement. The design goal should be a coherent logical description of the software design, which runs from product summaries at the top to implementation details at the bottom.

In the Cleanroom method, software design uses a function-based technique for creating and recording a structure of logical constructs and function specifications. The model for software is the mathematical function, which defines the input and output relationship of the software. The function is expanded through successive levels by a process of stepwise refinement or elaboration. Each refinement step results in an expansion of one or more functions into smaller units (design constructs from structured programming) of manageable size. With each step, new subfunctions for subsequent refinement are introduced resulting in designs that are hierarchical by construction. The problem data is refined in a similar manner.

Stepwise refinement is not a mechanical process and an understanding of the software requirements and the problem data is required prior to design. The depth of design will vary with complexity and stop when no further refinement is necessary.

4.3 SOFTWARE SPECIFICATION

An accepted but unresolved requirement for software development is the use of a formal language for documenting the requirements to be addressed by the software. Natural language has many drawbacks in attempting this role (ambiguity, inconsistency, and vagueness, to state a few) and, at the other extreme, programming languages remove most of these drawbacks but at the expense of too much detail and after-the-fact specification (documenting what was implemented rather than what was required). When starting a software development, there is no need for implementation detail and a requirements specification should strive to abstract the essential elements to be addressed in a design.

What is needed is a formal, or exact, language for expressing specifications, which should be considered as equivalent to the blueprint for architects and builders. The blueprint and the list of building materials combine to make an excellent specification of the structure to be built. The blueprint's advantage is that the specification is formal (i.e., there is little or no room for ambiguity, is a model of the final product, and defines what is needed but not how to get there).

Mathematics is the obvious choice for a specification language since it supports abstraction, allows the definition of a model for describing the key features of the software, and permits the proving of the implementation correctness. It has long been recognized that the best systems are built by one or two people but that the available specification and design techniques limit the size of the systems that can be built that way. Techniques that support greater abstraction may enable small teams to master larger systems that are beyond their current capabilities. Mathematics can support the building of a model as the specification is written, which allows the separation of concerns and the focusing on logical not physical considerations in the design. The physical considerations are ignored not because they are unimportant but rather because they are factored into the design solution at a subsequent step.

Correctness only makes sense in terms of proving that the implementation satisfies the specification. Since software is implemented with languages with formal structure and syntax, correctness proving requires equal formality and structure in the specification language. In trying to use mathematics as the specification language, mathematical notation can be used to express the properties of the requirements, which is an elegant but difficult-to-use and generally unacceptable specification approach. An alternate and reasonably accepted approach is to use mathematics for building a model of the software to be implemented, which requires the specifier to be mathematically conversant but only to the same level of sophistication as required with the alternate approach. What is needed is a well-defined notation and defined rules for manipulating the notation, which have a basis in mathematical theory.

The advantages of formal specifications over informal ones are that they anchor the software development in mathematics (e.g., formal logic, algebra, and so on) and that they offer the first real opportunity for proving implementation correctness. Both are critical considerations with the ever-growing reliance on software with unquestioned quality and reliability. While the reasoning is impeccable, formal methods are not in popular use for specifying requirements. One reason for this lack of acceptance is the increased level of mathematical sophistication required in the software staff—hard to come by and with unjustified payback in terms of productivity and quality. The second reason is the unsettled state of formal methods—uncertainties about their widespread applicability and questionable results on their ease of use. In spite of these negatives, at least three methods are emerging as viable techniques for formally specifying and designing software: the Vienna Design Method (VDM) [4], the Z specification notation [5], and the box structure methodology [6].

The box structure methodology suggests that the behavior of a system can be rigorously described by a hierarchy of three distinct box structure forms: the black box, state machine, and clear box of the system. The black box gives an external view of a system, which provides a system description without details on the internal structure and operations but with a description of the user visible system inputs and responses. The state machine gives an intermediate system view by decomposing the internal state structure from the black box description of the system. The clear box gives the internal view of the system operations on inputs and internal state data. Each of the box structures define the identical behavior of the system but with increased visibility into the hierarchy of the internal structure, which specifies the requirements for the system implementation.

VDM was developed by the IBM Vienna Laboratory in the early 1970s and provides a framework for systems development in which mathematical notation is used for formally defining system behavior. VDM supports the creation of a precise, consistent, and unambiguous specification, which can be validated by formal or informal verification methods. This method uses mathematical logic and set theory to produce a rigorous mathematical specification on which system development can be based. The essential decisions on system functions and operations can be made during the specification process through iterative interaction with the system customer (user).

Z was developed by the Programming Research Group at Oxford University during the 1980s and is a diagrammatic notation for developing software specifications. The Z notation uses a kernel boxlike structure, called a schema, and relies on methods from mathematical logic and set theory for specification descriptions. The

Z specifications strive to be rigorous, unambiguous, partitioned, free of implementation or extraneous detail, and still understandable by the system customer (user).

Current Cleanroom experience has only recently started using these formal specification methods whose detailed capabilities are well defined in the reference documents. Rather most Cleanroom experience has relied on natural language specifications, supplemented with formal grammars and tabular notations to add conciseness and precision. Formal grammars which have most commonly been used in specifying and developing compilers for programming languages can afford the same benefits to the specification of other applications, by providing the syntax and the syntax rules needed for specifying requirements. Grammars provide precise language representations for reaching agreement on requirements with users or customers and for giving unambiguous directions for the software design. A grammar typically defines a single top-level abstraction for the application in which it is used, whether that is the definition of the compilable unit (i.e., modules or programs) or the structure of a query in a data base system. From that starting point, the syntax rules can be used to elaborate intermediate abstractions to the necessary level of detail. The hierarchical structure of grammars offers a natural method for separating and addressing complexity during the elaboration of the requirements for an application.

4.4 SOFTWARE DESIGN

With conventional software design methods, the focus tends to be exclusively on functional requirements and their detailing into software logic with little upfront consideration of the software's data requirements. This is a natural outgrowth of the traditional requirements specification approach, where the emphasis is placed on identifying all the operations to be performed by the software and on bounding the extent of the software's functional capabilities. This functional approach to requirements specification has been preferred since it permits an assessment of the software's worth to the customer or user and the definition of the software's roles in the customer's workplace. The concentration on function allows the easy trade-off of more or less software capability, in order to gain software acceptance by the intended customer set.

The emphasis in conventional design methods is on detailing the software logic and not on the rigorous decomposition of requirements. Software design becomes a hunt for software with similar functional capability, whose design can be used as a model or whose code can be directly inserted as a component. In the conventional design process, correctness is not an active consideration but more an after-the-fact check of the documented design to uncover errors. Design languages are used exactly like programming languages, that is, to detail the software logic rather than to support a rigorous decomposition of requirements and elaboration of design. The introduction of mathematically based methods (e.g., structured programming) without a change in the conventional design focus (i.e., detailing design logic) will not have a marked impact on design quality but more a cosmetic change in the form of the design documentation.

4.4.1 Theoretical Basis for Formal Software Development

Formal software development requires a systematic method for design elaboration and a design model anchored in mathematics that focuses design consideration on the software function and the software data. The structured programming ideas [7] introduced this needed thoughtful approach to software construction. The ideas drew a correspondence between the static software text and the dynamics of its execution, which permitted higher levels of precision in software design.

A formal design approach [2] was formulated from this work which combined the ideas on formulating structured programming with a theory on software correctness. This mathematics-based design approach, adopted by the Cleanroom method, demonstrates that correct programming involves only combinatorial selection of the structured programming constructs and does not require absolutely perfect precision on a continuous scale. It offers the real opportunity to move software design from a trial-and-error activity to a systematic and quality-controlled industrial process.

Software design was defined as a stepwise expansion of mathematical functions into structures of logical connectives and subfunctions, where the expansion was carried out until all identified subfunctions could be directly stated in the programming language used for implementation. Four mathematical results are the underpinning of the definition. The **structure theorem [8]** guarantees that any flowchartable software program logic can be represented by expansions of as few as three types of structures (e.g., compositions, selections, and iterations). This is in stark contrast to nonstructured programming practice of flow charting arbitrary control logic with unrestricted branching operations. The second mathematical result is the **top down corollary [9]** which guarantees that a structured program can be written and read top down, such that the correctness of each segment of a program depends only on segments that have already been written or read and on the specification of function in other segments referenced by name. This is a different approach to the conventional bottom-up design approach which completely resolves those functions that are understood and fills in the others as time and knowledge permit. The third mathematical result is the **correctness theorem [10]** which reduces the problem of correctness to a consideration of function-theoretic questions to which standard mathematical practice can be applied. The questions are aimed at demonstrating the equivalence between a stated function and the structure of logical connectives and subfunctions, which are the design expansion. The questions are formulated on a systematic basis (i.e., driven by the construct hierarchy) but technical judgment must be used in deciding the level of validation that is needed or desirable for a given design. The fourth mathematical result is the **expansion theorem [9]** which defines the designer's freedom for expanding a function specification into a structure of logical connectives and subfunctions. This surprising result is that the designer has very little freedom in deciding the correct expansion of a top-down design, which leads to the conclusion that design is more of an analysis than synthesis activity. Top-down design reduces to a sequence of decompositions and partitions of function and subfunction specifications, each of which produced further subfunction specifications, until the level of programming language description is reached. This is different from the more conventional synthesis of programming language statements to implement a function specification and leads to the observation that design is a combinatorial activity.

Other software design methods [4,5] could prove equally effective for the Cleanroom method, as long as they enforce rigorous design elaboration with embedded correctness verification at each step in the elaboration.

4.4.1.1 *Liberties Taken with Structured Programming Theory* The introduction of structured programming practice during the 1970s spawned the definition of many software design methods which, while they included the word "structured" in their title, were simplified, generally nonmathematical, and usually graphical approaches for software design. The methods were easily taught and introduced into a software development environment. They frequently defined a hierarchical design approach, which would vaguely map to the structured programming constructs but were no more than graphical icons. They could be used to describe aspects of the design but had no connotation of a rigorous and complete function specification as required with the Cleanroom method.

Designing with methods which generate graphical descriptions of software designs that exhibit a hierarchical structure of the design elements has appeal to software professionals and their management. There is little to learn about the method and it has the semblance of formality. The design, since it does not rigorously define the problem solution, offers the implementors the opportunity to be creative in detailing the real design during code implementation. Since the designer is not burdened with rigor and thoroughness and the implementor is not stifled in coding, there is an apparent benefit in the use of these methods. The pitfall is that the development project is lulled into a sense of design completeness and correctness, which does not exist and will not be achieved until code is written and debugged.

In general, these methods that have no mathematical underpinning but have the trappings of structure and formality should be avoided for serious software design. In no way should they be considered for the software design function with the Cleanroom method, which expects the elaboration of a design whose correctness can be established and verified at each step of the elaboration.

4.5 SOFTWARE IMPLEMENTATION

Software design should be a top-down iterative decomposition of the software requirements with an elaboration of the design solution to those requirements. In the stepwise elaboration, the designer should consciously identify possible data abstractions that would allow data operations to be viewed at the higher problem level and for which corresponding data operators could be defined. Abstracting

Design Activity	Recording	Design Level
Specifying	mod a **spec**	1
Designing Specifying	begin uses b uses c end a proc b mod c : **spec**	2
Designing Specifying	begin uses d end c mod d **spec**	3
	: ETC.	

Figure 4.4   Stepwise Refinement Example

permits the separation of the particular data requirements from the rest of the problem for their independent design and development. At the same time, it allows the other parts of the design to work with the particular data requirements, not at a detailed implementation level but through the defined data operators. The form of the actual implementation of the data operators is of no concern to the other parts of the design as long as the stated functions and interfaces are maintained.

4.5.1   Stepwise Design Refinement

Design starts with the requirements specified for the software, which can be a reference to a separate software requirements specification (SRS) or can be an abstraction of the real requirements from the SRS. An abstraction would identify the specified functions and the principal elements of data to be factored into the design. In the refinement step, the specified function is expanded into a structure of logic connections and specifications for subfunctions, which are collectively simpler than the starting function specification. The subfunction specifications are themselves refined and re-expressed as structures of logic connections and specifications for even lower level subfunctions. Figure 4.4 depicts, with the use of a design language (i.e., PDL), the typical refinement steps for a hypothetical software module.

To elaborate the design for a refinement step, the appropriate structured programming construct(s) is selected which reflects the design logic needed for the specified function (i.e., composition, selection, or iteration). The selected construct should provide the structure for connecting the design logic (with necessary data interaction) and the specifications for the next level subfunctions. The design for the subfunctions will trigger selection of further structured programming constructs to provide the necessary design structure. For the hypothetical case in Figure 4.4, the top-level design is a composition of component b and component c and the design for component c is also a composition of component d.

In this stepwise process, the designer looks far enough ahead (i.e., additional refinement steps) to be comfortable with the elaboration being considered for the current refinement step. If the specification is for a known operation (i.e., sorting a small table), further thought and elaboration may not be necessary. If the specification covers an unknown function, the look-ahead or elaboration should be carried to the point where an obvious solution is apparent. A rule of thumb is to look ahead two to three levels of refinement to become comfortable with the refinement proposed for the current level. As the analysis is performed, the design elaboration should be recorded with a design language (e.g., PDL) after every three or four elaboration steps. This allows sufficient freedom in organizing the design (three to four levels with a possible two to three levels of look-ahead) but ensures that the stepwise elaboration is not lost and really recorded in small increments (avoiding the great leaps of faith in the design).

The stepwise refinement results in a natural development plan for allocating effort to those parts of the problem most in need of thought and elaboration. Without this systematic approach, human inclination would be to completely design (and possibly implement) those parts of the problem whose solution was known but to defer the consideration of the hard parts. By forcing a different design strategy, the thoroughness of the design is improved and the correctness of the design can be considered. Each refinement offers a working hypothesis on the design of the software's function or subfunctions, which must be accepted as sound or reworked before proceeding. The accumulation of these hypotheses confirmations, collected on a top-down basis, ensures a complete and correct decomposition of the software requirements, within the bounds of intellectual reasoning.

For large and complex problems, the design becomes organized as a tree structure with this top-down refinement strategy. Each node in the tree represents a subfunction specification which is self-contained with explicitly defined interfaces to the other parts of the design to avoid problems with function side effects. The tree structure can support many designers, concurrently elaborating different parts of the design, and also provide a structure for monitoring status and total design content as the subfunction designs are completed.

4.5.1.1 *Elaborating Subfunction Specification*   One key to effective stepwise refinement of a software design is the specification of the function and subfunctions for each step of the refinement. Producing a complete and correct specification on the first attempt is generally difficult. The highest level function specification must capture an abstraction of the total requirement and adequately define all data with the scope of their values, a crisp set of rules for the function operation, and whatever other considerations need mentioning (e.g., constraints, performance budgets, and so on). The subfunction specifications must satisfy all of the function specification requirements, while, at the same time, isolating and extracting only a subset of the function requirements being decomposed in the

current refinement step. The clean splitting of a function may be difficult to accomplish but the refinement practice gives immediate feedback on the decomposition effectiveness, since the sum of the subfunctions must equal exactly the function or subfunction being refined. When this consistency in function requirements can not be established, then the definition of the subfunctions within the step must be revisited.

The specifications should state only the "what" and not the "how" of the function to be designed. At a minimum, the specification must define input, output, and function rule, where the rule defines the relationship that must be maintained between the input and output. The input specification needs to address each data variable which can be an input and the domain of values which must be accommodated by the function rule. The specification must contain sufficient data for verifying the correctness of the refinement step.

Natural language is adequate for specifying the function or subfunction if written with thoughtfulness and care. The belief that highly mathematical notation is always required is wrong though such notation has advantages in expressing the function relationships and in introducing conciseness, rigor, and precision into the specification. The emphasis should be on the effectiveness of the decomposition and not the style of the description. An elegantly formal specification that contains incorrect information is worse than useless.

Two concerns that software designers have in coming up with specifications are how formally should they be written and how much description reuse should be practiced. With regard to formality, intellectual control and effective communication of the design are the objectives, so the designs and the specifications must be readable as well as writable. The goal should be that each part of a design should stand by itself, without need for supporting documentation and, more importantly subject to only one interpretation. Formality and precision should not be confused as being synonymous. Though formality tends to encourage precision, formality needs to be introduced only in those cases where the necessary level of precision can not be described without formal notation.

Tabular notation is particularly useful for specifying a function rule that might otherwise require a lengthy and/or nested conditional expression. In many problems, decision logic for a function needs to be specified as combinations of modes, conditions, events, and data where a tabular form tends to produce crisper, clearer, and more precise specifications. The excerpt shown in Figure 4.5 illustrates the use of a tabular form for specifying the computation of the azimuth steering line angle to be displayed in a complex avionics application [11]. This table defines the different operating modes which must be considered and up to three situations which must be considered for each mode. Note the conciseness obtained by grouping modes which have similar actions. To show the interpretation of this particular table, consider the following examples:

If the mode is Grtest, then HUD vertical is displayed.
If the mode is CCIP and the impact angle is less than or equal to 20 degrees below aircraft boresight, then the angle of the bomb fall line is displayed.

Modes		Conditions	
Nattack Noffset BOC BOCFltto 0 BOCoffset	N/A	Always	N/A
CCIP	N/A	impact angle elevation > 20 degrees below aircraft boresight	impact angle elevation <= 20 degrees below aircraft boresight
Grtest	Always	N/A	N/A
Output: Azimuth Steering Line Angle	HUD vertical	perpendicular to pitch lines	angle of bomb fall line

Figure 4.5 Example of Tabular Format for Function Specification

Clearly, the table format is much crisper than the wordy conditional statements.

4.5.2 Elements of Structured Design

The early work on structured programming theory [2] indicated that a small number of constructs would suffice for formulating designs of any size and/or complexity. These constructs are commonly referenced as the structured primes and offer to software design what Boolean algebra provides to hardware design. In particular the minimum set has module, program, composition, selection, and iteration constructs as shown in Figure 4.6. It should be noted that only single predicate constructs are identified since it has been demonstrated [2] that any design described with a multiple predicate construct can be redesigned and redescribed with equivalent single predicate constructs.

From a packaging viewpoint, the designer must be able to package separately the major components of an application and the procedural logic within each component. The module and program are used for packaging the software components. The module is a collection of programs, each of which performs some similar or common application function. In a banking system, all the software connected with checking or savings accounts might be collected into two modules, one for checking and one for savings. Similarly, all of the software common to accessing a customer's account (opening, closing, updating, auditing, and so on) might be collected into an account accessing module.

The program is used for organizing the software logic of a component, which describes the translation of inputs to outputs as defined in the function specification. The model for the program is a deterministic algorithm to perform the translation, the domain of input values that can be processed, and the range of output values into which the input values must be mapped. In the banking example, a

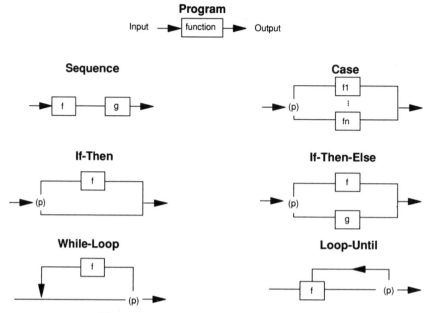

Figure 4.6 Structured Programming Constructs

program might be defined for computing mortgage schedules which would use a prescribed set of interest-computing algorithms, an input set of interest rates, mortgage periods, and mortgage amounts, and outputs reflecting a 15- or 30-year schedule. Two different programs might be defined for fixed- and variable-rate mortgage commitments, since the algorithms are different even though the inputs and outputs are basically the same.

The logic within programs is designed with the use of the composition, selection, and iteration constructs from structured programming theory. The composition constructs are intended for grouping multiple pieces of logic which are performed in a fixed sequence. The simple sequence defines a single excursion through the set of logic pieces, whereas the indexed sequence defines a fixed number of excursions through the set. The selection constructs are intended for identifying choices in software logic, where the decision on which logic choice to follow is determined by the value of some predicate. The if-then construct is used to define the inclusion or exclusion of some logic, the if-then-else to define the execution of one of two choices, and the case to define the execution of one of many choices. The iteration constructs are intended to permit variable execution of a logic sequence, where the variability is controlled by the value of some predicate. The difference between the while-loop and loop-until constructs lies with whether the predicate is evaluated at the beginning or the end of the logic within the loop.

The use of the structured programming constructs in formulating software designs has been well documented in the professional literature. There is also reported evidence [12] of their effective use and scale-up in software applications for which the designed solution required millions of lines of code.

4.5.2.1 *Structured Data Design* A systematic approach to data design is as necessary as it is for logic design. Three ideas from software engineering practice are particularly useful in defining a data design method: data encapsulation, data typing, and data abstraction. The combined use of these ideas dramatically simplifies the data considerations in a design, reduces overall design complexity, and makes the design more amenable to correctness verification.

Data encapsulation is a vintage programming term which has taken on a new significance with the drive for design correctness. Restricting the visibility into data variables to the smallest possible audience has taken on added importance for two reasons: to localize the data design into one (or a small number of) design component and to mask the implementation and its changes from the other components that reference the data. The module and program constructs are particularly effective in supporting the data encapsulation concept.

Data typing is another term that has taken on new significance in software engineering and refers to the segregating of each data variable in a design into a particular data class. Each class and, therefore each data variable, is assigned a specific set of characteristics and a defined set of data operators that bound the processing performed on data variables within the class. Most programming languages make use of the concept but have been very forgiving about its misuse. Generally, explicit data typing has not been required from the programmer since default definitions can be automatically supplied by the compiler. Mixed mode operations, data conversions, and so forth are generally supported in most programming languages but are now recognized as the causes for correctness and design problems. In modern programming languages, explicit data typing is mandatory and forces the designer to understand the problem data (i.e., their characteristics and limitations) to the same depth as the problem function.

Data abstraction is a third term that has not been exploited to its fullest potential but could provide significant support for the construction of correct designs. It refers to elevating the consideration of data from the bit implementation (machine) level to the level appropriate for the problem. Programming languages generally offer some capability in this area, by providing data structures, such as files, arrays, and records, for grouping problem data into meaningful collections. The new correctness-driven thrust is directed at relaxing restrictions with current abstraction offerings and providing an open-ended capability. Modern programming languages support a more open-ended data abstraction capability through their data typing and module definition facilities. Particularly useful data abstractions described in the literature [13] are the set, stack, queue, list, and tree. These language extensions allow the software designer to define further data abstractions which more accurately describe the problem characteristics. The only drawback is that the software designer must define the mapping from the abstract form (i.e., data and operations) to an acceptable programming language (i.e., implementation) form.

4.5.3 Software Design Expression

With typical software developments extending over long periods of time, the designers and users must have some method for communicating effectively about the existing design structure and the impact of proposed changes to that structure. Natural language is an effective communication vehicle to a point but lacks the structural form and building blocks for describing complex function interactions crisply. Programming languages can provide the structural form but introduce a uniformly low level of expression, which can bog down a design description in a sea of detail. Generally, the use of programming language syntax and semantics for elaborating software designs tends to add more obscurity than clarity to the design description.

Several languages have been defined specifically for inventing and communicating software designs in a textual form. These languages should be viewed as open-ended specializations of natural language and mathematics rather than closed language forms like most programming languages. The structure of these design languages is intended to assist with the description of designs from a logical viewpoint and to sharpen the precision of the human communication on the designs. Figure 4.7 illustrates the syntax for a typical design language [2] that has been used for design in many Cleanroom projects.

The constructs for which syntax is included within Figure 4.7 are the program, simple sequence, for-do sequence, case selection, if-then-else selection, if-then selections, while-loop iteration, and loop-until iteration. For each construct, a function specification is identified, which defines the requirements to be addressed in the construct. Within each construct, <statements> refers to the body of the construct for which other constructs, mathematical notation, or natural language can be used to define the design logic. Predicates where needed can be expressed in mathematical notation or natural language, whichever is appropriate for the level of design and allows the consideration of the allowable choices. In the case construct description, bracketed items indicate that there can be any number of parts coinciding with the choices and that the else clause is optional to handle all non-specified situations (i.e., no case-part provided).

These languages are typically less stringent in their syntax requirements (e.g., reserved terms, punctuation markers, and so on) than programming languages which need to be demanding for compilation reasons. Compilation of design descriptions is not a necessary nor useful objective, whereas the research effort on compilation of software requirements specifications could have long-term benefits for the development of quality software. Availability of a translatable specification capability for general industry use is at least a decade off and probably longer.

```
┌─────────────────────────────────────┐      ┌─────────────────────────────────┐
│<function specification>              │      │DO <function specification>      │
│PROC <program-name> <parameter-list>│       │   <statements>                  │
│   <data-declarations>                │      │END                              │
│   <statements>                       │      └─────────────────────────────────┘
│END                                   │
├══════════════════════════════════════┤     ┌─────────────────────────────────┐
│<function specification>              │      │<function specification>         │
│FOR <index-name> = <index-expression>│       │CASE <predicate-prefix>          │
│LOOP <function specification>         │      │  +{PART <case=predicate><function specification>│
│   <statements>                       │      │      <statements>}              │
│END                                   │      │   {ELSE <function specification>│
├══════════════════════════════════════┤     │      <statements>               │
│<function specification>              │      │END                              │
│IF <predicate>                        │      └─────────────────────────────────┘
│   THEN <function specification>      │
│      <statements>                    │      ┌─────────────────────────────────┐
│   ELSE <function specification>      │      │<function specification>         │
│      <statements>                    │      │IF <predicate>                   │
│END                                   │      │   THEN <function specification> │
├══════════════════════════════════════┤     │      <statements>               │
│<function specification>              │      │END                              │
│WHILE <predicate>                     │      └─────────────────────────────────┘
│LOOP <function specification>         │
│   <statements>                       │      ┌─────────────────────────────────┐
│END                                   │      │LOOP <function specification>    │
└─────────────────────────────────────┘      │   <statements>                  │
                                              │UNTIL <predicate>                │
                                              │END                              │
                                              └─────────────────────────────────┘
```

Figure 4.7   Example of Design Language Syntax

4.5.4 Example of Software Design Elaboration

To illustrate the use of design practice with the Cleanroom method, an example is used which is also used for illustration in the subsequent correctness verification, statistical testing, and reliability analysis chapters. The example addresses the development of a component of the flight software for an avionics application. The flight software provides the necessary navigation and control functions for the operation of the aircraft and includes such functions as flight plan processing, aircraft navigation, aircraft system diagnostics, and flight personnel controls/displays. The particular flight software application was written in the JOVIAL J3 programming language, required approximately thirty thousand JOVIAL J3 source language statements (30 ksloc), and executed on a specialized computer on board the aircraft.

4.5.4.1 Specification of the Software Component   The requirements for the particular flight software application were documented in a separate SRS, which was written in natural language but made extensive use of tables to crisply and concisely identify required function. The number of requirements, when measured in terms of the use of the English verb ''shall,'' was in the order of twenty-five hundred discrete requirements to specify the flight software function. In order to support the correctness verification of the flight software design, exten-

TABLE 4.1   Component Hierarchy

CCNID	
CCDATA	Data declarations
CCNVID	
CCINIT	Software initialization
CCACTRAC	Active radio initialization
CCTIMERS	Equipment timers management
CCADFTIM	ADF controls for UHF and VHF
CCMMUHF	UHF radio
CCMMVHF	VHF radio
CCMMHF	HF radio
CCRNAV	Navigation equipment
CCIDENT	A/C identification equipment
CCMAYDAY	May-day function

sive use was made of design language commentary for specifying the functions and subfunctions required at each step in the design refinement. Rather than copy or summarize the SRS into the design language description, the appropriate sections, paragraphs, sentences, and phrases from the SRS were referenced instead. These references were given further elaboration, as necessary, to clarify the details on elaborated subfunctions which were identified as the flight software requirements were decomposed.

The particular component within the flight software application that has been selected for illustration is the software component which manages the aircraft's radio equipment (HF, VHF, and UHF), navigation equipment (TACAN and ADF), and aircraft identification equipment (IFF). The aircraft personnel interface with this particular component through a set of four programmable displays, each of which have 20 programmable function keys and two separate data entry keyboards. The meaning and interpretation of the programmable function keys is dictated by the content of the panel, displayed at any particular time. As a specific panel is displayed, each function key (e.g., the top-left-side key) takes on a specific role, whose interpretation is local to the particular panel. The same function key when a different panel is displayed will play a different role.

4.5.4.2   *Top-Level Design of the Software Component*   To package the design for this particular component of the flight software, the designer structured a module (CCNID) which collected the equipment control and common processing requirements allocated to the component. The module included a set of programs which handled the definition of the different data structures used by the component, a variety of processing functions common to the specific equipment, the management of the three major equipment types, and the handling of the specialized may-day function. The module contents that reflected the top-level design structure are shown in Table 4.1.

```
proc CCNVID
 -< **** CCNVID - Comm/Nav/Id control
 -<Compliance section: SRS para. 3.2.10.1
 -<                  3.2.10.2
 -<                  3.2.10.3
 -<Called by CCNID
 do
   if (mayday indicator = ON)
     then
       CCMAYDAY  <execute may-day function>
     end
   if (exec is requesting initialization)
     then
       CCINIT   <initialize>
     else
       do
         CCACTRAD  <set active radio indicators>
         CCTIMERS  <check communication timers>
         CCADFTIM  <do ADF processing>
         for (number of displays)
           loop
             CCMMUHF (display id)  <do UHF functions>
             CCMMVHF (display id)  <do VHF functions>
             CCMMHF  (display id)  <do HF functions>
           end
       end
     end
   CCRNAV   <TACAN & LF ADF functions>
   CCIDENT  <A/C identification functions>
 end
end
```

Figure 4.8   Design for Main Entry Point Program

The execution for the module was controlled through the CCNVID entry point and program. This program decided what module function was to be performed at each entry, whether the may-day function was to override all other processing and for initial entry into the module what software initialization was required. This was the minicontrol program for the specified function which was entered on a periodic basis by the system executive. The design for this program is illustrated in Figure 4.8 which shows that the top-level design for this program is a sequence of an if-then and an if-then-else construct. The if-then construct defines the special may-day processing logic and the if-then-else construct defines the normal logic path through the program. In setting up the design the designer wanted to ensure that priority treatment was given to the may-day function which is why it is separated from the other functions and placed at the start of the program's processing.

The specified function for the program is identified as all requirements in the

```
proc CCMAYDAY
  -< **** CCMAYDAY - mayday processing ****
  -<Compliance section: SRS para. 3.2.10.10.1.2.1.4
  -<                    3.2.10.1.2.2.3
  -<                    3.2.10.3.2.10
  -<Called by CCNVID
  begin
    -<Save VHF1 Frequency as Channel 0
    VHF1CHAN0 = DISPVHF1.FREQ
    -<Set VHF1 Frequency to 121.500
    DISPVHF1.FREQ = 121.500
    RTUVHF1.FREQ = 121.500
    -<Set VHF1 Voice Mode to Clear
    DISPVHF1.VOICE1 = CLR
    RTUVHF1.VOICE1 = CLR
    -<Deactivate VHF1 ADF if active
    if (DISPVHF1.ADF = ON)
      then
          RTUVHF1.ADFRELAY = TR
    end
    call CCIEMER
  end
end
```

Figure 4.9 Design for May-Day Processing Subfunction

```
proc CCINIT
  -< **** CCINIT - Comm/Nav/ld initialization
  -<Compliance section: SRS para. 3.2.10.1.2.4
  -<                    3.2.10.2.2.9
  -<                    3.2.10.3.2.15
  -<Called by CCNVID
  begin
    -<Initialize UHF radio data
    Assign defaults to DISPUHF & RTUUHF tables
    UHFCHAN0 = 200.000
    -<Initialize VFH radio data
    Assign defaults to DISPVHF & RTUVHF tables
    VHF1CHAN0 = 30.000   VHF2CHAN0 = 116.000
    -<Initialize HF radio data
    Assign defaults to DISPHF & RTUHF tables
    -<Initialize radio NAVAIDS data
    Assign defaults to DISPRNAV & RTURNAV tables
    -<Initialize aircraft identification data
    Assign defaults to DISPIDNT & RTUIDNT tables
  end
end
```

Figure 4.10 Design for Initialization Subfunction

```
proc CCMMUHF
    -< **** CCMMUFH - UFH radio communications control
    -<Compliance section: SRS para. 3.2.10.1.2.1
    -<UHF requency list data entry is handled by the entrypad
    -<sub-function in the controls/display component.
    -<Called by CCNVID
    begin
       -<Save function key which was depressed
       KEY = OFPINPT(DISPLAY)
       -<Determine if UHF function keys were depressed
       if (display panel and function key is for UHF)
         then
            if (UHF radio data currently useable)
              then
                 if (Have-quick-entry indicator is inactive)
                   then
                      -<Select appropriate UHF sub-function based on function key
                      case KEY
                         part (top left key)
                            CCRVOICE (UHF)   <UHF clear/secure sub-function>
                         part (second top left key)
                            CCRSQUEL (UHF)   <UHF squelch sub-function>
                      end
                      -<Entrypad data collection sub-function
                      Check if UHF channel or frequency data & call appropriate program
                 end
              else -<Illegal data case
                      Set illegal entry alert
            end
         else -<illegal function key
            Set function inoperable alert
       end
    end
end
```

Figure 4.11   Design for UHF Radio Subfunction

indicated paragraphs of the SRS with some further clarification on the initialization mechanism. This function is decomposed into two subfunctions for the two parts of the sequence. The subfunctions allocate the may-day requirements to one part and all other requirements to the other part. The may-day subfunction is handled by a single program (CCMAYDAY) and any further decomposition would be handled within that program design as seen in Figure 4.9 which gives the design of CCMAYDAY.

The other subfunction is more complicated and is further decomposed within the CCNVID design. The first decomposition is to separate the initialization requirements from the normal execution requirements. This is done in the then-part and the else-part of the if-then-else construct respectively.

A second level of decomposition is required for the else-part construct which is a sequence of six parts, one of which is itself a for-loop sequence. This is needed to allocate the normal execution subfunctions to appropriate programs. Further decomposition was not needed for the then-part, since any further decomposition of subfunctions would be handled by the single program (CCINIT) which handles all initialization functions as shown in Figure 4.10.

The subfunctions allocated to the equipment management components within this design involve significant numbers of requirements whose processing is controlled through the programmable function keys on specific display panels. The design for one such component (CCMMUHF) is shown in Figure 4.11, which identifies a top-level decomposition of requirements into two subfunctions that are handled in the design by an assignment and a very involved if-then-else construct. The subfunction for the if-then-else construct is further decomposed, within the then-part subfunction with several levels of additional decomposition to separate the requirements into designable pieces.

References

1. M. Dyer et al., "The Management of Software Engineering," *IBM Systems Journal,* Vol. 19, No. 4, 1980.
2. R.C. Linger, H.D. Mills, and B.I. Witt, *Structured Programming: Theory and Practice,* Addison-Wesley, 1979.
3. P.A. Currit, M. Dyer, and H.D. Mills, "Certifying the Reliability of Software," *IEEE TSE,* Vol. 12, No. 1, 1986.
4. C.B. Jones, *Systematic Software Development Using VDM,* Prentice Hall, 1986.
5. M. Spivey, "The Z Notation: A Reference Manual," Oxford University Research Group, 1987.
6. H.D. Mills, R.C. Linger, and A.R. Hevner, *Information Systems Analysis and Design,* Academic Press, 1986.
7. E.W. Dijkstra, *Notes on Structured Programming,* Academic Press, 1972.
8. C. Bohm and G. Jacopini, "Flow Diagrams, Turing Machines and Languages," *CACM,* Vol. 9, 1966.
9. H.D. Mills, "Top Down Programming in Large Systems," Proceedings of Courant Computer Symposium, 1971.
10. H.D. Mills, "The New Math of Computer Programming," *CACM,* Vol. 18, No. 1, 1975.
11. K.L. Henninger, et al., "Software Requirements for the A-7E Aircraft," NRL Report 3876, 1978.
12. A.J. Jordano, "DSM Software Architecture and Development," *IBM Technical Directions,* Vol. 10, No. 3, 1984.
13. H.D. Mills and R.C. Linger, "Data-Structured Programming," *IEEE TSE,* 1986.

CHAPTER 5

The How To's of Correctness Verification

Testing has been the accepted step in software development where errors introduced during the software design and implementation can be detected and removed. Within the development life cycle, many testing points are identified, each with a specific purpose and role, but the tester's underlying objective is to execute the software in whatever ways will uncover errors. Testing tends to account for some 40% of a software development budget and, when postdelivery software maintenance is considered, for as much as 70% of the total life cycle budget.

Testing does require the software to be designed and implemented, in order to have something to execute, whereas development experience indicates that finding and fixing errors closer to the point of their introduction is clearly more cost effective. This finding is seemingly at odds with the testing role, particularly, when published data [1] indicates that the cost of repairing a software design error can be a hundred times more costly when that design error is found after software delivery rather than during software design. Since testing must wait until code is implemented, there is by definition a minimum 20 to 1 difference in cost effectiveness between testing and other error detection methods, which can operate during software design.

The formal software inspection [2] was defined exactly to fill this void and to introduce systematic error detection into the software design and implementation processes. Design inspections provide a check on the translation of those requirements into a software design. Code inspections provide a check on the translation of that design into a program implementation. The formal inspection has had a measurable impact on the quality of software and recent extensions (e.g., causal analysis [3] and defect prevention process [4]) to the inspection idea are aimed at achieving comparable impacts on the software process.

Correctness verification is an old but more recently introduced idea to prevent the introduction of errors, at their source, namely, as the software design is constructed. If verification is woven into the formal design methods, then genuine error prevention can be realized in software development. *Developing correct designs (not just correctness proving) is the rationale and real benefit from software verification.* The use of software verification during the design process compounds the benefits realized in software quality, since fewer errors are introduced which must be subsequently detected and removed.

5.1 CORRECTNESS VERIFICATION OVERVIEW

In elaborating a software design, the choice of the design and the verification methods must both be based on a formal model if correctness is to have any real meaning. Structured programming theory [5] provides that rigorous underpinning for the design method in Cleanroom. The functional correctness model [6] provides the rigorous underpinning for software verification in Cleanroom.

In the Cleanroom method, software correctness is defined to be the correspondence between a software design and its requirements specification. As a software design is elaborated, the function to be performed by each step in the design elaboration must be identified as some subset of the specification for the software product. At each step, the design, expressed in terms of structured programming constructs and problem data, is hypothesized as providing a solution for the function implementation. The role of correctness verification is to validate that hypothesis by demonstrating that the software design (logical conclusion) implements the specified function (logical hypothesis).

Verification comes down to answering one of two questions: is the design identical to the function at each step (complete correctness) or is some subset of the design equivalent to the function (sufficient correctness)? For complete correctness, a design should produce results only for the input values defined by the function. With sufficient correctness, a design might also correctly produce results for input values not defined by the function. Complete correctness is generally what is sought but considerations about design reusability might dictate the acceptability of sufficient correctness in given instances. The problem with sufficient correctness is the unknown errors or side effects in those aspects of the design not verified but carried along for reusability considerations.

The basis for correctness does not rely on the infallibility of the software designer, his being more careful, or working harder. Rather it stems from the recognition of programs as mathematical objects, subject to logic and reasoning, with defined rules for their orderly combination based on structured programming principles. Verification of complex software, like its design, can be reduced to checking the correctness of the component parts of the design, which are composed of the structured programming constructs. The practice of software verification may exceed a software designer's time and patience but not his knowledge, since it is grounded in the familiar constructs of structured programming. For example, the logical model for a software program is a mathematical function so that the associated proof rule should be and is concerned with the correctness of the transformation of the program's input to its output.

The verification should be carried out to a desired degree of rigor, as the design is constructed, and should be based on correctness proofs that identify the steps to be followed in the proof and provide mathematical justification for the proof arguments. Mathematical notation can be introduced for added formality and conciseness in the proof. Mathematics should not be necessary to ensure the precision and rigor of the proof nor needed for the application of the proof. In the functional correctness model, when mathematical notation is used, the verification is referred to as a formal proof application, and when not, as an informal proof application.

5.2 FUNCTIONAL CORRECTNESS VERIFICATION

In the functional correctness model, a software design is shown to be correct by demonstrating, first, that its execution terminates and, second, it is equivalent to the specified function, which it is intended to satisfy. This correctness demonstration must be incorporated into the software design method so that software designs can be shown to be correct at each step of the design elaboration. Formal proofs of correctness [6] have been defined for each of the structured programming constructs suggested for software designs in the Cleanroom method. These proofs are used in an identical manner whenever the construct is used regardless of the design content being addressed in the construct. If a loop construct is used to design the work selection function in an operating system or to describe the table look up of a telephone directory, the same proof procedure is followed with obviously different arguments. This independence from the application content offers a consistent and scalable approach to verification where being conversant in the proof rules is more important than in the application content.

The structure for the formal proof of a given structured programming construct can be given in tabular form, using the following format:

FUNCTION
   Statement of the specified function to be implemented.
DESIGN
   Details of the proposed design of that function.
PROOF
   Application of the appropriate correctness proofs for that design.

The formal proofs use trace tables and logical analyses to identify and record the proof arguments for a particular design. A detailed explanation of these formal proofs can be found in the literature [7] and is not repeated here because of the minimum use made of formal proofs in the Cleanroom method.

Instead, a set of informal proofs have been defined that involve the asking and answering of correctness questions, which track the correctness condi-

TABLE 5.1 Functional Correctness Model: Informal Approach

Construct	Construct Syntax	Correctness Questions
Sequence	sequence = firstpart : secondpart	Does sequence equal firstpart followed by secondpart?
Forloop	forloop = for indexlist loop looppart end	Does forloop equal firstpart followed by secondpart . . . followed by lastpart?
If-then	if-then = if iftest then thenpart end	When iftest is true, does if-then equal thenpart? *And* When iftest is false, does if-then equal identity?
If-then-else	if-then-else = if iftest then thenpart else elsepart end	When iftest is true, does if-then equal thenpart? *And* When iftest is false, does if-then equal elsepart?

TABLE 5.1 (*Continued*)

Construct	Construct Syntax	Correctness Questions
Case	case = case predicate when cl1 casepart1 . . . . when cln casepartn when others elsepart end	When predicate equals cl1, does case equal casepart1? *And* . . . . *And* When predicate equals cln, does case equal casepartn? *And* When predicate not equal any clx's, does case equal elsepart?
While-loop	while-loop = while whiletest loop looppart end	Is loop termination guaranteed for any argument of whiletest? *And* When whiletest is true, does while-loop equal looppart followed by while-loop? *And* When whiletest is false, does while-loop equal identity?
Loop-until	loop-untils = loop looppart until untiltest end	Is loop termination guaranteed for any argument of untiltest? *And* When untiltest after looppart is false, does loop-until equal looppart followed by loop-until? *And* When untiltest after looppart is true, does loop-until equal looppart?

tions addressed in the formal proofs. Informality does not mean any relaxation of rigor since the necessary correctness conditions must still be proven to be identical. The questions that are defined for each structured programming construct are identified in Table 5.1, together with the definitions of the corresponding construct syntax.

When the structured programming principles are applied with care and concentration, correct software designs can be consistently created. The same situation holds for carrying out correctness proofs, either as a design is constructed or subsequently, as a design's correctness is confirmed. In either case, the objective of the designer is to be able to convince himself or others that the elaborated design is equivalent to the specified function. If the intent of a design is self-evident, direct inspection of the design and the specified function should suffice. If the design intent is not self-evident, then a more deliberate proof demonstration is required. Judgment must be used in communicating correctness arguments. A convincing proof must attract the interest of the listener since many different conclusions can be drawn from the same hypothesis. If the proof has too few steps, the jump in intuition may be too large; if there are too many, then distraction or fatigue may result.

The proof can be carried out in conversation or in writing. In any proof, mathematics should play a supporting (indirect) role, offering notation to facilitate human communication. The notation should facilitate reaching agreement on the succession of claims in a proof by helping to extend the reviewer's memory for details and by allowing both parties to cover more ground with less effort.

Knowledge of the correctness proofs for the design constructs allow verification to be performed to any level of design detail as has been shown in the Cleanroom experience. Equally important is the influence that this knowledge has on the design process itself, where the goal quickly becomes one of creating designs that are self-evident and for which extended correctness demonstrations are not required. When direct inspections of designs against their specified functions are not possible, redesigning for greater simplicity is preferred to attempting an involved proof.

5.2.1   Software Verification Practice

In the Cleanroom method, verification is woven into the software design process. A stepwise elaboration of design is recommended where each step is an iterative mental process of decomposing a specified function into a set of component functions. The elaboration is performed until a direct mapping of component functions to the programming language selected for implementation is reached. In this elaboration, the functional correctness model [6] provides guidance with a uniform and scalable strategy for design elaboration, since the model must organize a comprehensive proof for the total elaboration. Without this correctness roadmap for guidance, the stepwise design elaboration would generally be performed in a more heuristic and subjective way.

In addition to its strategic importance, the functional correctness model also plays a tactical role in the design elaboration. Before settling on a particular design elaboration, the feasibility of subsequent elaboration should be resolved and the functional equivalence between that proposed design and the specified function demonstrated. At each step, the proof of the correctness of the elaboration made by the designer should be the basis for decisions to continue the elaboration or to redesign the current step. Completion of the proof provides the designer with an objective method for deciding how to proceed with the elaboration. By testing the validity of the design elaboration at each step, the designer can proceed with the certainty that previous steps in the elaboration have been demonstrated to be correct. The designer's attention can be focused on those requirements still in need of decomposition.

A four-step practice should be followed in performing each step of the design elaboration, which involves:

1. Specifying the function.
2. Selecting the appropriate design construct(s).
3. Using the construct(s) proof to show equivalence.
4. Deciding to iterate or proceed.

5.2.1.1 *Software Verification Example* To illustrate how the functional correctness model would be used to verify a software design as the design was elaborated, a problem which is found in most software testing literature will be used. The problem is one of going through a set of data values, taking out three values at a time, deciding whether the three values could form the sides of a triangle, and printing a message indicating which type of triangle. A flowchart of one possible solution to this problem is shown in Figure 5.1 and gives the assumptions for the solution (i.e., only positive integer values are considered, values are input three at a time, separate end-of-file indicator appears at the end of data, and triangles are defined as scalar, isosceles, and equilateral).

To start the design of a solution to this problem, the function to be performed needs to be specified and, then, a design formulated to perform that function. As shown in Figure 5.2, a program is defined to package the solution which at the highest level is a two component sequence for data definition and for the triangle decision logic. Correctness would be verified by applying the sequence correctness rule, as shown in Figure 5.2, and would determine whether to proceed to the second elaboration step.

At the second design step, the detailed design for the data definition component is considered self-evident and needs no further elaboration. The detailed design for the triangle decision logic is not considered self-evident and needs elaboration as shown in Figure 5.3. For this elaboration, another two-component sequence is selected to input an initial triple of values and to perform the analysis for triangle selection. Correctness would again be verified by applying the sequence correctness rule, as shown in Figure 5.3, and would determine whether to proceed to the third elaboration step.

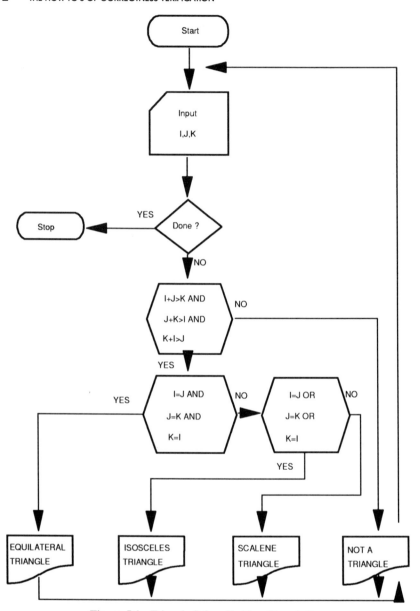

Figure 5.1   Triangle Solver Problem Description

At the third design step, the detailed design for the component to input an initial set of values is considered self-evident and needs no further elaboration. The detailed design for performing the analysis for triangle selection is not considered self-evident and needs elaboration as shown in Figure 5.4. For this elaboration, a while-loop is selected to package the iterative processing of value triples to make the triangle selection. Correctness would be verified by applying the while-loop

Proposed Design:

1. --<Determine if data value triple forms triangle and print type>

2. proc TRIANGLE

3. --<I,J,K are data triple variables and DONE is EOF indicator>

4. var I,J,K: Real

5.   DONE: Boolean

6. --<Input data triple and test for EOF. Exit when EOF reached.

7.   Determine if data triple represents sides of a triangle,

8.   classify and print as equilateral,isosceles or scalene. >

9. begin

10. end

11. end

Correctness Proof:

Does the combination of specifications on lines 3 and 6 satisfy the specification on line 1?

Figure 5.2   First Step in Design Elaboration

correctness rule, as shown in Figure 5.4, and would determine whether to proceed to the fourth and subsequent elaboration steps.

As can be seen from Figure 5.5, another four elaborations would be performed to reach a point where all further detailed design would be considered self-evident. In the figure, the parts of the structured programming constructs used in the design steps are bracketed and the statement numbers which bound the constructs and their commentary are highlighted. These additional elaborations would define the logic for analyzing the triplets of data values. A structure of nested if-then-else constructs is used in describing this logic, which first determines whether the data values can form any type of triangle and then looks for repeated (equal) values to decide which type of triangle. As the analysis progresses, there are several instances where the design of the intended function is self-evident and needs no further elaboration (e.g., generating an appropriate printout when the type of triangle is identified).

This example, while small and straightforward, does illustrate how systematic verification would support the top-down elaboration of this design. If software verification were not used, the designer would most likely define the different checks on the data value triplet first, since that would be considered the key aspect of the analysis problem. The checking would probably be done in the order of all

Design Elaboration

```
6.   --<Input data triple and test for EOF. Exit when EOF reached.
7.     Determine if data triple represents sides of a triangle,
8.     classify and print as equilateral,isosceles or scalene. >
9.   begin
10.    --<Input first data triple or EOF from system file. >
11.      read I,J,K
12.      read DONE
13.    --<When EOF read,exit procedure; otherwise check if inputs
14.      are sides of triangle, then classify and print type. >
15.      while (Not DONE)
16.        loop
17.        end
```

Correctness Proof:

Does the combination of specifications on lines 10 and 13
satisfy the function specified on line 6 ?

Figure 5.3   Second Step in Design Elaboration

values equal, two values equal, and can the three values form a triangle, since this is an easy checking scheme. As shown in Chapter 4 (Figures 4.1 and 4.2), some very complex designs might result with this approach because an optimum checking strategy is not employed.

The consideration of getting an input triplet, looping through a file of data values, terminating the analysis, and declaring appropriate data structures would, probably, be handled as afterthoughts. Unfortunately, these considerations are the kernel of an analysis, where the details of the specific steps can be inserted at any point. Correctness verification ensures that the structured programming-based design method proceeds top-down with a consistent decomposition of requirements, which generally provides the optimum and simplest solution.

5.3 VERIFICATION-BASED INSPECTIONS

Conventional development practice assumes that software is developed with errors and relies on testing (primarily) and inspections (to a lesser degree) to discover and diagnose these errors. With the mathematics-based design methods in Cleanroom, software can be developed more correctly and with dramatically fewer defects. This expectation of correct software has recast the role of inspections in the development process from one of error detection to one of independent confirmation

Design Elaboration:

13.   --<When EOF read,exit procedure; otherwise check if inputs
14.   are sides of triangle, then classify and print type. >
15.   while (Not DONE)
16.   --<DONE = false; determine if current input triple forms
17.   triangle, classify/print and read next input triple. >
18.   loop
19.   end

Correctness Proof:

Is loop termination guaranteed for any argument
of the predicate on line 15 ?
AND
Is the specification on line 13 satisfied
by the execution of the function on line 16 followed
by the execution of the function on line 13
when the argument on line 15 is true ?
AND
Does the specification on line 13 equal identity
when the argument on line 15 is false ?

Figure 5.4   Third Step of Design Elaboration

of software correctness. The change in inspection focus requires the introduction of correctness methods into the inspection practice. The Cleanroom experience has used the functional correctness model exclusively but other correctness models might also be applicable.

For the correctness focus in inspections to work, correctness verification must first be an integral part of the software design process and applied in a stepwise fashion as the design is elaborated or refined. The verification-based inspections are then a confirmation of the verification performed by the designer in constructing the design and a second opportunity to ensure the development of correct designs.

The verification-based inspection could also be used with conventional development practice and be an effective agent for introducing correctness verification into the development. By forcing a correctness-proving focus during inspection, the designer in this case would think about correctness after the fact but would soon recognize the benefit from using the same proof arguments during design construction. The functional correctness model provides a systematic method for checking the completeness, consistency, and goodness of designs as they evolve. Software designers should recognize the ease and effectiveness of

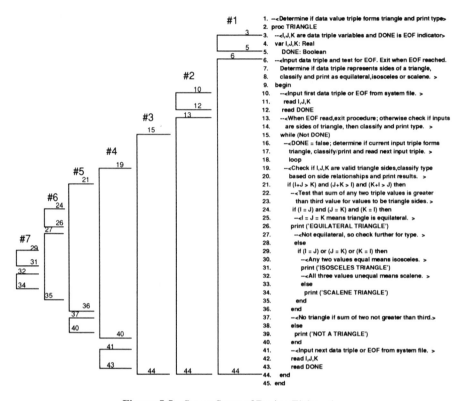

Figure 5.5 Seven Steps of Design Elaboration

using the verification ideas, which simplify their bookkeeping chores and ensure their addressing of the complete set of requirements.

5.3.1 Importance of Formal Inspections to the Baseline Capability

The formal inspection [2] is a technical assessment of a software workproduct in order to detect and resolve errors as soon as possible after their introduction into the workproduct. The formal inspection is performed by a specially constituted team whose members bring different engineering disciplines and different insights to identifying workproduct errors. Defined checklists are used in the process to focus the inspectors on the more likely types of errors which are made within the particular development organization. The combination of these two features (well-structured teams and checklists) is what sets formal inspections apart from other types of software reviews.

Prior to formal inspections, different forms of informal reviews were performed in the typical development process. Desk checking, peer reviews, walkthroughs, audits, and so forth were commonly practiced by most development organizations.

TABLE 5.2 Example of Formal Inspection Guidelines

Design Inspection Topics	Code Inspection Topics
Logic flow	Logic flow
Decisions and paths	Decisions and loops
Data usage	Data usage
Return codes and messages	Register usage
Module-program attributes	Storage usage
External linkages	External linkages
Higher-level design	Design problems
Standards adherence	Language constraints
User interfaces	Code commentary
Performance	Performance
Maintainability	Code maintainability
Other	Other

They tended to be performed with varying frequency, thoroughness, and consistency so that they had unpredictable impact on the development process. Formal inspections introduced a formality which allowed technical assessment to be repeatable and consistent and defined a procedure which could be scheduled into the development.

Formal inspections are suggested and generally performed against the software workproducts (design descriptions and implemented code) and, more recently, against the other engineering workproducts, such as specifications and test materials. Guidelines are prepared for the different types of inspections to focus the analysis that should be performed by the inspectors. The guidelines address considerations such as adherence to organizational standards, software interfaces, error detection logic, and the like. Checklists are generally prepared to support these guidelines, as shown in Table 5.2, and used to collect and categorize the errors found during inspections.

5.3.1.1 *Formal Inspection for Software*

The software inspections focus on detecting errors in the software design and implementation before attempting any execution. The software design is inspected to check its readiness for implementation and the software code is inspected to check its readiness for execution. The inspectors are asked to focus on differences between the design and the approved requirements specification, in the first case, and between the code and the approved design, in the second case.

Three different formal inspections have been identified for software, which should be scheduled into the development process and should be the basis for proceeding through the development process. These three inspections have been named the I_0 inspection of the high-level design, the I_1 inspection of the detailed-level design, and the I_2 inspection of the implemented code. Reinspections are performed, as needed, at any of the three points to ensure that previously identified errors were repaired and that the revised design or code is acceptable to the inspection team.

The purpose of the I_0 is to verify that the software requirements have been correctly decomposed into a software design. At this design level the design is typically represented by a set of connected and interacting programs and modules, where modules are collections of programs performing similar functions. The I_0 inspection examines the functional content of the identified modules and programs to ensure they perform their stated function. The I_0 inspection assesses that the combination of the module and program functions is consistent with the specified software requirements. Tracing the intermodule data flows is helpful in performing this consistency and completeness check on requirements and, where asynchronous or real-time software execution is specified, in resolving questions on processing deadlock and data coherence.

The purpose of the I_1 inspection is to verify that the modules and programs, defined in the high-level design, are correctly designed in terms of structured programming constructs and appropriate representations of problem data. The I_1 inspection examines the internal module and program logic (the decision points and functional content of different conditional paths) to ensure the capture of the complete module or program function. Tracing the logic flow is helpful in performing the completeness check on requirements and in isolating the macro designs of the detailed processing logic.

The purpose of the I_2 inspection is to verify the translation of the detailed design description into an appropriate programming language. The I_2 inspection examines the code for compliance with organizational standards as well as correct design translation.

5.3.1.2 Formal Inspection Process

A systematic process has been defined for formal inspections, which addresses the preparation and the resolution effort needed in addition to the conduct of the inspection. A set of preparation activities is defined which must be performed prior to the actual inspection. This includes the identification of an inspection moderator who organizes the material on the particular workproduct and distributes that material to the inspection team. The inspection team is expected to assess this material against the appropriate checklist to confirm its technical accuracy and agreement with specifications. At the same time, the team identifies any errors or questionable areas in the design or implementation, which need to be discussed during the inspection.

The formal inspection is conducted at a meeting of the inspection team with the originators of the particular workproduct. The identification and recording of errors is the prime objective of the inspection meeting and not the resolution of these errors. Reworking the design or code to address particular errors is done after the meeting by the workproduct originators. All issues, concerns, and errors in the workproduct are expected to be resolved.

The inspection follow-up is defined to verify that the necessary rework was performed and completed, so that the actual resolution can be recorded within the

TABLE 5.3   Profile of Error Detection Efficiencies

Project	Formal Inspections				Unit Test	System Test
	I_0	I_1	I_2	Subtotal		
1			50	50	25	25
2			60	60	24	16
3			58	58	21	21
4	4	13	49	66	17	17
5	5	16	39	60	19	21
6	20	27	10	57	20	23
7	6	18	22	46	18	36
8	8	8	30	46	24	30
9	6	20	26	52	22	26
10	10	18	24	52	24	24

inspection report. When a significant portion of the workproduct must be reworked (greater than 25%), a reinspection is generally required.

The inspection meeting is restricted to 2 to 3 hours, which is considered the optimum period for maintaining a high level of concentration on the workproduct being inspected. For effective inspection it is expected that each team member spends a comparable amount of time preparing for the inspection. Rules of thumb on the amount of material to be considered during each hour of a specific insp c-tion are 10 pages of high-level design, 5 pages of detailed-level design, and 100 to 200 programming language statements. Where design languages are used to document design—an equivalence of 25 design language statements per page of design seems to hold.

5.3.1.3   Benefits of Formal Inspections

The management benefit from formal inspections is early visibility into the status and quality of the software development with ample time to take corrective action if progress and quality are not at acceptable levels. Since the inspections can be worked into project plans, they can be used as milestones for judging schedule status, checkpoints for judging product sizes and production rates, and opportunities for removing product errors.

Available evidence indicates that formal inspections have had significant positive impact on the quality of the developed software. Formal inspections provide the opportunity to discover and remove large numbers of software errors before they are embodied in the executing code. Reported inspection data [8,9,10] indicate that more than 50% of the errors can be removed and that design and code inspections are equally effective at error detection. The same trend is shown in Table 5.3, which gives the error removal profiles for some recent IBM software developments. These profiles show the percentage of software errors uncovered by the different detection steps in the development process and clearly show the significant contribution (removal of 50 to 70% of the software errors) of formal inspections to error detection and removal.

5.3.2   Merger of Functional Correctness and Formal Inspection Models

In the Cleanroom method, verification-based inspections [11] are primarily defined to support the design of correct software by providing an independent confirmation of software correctness during the design process. They assume design using the constructs from structured programming theory, written in a design language and organized under a top-down incremental development strategy. The inspection approach can provide two other benefits: (1) improved effectiveness in existing formal inspection practice and (2) a medium for the indirect introduction of correctness verification into software design practice.

Existing published material on formal software inspections tends to concentrate on their administration (i.e., staffing, reporting, and so forth) with very limited focus on their technical content. Available guidance on how to technically inspect designs and code tends to boil down to mentally simulating code execution with selective inputs or to looking for specific classes of software errors. The most difficult choices facing an inspector are how to get started on an inspection and on what key technical parts of the application solution to focus. Without experience in the application, the typical inspector generally starts at the front of the material to be inspected and proceeds to march through the material. *A significant benefit from the verification-based inspection is the organization of the questions and their sequence, which are to be used in an inspection. This takes away the inspector's guesswork on what questions to ask and how to step through an inspection.*

The use of mathematics-based correctness models for software verification has not been readily accepted by the software community, where it is considered too complex, mathematical, and demanding for practical use. Verification-based inspection attempts to demonstrate that there is no mystique in performing software verification with the functional correctness model and that, with limited tool assistance, software verification can become part of the design process. The analysis (and output) of the verification-based inspection can be used by the software designer to guide software verification as designs are constructed. The verification-based inspection script forces the design inspectors to confirm design correctness rather than to focus on just finding software errors.

The thrust of the verification-based inspection is to contribute to improved software quality without causing a detrimental impact on software productivity. Based on experimental evidence [7,12], once there is a recognition that correctness verification leads to better software designs and achieves more quality objectives than conventional software testing, the testing activity and cost tend to drop off dramatically. The active use of software verification exploits the full potential of modern software design methods and, as was intended, allays misapprehensions about the feasibility of its application to software of any size and complexity.

5.3.3 Verification-Based Inspection Practice

Confirming the correctness of software designs is a significantly different focus than inspecting software material for errors, which needs to be performed with more care and attention. Unlike the rules of thumb given for the I_0, I_1, and I_2 formal inspections, the rules for verification-based inspections are that they be performed frequently and never consider more than a half dozen pages of design description (about 100 to 150 design language statements). This represents a significant amount of design to consider but small enough to discard or redo, when correctness can not be confirmed. Based on the average of one step in a correctness proof for every six design language statements, as identified in reference [11], an average verification-based inspection meeting could take on the order of an hour assuming a few minutes on each step on a proof. This is a reasonable time period for maintaining attention and comprehension.

The estimate of only several minutes per proof is based on the fact that the functional correctness model only requires localized reasoning about a proof. Since the verification procedure assures the correctness of all previously considered steps in the design and organizes proofs on the basis of self-contained design constructs, there is no need to look elsewhere in the design to reason about the proof for a given construct. The several-minute estimate has been confirmed in the Cleanroom experience.

In generating the questions for verification-based inspections, a point should be made on the difficulty of specifying functions at each level of the requirements decomposition, which is really a question on the necessary level of formal description. *The current unacceptance of verification seems to stem from the mistaken belief that absolute precision, complete specification, and intricate mathematical notation is always required, which is definitely not the case.* If the function specifications are intended to drive an automated verification system which produces code, directly from specifications (an ongoing research direction), then absolute precision would be required and highly mathematical notation needed to specify the requirements, unambiguously and completely, to the automated system. If, however, the specifications are to be used in an environment that combines human reasoning with automation, then less formal description in function specifications can be tolerated and the need for mathematical notation, absolute precision, and full completeness can be relaxed. Humans are more tolerant with unstated assumptions, implied experience, and the like than machines, which require the explicit statement of all problem parameters.

In this latter case, where human reasoning is involved, there is another range of possibilities for blending the automation and human participation. At one end of the spectrum, if tools were used to perform automated semantic analysis, these tools would require, as input, fairly precise and complete specifications that are expressed in a symbolic or mathematical notation. At the other end, if tools were used only to analyze the structure of a design solution without looking at the semantics of the underlying specifications, then these tools could get along with significant relaxation in the formality of the specification description. For designs of small problems, where only structural analysis is of interest, human reasoning without any tool support would probably be the norm and place the minimum demand on formality.

For the tools which currently support the Cleanroom method, the automation support is limited to the analysis of design structure and driven by the prime program rules defined in the functional correctness model. The designers and inspectors are directed to lines in the design language descriptions only. The lines contain either function specifications (recorded as commentary) or the start of corresponding design constructs which presumably implement the function. The inspection practice asks the human to understand the semantics of the specification and design and to make the equivalence comparison, both of which are reasonable intellectual tasks. The alternate approach of attempting to automate the semantic analysis and comparison involve nontrivial computer analyses.

This current practice strikes a compromise between formality in specification description and thoroughness of verification. Targeting for rigorous but not over-exacting levels of description formality seems to be a more sensible approach to gaining acceptance for verification within the software community. As acceptance is gained, expanding the levels of formal description and introducing further complexity in the automation support should be considered in order to move software development toward a specification-driven process.

5.3.4 Verification-Based Inspection Example

To illustrate the use of the verification-based inspection, the triangle solver problem shown in Figure 5.1 is used. The design language description for a possible solution is given in Figure 5.5, which shows a refinement of seven steps to get the design to a level where all parts are self-evident.

To start the inspection process, an analysis tool, like the one currently used within IBM for the Cleanroom method, is run to organize a script, similar to the one shown in Figure 5.6. The script prepared by the analysis tool would lay out the questions to be asked by the inspectors and the sequence in which the questions should be asked. With the Cleanroom method, it would be assumed that the correctness of the design had been verified by the designer as part of the design construction as discussed earlier in section 5.2.1.1. The role of the verification-based inspection is a confirmation of that correctness and, where correctness is difficult to demonstrate, a request for design simplification. The prepared script would be generated to guide the inspectors in confirming the correctness of the design.

The script is automatically produced by the analysis tool, based on its analysis of the design language description of the problem solution, shown in Figure 5.5. The organization of the questions included in the script is based strictly on a top-down analysis of the particular logical structure of the design (i.e., the hierarchy of nested structured programming constructs). For this case, a seven-level hierarchy

1   Does the combination of behavior specs on lines 3 and 6 satisfy the intended function on line 1.

2   Does the combination of behavior specs on lines 10 and 13 satisfy the behavior spec on line 6.

3   Is loop termination guaranteed for any argument of the predicate on line 15 (ie. DONE)
     AND
     Does the behavior spec on line 13 equal the behavior spec on line 16 followed by the behavior spec on line 13 when the predicate on line 15 (ie. DONE) is true.
     AND
     Does the behavior spec on line 13 equal identity when the predicate on line 15 (ie. DONE) is false.

4   Does the combination of behavior specs on lines 19 and 41 satisfy the behavior spec on line 16.

5   Does the behavior spec on line 22 satisfy the behavior spec on line 19 when the predicate on line 21 (ie. (I+J>K) and (J+K>I) and (K+I>J)) is true.
     AND
     Does the behavior spec on line 37 satisfy the behavior spec on line 19 when the predicate on line 21 (ie. (I+J>K) and (J+K>I) and (K+I>J)) is false.

6   Does the behavior spec on line 25 satisfy the behavior spec on line 22 when the predicate on line 24 (ie. (I=J) and (J=K) and (K=I)) is true.
     AND
     Does the behavior spec on line 27 satisfy the behavior spec on line 22 when the predicate on line 24 (ie. (I=J) and (J=K) and (K=I)) is false.

7   Does the behavior spec on line 30 satisfy the behavior spec on line 27 when the predicate on line 29 (ie. (I=J) or (J=K) or (K=I)) is true.
     AND
     Does the behavior spec on line 32 satisfy the bevavior spec on line 27 when the predicate on line 29 (ie. (I=J) or (J=K) or (K=I)) is false.

Figure 5.6   Verification-Based Inspection Questions for the Triangle Solver Problem

was used in elaborating the design, as shown in Figure 5.5. The structured programming constructs used at each level of this particular hierarchy are:

1. Two-part sequence—lines 3 to 5 and lines 6 to 44.
2. Two-part sequence—lines 10 to 12 and lines 13 to 44.
3. While-loop—lines 16 to 44.
4. Two-part sequence—lines 19 to 40 and lines 41 to 43.
5. If-then-else—lines 21 to 40.

   6. If-then-else—lines 24 to 35.

   7. If-then-else—lines 29 to 34.

The generated script maps this structure by prompting the inspector with the informal proof questions for a sequence, for another sequence, for a while-loop, for a third sequence, for an if-then-else, for another if-then-else, and, finally, for a third if-then-else. Obviously, if a different design description had been created, a script with different questions and different ordering would be created.

   The format of the specific questions suggested at each step of the inspection are dictated by the informal proof which has been defined for the particular structured programming construct within the functional correctness model. In this particular example, the informal proof for a sequence construct would be used for steps 1, 2, and 4, the informal proof for an if-then-else construct for steps 5, 6, and 7, and the informal proof for a while-loop construct for step 3. While there are three distinct instances of the informal proofs for both the sequence and if-then-else constructs, the proof in each instance is tailored to a different scope of the design description and addresses, at least, different line numbers and predicates. For the sequence proofs, the first focuses on lines 1, 3, and 6; the second on lines 6, 10, and 13; and the third on lines 16, 19, and 41. For the if-then-else proofs, the first focuses on lines 19, 22, and 27 and on the predicate on line 21; the second on lines 22, 25, and 27 and on the predicate on line 24; and the third on lines 27, 30, and 32 and on the predicate on line 29. For a very simple case, this example highlights the power of the functional correctness model—*only a small number of distinct proofs are defined (one per structured programming construct) which can be applied wherever the construct is used in a design.*

   The details on each of the informal correctness proofs for the structured programming constructs are summarized in Table 5.1. Additional discussion of the functional correctness model and the formal and informal proof definitions can be found in references [5,6].

   Note that in this case the content of the commentary (function specification) is a mixture of natural language and symbolic text, which, to the designer, provides a sufficiently rigorous function specification to support correctness verification. The designer might have elected to use more mathematical, set theoretic, or box structure notation to more concisely and precisely specify the function. Moreover, the designer might have elected to not include function specifications (commentary) for the obvious or self-evident design cases (i.e., the commentary on lines 3, 25, 30, 32, and 37). In essence, printing the type of triangle was inferred from earlier specifications as an alternative and did not necessarily have to be explicitly stated. The important point is that, while the designer might be prompted to consider a function specification by the analysis tool, the designer makes the final decision on whether to include or exclude a specification. If the designer views the function to be self-evident, then its specification can and should be excluded.

   While this particular example (triangle solver problem) and the small number of steps in the correctness proof (seven) might seem atypical, current research [11] indicates that proofs with the functional correctness model are generally compact.

As a particular illustration of the compactness of proofs, two other variants on the design for the triangle solver program were identified, earlier, in Figures 4.1 and 4.2. For these variants, it was noted that the number of logic paths in these designs was 89 and 26, respectively. The number of steps in the correctness proofs for each of these designs turns out to be 18 and 11, respectively, which is a further confirmation of the compactness of the correctness proofs with the functional correctness model. This compactness probably results from the use of structured programming theory and from the limitation on the levels of problem abstraction which can be comfortably handled by the human mind.

The triangle solver problem is given particular mention in reference [12], as a seemingly straightforward requirement for which the typical software tester misses running half of the tests needed for validating the solution. Rather than the illustrated seven-step proof, a minimum of 16 discrete tests are suggested to provide an adequate but incomplete validation of a single pass through the design. The iteration explicit in the specification would not be addressed by the 16 tests though all correctness conditions (including iteration) are addressed in the seven-step proof.

5.3.5 An Example of a Larger Application

Verification-based inspections are particularly effective for inspecting and confirming the correctness of large-size designs which, by necessity, must be developed in pieces. The inspections would be ordered in a top-down sequence because of the functional correctness model orientation, which would ensure that each inspection could count on the correctness of all logically preceding inspected components.

To demonstrate how this works, the verification-based inspection practice followed for the flight software in an avionics system, which was developed with the Cleanroom method, is illustrated. In particular, a component of that software was concerned with managing the radio, navigation, and aircraft identification equipment that was carried on the aircraft. In each category, there were several discrete pieces of equipment (e.g., UHF, VHF, and HF radios) that provided different capabilities and could be used in various combinations during a given mission. The requirements for this component were documented in some 20 pages of English text, within the SRS for the flight software. The external interfacing functions for this component were handled by a separate and generalized controls-and-display component, which handled all interfaces with four programmable displays, their function keyboards, and two separate data entry keyboards.

The high-level design for this component was documented in some 45 pages of design language description, which was composed of high-level assignment statements, structured programming constructs, and some English text. The English text was used to identify known logic whose design was self-evident and acted as placeholders in the description. The actual details of this self-evident design were defined during subsequent coding steps with the programming language used for implementation. The design constructs which were used for this component in-

CCNID	Comm/Nav/Id Module
CCDATA	Data Declarations
CCRADDAT	Communications Data
CCRNVDAT	Navigation Radio Data
CCIDDAT	A/C Identification Data
CCNVID	Comm/Nav/Id Control
CCINIT	Initialization
CCACTRAD	Active Radio Indicators
CCTIMERS	Timer Control
CCADFTIM	ADF Control
CCMMUHF	UHF Radio Control
CCRVOICE	Voice Mode Control
CCRSQUEL	Squelch Control
CCRTONE	Tone Control
CCRCHAN	Channel Selection
CCRFREQ	Frequency Selection
CCADFKEY	ADF Processing
CCUHFMOD	Radio Mode Control
CCUHFGRD	Mode Sequencing
CCHAVEQA	Have-Quick-A Control
CCHAVEQT	Have-Quick-T Control
CCMMVHF	VFH Radio Control
call CCRVOICE, etc.	

CCMMHF   HF Radio Control
 call CCRVOICE, etc.

CCRNAV   Navigation Radio Control

CCIDENT   A/C Identification Control

CCMAYDAY   Mayday Processing

Figure 5.7   Component Hierarchy

cluded the sequence, forloop, if-then, if-then-else, and case constructs. Since loops were not used in the design of this component, the verification-based inspection was reasonably straightforward. The resulting design was simple (conservative) and could be reliably inspected, implemented, and maintained. Figure 5.7 shows the structure of this component in terms of the internal programs and procedures.

Verification-based inspection of this material could be characterized as checking the design in layers, relying on the commentary for the specification of function, and structuring the verification based on the nested use of the structured programming design constructs. Checking the design in layers would mean that the CCDATA and CCNVID components would be confirmed first, then the 13 components at the next design level (CCRADDAT through CCMAYDAY), and then

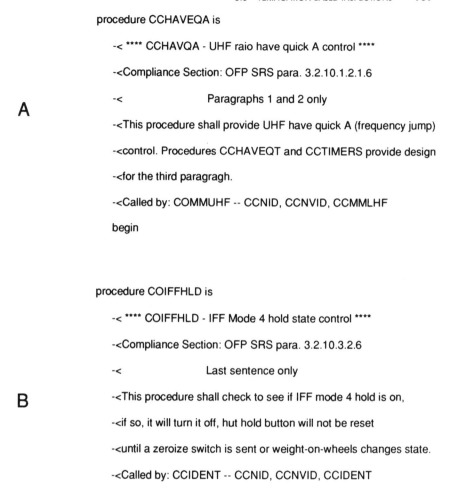

procedure CCHAVEQA is

-< **** CCHAVQA - UHF raio have quick A control ****

-<Compliance Section: OFP SRS para. 3.2.10.1.2.1.6

-<   Paragraphs 1 and 2 only

-<This procedure shall provide UHF have quick A (frequency jump)

-<control. Procedures CCHAVEQT and CCTIMERS provide design

-<for the third paragragh.

-<Called by: COMMUHF -- CCNID, CCNVID, CCMMLHF

begin

procedure COIFFHLD is

-< **** COIFFHLD - IFF Mode 4 hold state control ****

-<Compliance Section: OFP SRS para. 3.2.10.3.2.6

-<   Last sentence only

-<This procedure shall check to see if IFF mode 4 hold is on,

-<if so, it will turn it off, hut hold button will not be reset

-<until a zeroize switch is sent or weight-on-wheels changes state.

-<Called by: CCIDENT -- CCNID, CCNVID, CCIDENT

begin

Figure 5.8   Examples of Commentary for Specifying Component Function

the detailed components within CCMMUHF, CCMMVHF, CCMMHF, CCRNAV, CCIDENT, and CCMAYDAY. Systematically inspecting successive layers in the design hierarchy, exhibited in Figure 5.7, permits the confirmation in discrete steps, where the data for inspection is self-contained for each step. Correctness is confirmed or challenged at each layer before proceeding to the details of subsequent layers. This systematic approach to correctness confirmation is a key benefit derived from using the functional correctness model and takes the guesswork out of deciding how to attack the inspection of 45 pages of design.

Without the guidance from the functional correctness model, an inspector might take the approach of tracing down each branch of the hierarchy completely and resolving all aspects of a particular function. As an example, the inspector might first take the path CCNID, CCNVID, CCMMUHF, CCUHFMOD, and CCUFHGRD, which would be one of the many threads through the UHF radio function. That approach would introduce unnecessary levels of localized detail and necessitate the handling of a potentially large number of incomplete correctness proofs, since consideration of the alternate branches along the nested branches of the hierarchy is being deferred.

This approach of tracing design threads to their full detail might be viable for small designs whose correctness could be confirmed in one 1 to 2 hour session. The approach would be infeasible for this particular avionics case which required some 20 hours of inspection time, spread over an approximate two-week time period. Too many correctness points would be left unresolved between sessions (alternate branches of nested decisions) and no clear boundaries would exist of which parts of the design have been confirmed correct and which parts remain to be completely or partially confirmed. Specifically for the case cited, only the aspects of CCNVID initialization (CCINIT) needed for the particular path would be checked and the rest of the CCINIT design would be assumed to be correct. As different paths through CCNVID were checked, it might become unclear what parts had and had not been checked in CCINIT.

Commentary within the design language description was used to specify the function allocation of the SRS to the software components. In particular, compliance commentary was used in each component description which referenced the appropriate paragraphs and subparagraphs with the SRS which defined the component's function. As shown in Figure 5.8, the compliance commentary identified sections, paragraphs, sentences, and phrases within the SRS to explicitly define which software requirements were allocated to each design component. For further illustration, Figure 5.8A shows a case where only certain paragraphs within a section apply and Figure 5.8B shows a case where only the last sentence of a particular paragraph applies.

The design excerpt shown in Figure 5.9 is an if-then construct whose then part also contains an if-then construct, so that verification based on the functional correctness model would use a set of four proofs for this segment. The first would be an if-then proof for the if-then which checks if the ''have quick T'' indicator is on. The second would be a sequence proof for the thenpart which is composed of an assignment and an if-then. The third would be another if-then proof for the nested if-then which makes the five-second test. The fourth proof would be another sequence proof for the four assignment statements in the thenpart of the nested if-then. The analysis support tool could organize scripts to map the inspection of this excerpt, as well as the program (CCTIMERS) and the design components (CCNVID and CCNID) of which it was an element. The tool would also format the correctness questions which must be answered at each step of the inspection.

In this particular avionics application, status of the verification-based inspection was indicated by annotating the scripts, where design issues, errors, and the like were also noted. The status of the software design was indicated by annotating the appropriate sections of the SRS, based on the allocation of requirements indicated in the design commentary by section, paragraph, sentence, and phrase.

```
procedure COTIMERS is

   -< ****** COTIMERS - communications timers control ******

   -<Compliance Section: OFP SRS para. 3.2.10.1.2.6

   -<                              3.2.10.1.2.1.7

   -<                              3.2.10.1.2.2.5

   -<              Timer reset portion of each section

   -<This procedure shall check to see if any of the communications

   -<timers are on. If so they are updated. If any have reached their

   -<maximum times, they shall be turned off.

   -<Called by: COMMUHF -- CCNID, CCNVID, CCMMLHF

begin

      -<Update have quick T timer each comp cycle it's on

      if DISPUHF.HAVET = ON then

         HAVETIME = HAVETIME + 1

         -<Turn have quick T off after 5 seconds

         if HAVETIME = ICC then

            DISPUHF.HAVET = OFF

            RTUHF.MODE = OFF

            -<Restore UHF radio mode

            DISPUHF.MODE = HAVENLDE

            RTUHF.MODE = HAVEMCDE

         endif

      endif
```

Figure 5.9 Excerpt of Component Design Confirmed with Verification-Based
Inspection

In the actual case, the inspection of this design component did require the
resolution of some issues before correctness could be confirmed. The majority of
issues dealt with new or revised requirements which were not adequately addressed in the design. Change-request authorizations were issued and the designs
were updated, generally through a more precise specification of the function to be
addressed. Eight of the 40-odd programs in this design required reinspection be-

cause of the discrepancy in specifying function. In the process, there was only one instance where the informal correctness proof was found inadequate and a formal proof was performed. The original design of the CCADFTIM program contained a section of fairly abstruse design description for which a formal proof was created which indicated a design error. In correcting the error, the designer opted to simplify that section of design, which could then be inspected using informal proofs.

References

1. B.W. Boehm, *Software Engineering Economics*, Prentice Hall, 1980.
2. M.E. Fagan, "Design and Code Inspections," *IBM Systems Journal*, Vol. 17, 1978.
3. R.T. Phillips, "An Approach to Software Causal Analysis," IEEE Globecom '86, No. 12, 1986.
4. R.G. Mays, et al., "Experiences with Defect Prevention," *IBM Systems Journal*, Vol. 29, No. 1, 1990.
5. R.C. Linger, H.D. Mills, and B.I. Witt, *Structured Programming: Theory and Practice*, Addison-Wesley, 1979.
6. H.D. Mills, "The New Math of Computer Programming," *CACM*, Vol. 18, No. 1, 1975.
7. R.C. Linger and H.D. Mills, "Case Study in Cleanroom Software Engineering," COMPSAC '88 Proceedings, 1988.
8. B.M. Knight, "On Software Quality and Productivity," IBM Technical Directions, No. 2, 1978.
9. R.B. Grady, "Role of Software Metrics in Managing Quality and Testing," Proceeding of the Sixth International Software Testing Conference, 1989.
10. J. McCall, "Introducing Software Metrics into Your Company," Proceedings of Achieving Quality Software Tutorials, 1991.
11. M. Dyer and A. Kouchakdjian, "Correctness Verification: Alternative to Software Structural Testing," *Information and Software Technology*, January-February 1990.
12. G.J. Myers, *The Art of Software Testing*, Wiley, 1979.

CHAPTER 6

The How To's of Cleanroom Testing

There is a dichotomy of opinion on the use of software testing versus correctness verification within the software development life cycle. Software testing has been the accepted method for detecting and removing software errors and has played the dominant role in error detection. Correctness verification has only recently matured into acceptable practice but shows the potential for playing an even more decisive role in error prevention during software development. The Cleanroom method integrates both ideas into an effective development practice.

Within the Cleanroom method, the functional correctness model [1] for software verification is introduced for software design. The available experience indicates that software is developed with sufficient quality to forgo the traditional structural or unit testing performed by the software developer. Statistical testing methods are also introduced in the Cleanroom method for functional or product testing. The experience in this case indicates that these methods do provide a formal and objective basis for validating that the software satisfies its intended requirements. The synergism between the correctness verification and statistical testing ideas results in the development of software with fewer errors. Moreover, these errors are easier to both detect and repair and the resulting software exhibits exceptional operating characteristics in terms of its quality. Error prevention, not detection, is the focus, which offers the only real potential for sustained quality growth in software.

6.1 TRADITIONAL TESTING FOCUS

Software testing techniques are generally classified into the two categories of structural and functional testing, which correlate with two possible starting points for software testing: the requirements specification or the software itself. *Structural testing* techniques [2] are generally used by software developers and are based on developing test data from the structure of the implemented software. The objective of the structural techniques is to verify that the implemented software matches its design. Within the development life cycle, structural testing is generally performed at the unit and module levels.

Functional testing techniques [3] are generally used by someone other than the developer (i.e., by testers and/or customers) and start with the software specification in which the required functions are identified. The objective of the functional techniques is to assess that the functions are provided and to validate that the software design and implementation yield the required capability. Within the development life cycle, functional testing is generally performed for the integration and acceptance of the software.

Software testing is performed during many steps of the software development life cycle. Establishing the testing hierarchy for a software development is common practice and can identify the opportunities during development for software error detection and for validation of the software capability.

6.1.1 Software Structural Testing

Structural testing is based on a detailed knowledge of the design and implementation of the software rather than on its required functions. Clear box and white box testing are other labels applied to this category of software testing. It is conducted at the unit level by the individual programmer to check the implementation of the piece of code for which the programmer is responsible. It is also conducted at the module level by the lead (chief) programmer to check the implementation of a collection of code units, which is intended to provide some identifiable capability. Demonstrating consistency between the software design and its implementation is viewed as a necessary first step before looking at requirements satisfaction. In those instances where functions are needed in a design but not addressed by the specification (e.g., file-accessing strategies for a data base), structural testing techniques may also be the only means for checking the satisfaction of the implied requirements.

Structural testing is the most widely used form of software testing, whose popularity is largely due to the simplicity of the concept and to the availability of numerous support tools. It involves execution of the software (unit or module) with the goal of tracking a particular execution path through the software or of achieving a level of execution coverage on the statements or branches in the software. It defines test data in terms of the control structure designed into the software, which simplifies use but is the major shortcoming of the approach because of the complexity of typical control structures.

Structural testing is generally conducted in an informal and loosely controlled manner. Unlike software functional testing, where plans and procedures must be documented and approved prior to test execution, structural testing tends to be conducted by developers with little preparation and essentially no reporting of results. Structural testing is viewed as the developer's opportunity to find and repair errors before the software goes public. The lack of structure raises questions about the effectiveness of the testing and the lack of reporting detracts from the quality level of the software.

The three basic approaches used in structural testing are statement (or segment), branch (or decision), and path testing. *Statement testing* attempts to check that each implemented software statement executes correctly when reached in the execution flow. *Branch testing* attempts to check each branch (or leg) in a transfer of control to ensure that each logic alternative from a decision executes correctly, if reached in the execution flow. *Path testing* attempts to check the different execution paths within the implemented software.

To illustrate the application of these techniques to a particular problem, the triangle solver program, as depicted in flowchart form in Figure 6.1, is used. This program is small in size, 22 design language statements as shown in Figure 6.2, but reasonably complex in logic with a loop and three nested branch statements in the 22. In creating structural tests and test data for this problem, at least six cases are needed to exercise both sides of the three branch statements on lines 21, 24, and 29. For the branch on line 21, this would require selecting three input values (e.g., 3, 4, and 5), such that the sum of any two is always greater than the third. For the same branch statement, another set of three values (e.g., 1, 2, and 3) would also be required for testing the opposing case where the sum of any two is not always greater than the third. For the branch on line 24, a test case with three equal values (e.g., all ones) and another with unequal values (e.g., 2, 2, and 1) would be required. Note that the case of 1, 1, and 2 would not be a good second choice since this set of values would not pass the branch statement on line 21. Finally, for the branch on line 29, two cases (e.g., 2, 3, 4 and 1, 2, 2) would be required to test each leg of the branch.

An additional two cases are needed for minimal testing of the loop statement (line 15): executing the loop without iteration and executing it with iteration (probably only two iterations). For the triangle solver problem, this would require two test cases, one with any three data values and the end-of-file indicator in the input file and a second with something like six or nine data values and the end-of-file indicator. If these eight cases did not force the execution of all 22 statements, then additional cases would be required to ensure all statements were executed. In the triangle solver case, it would appear that the eight test cases would also provide coverage for statement execution.

6.1.1.1 *Coverage versus Cost Dilemma*

The definition of a minimally thorough level of structural testing has eluded researchers (i.e., what is the minimum amount of testing needed to ensure confidence in the software's reliability). The combination of statement and branch testing gives only a start at thoroughness and path testing for software of any complexity is either impractical, impossible, or both. The first problem with path testing is the large number of paths that can typically be defined by the number of branch conditions and loops in software.

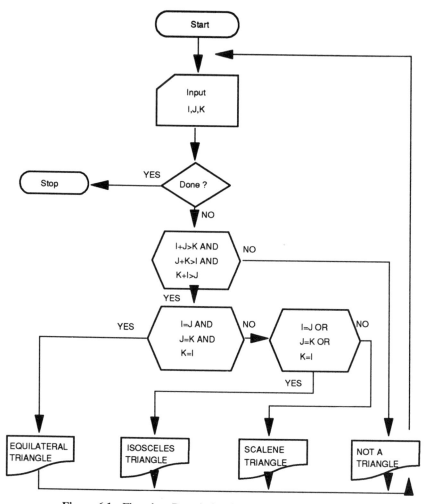

Figure 6.1   Flowchart Description for Triangle Solver Problem

Attempting to address all combinations of branch conditions generally results in a combinatorial explosion of the tests to be defined. Loops just add to this problem, particularly where loop variables are not fixed but set by inputs received during execution. The second problem with path testing is the identification of infeasible paths which can not be executed because of contradictions in the combination of conditional statements. The analysis to weed out the infeasible paths is nontrivial for software of any reasonable complexity.

For the simple triangle solver problem (Figure 6.1), attempting to use all combinations of three integer values would be impossible and trying to sort out inconsistencies in data values for the four levels of nesting would be nontrivial. A case, such as 1,1,1, might be a good test for the second branch (line 24) but would not

```
1.  --<Determine if data value triple forms triangle and print type>
2.  proc TRIANGLE
3.  --<I,J,K are data triple variables and DONE is EOF indicator>
4.  var I,J,K: Real
5.    DONE: Boolean
6.  --<Input data triple and test for EOF. Exit when EOF reached.
7.    Determine if data triple represents sides of a triangle,
8.    classify and print as equilateral,isosceles or scalene. >
9.  begin
10.   --<Input first data triple or EOF from system file. >
11.     read I,J,K
12.     read DONE
13.   --<When EOF read,exit procedure; otherwise check if inputs
14.     are sides of triangle, then classify and print type. >
15.     while ( DONE)
16.     --<DONE = false; determine if current input triple forms
17.       triangle, classify/print and read next input triple. >
18.       loop
19.     --<Check if I,J,K are valid triangle sides,classify type
20.       based on side relationships and print results.  >
21.       if (I+J > K) and (J+K > I) and (K+I > J) then
22.         --<Test that sum of any two triple values is greater
23.           than third value for values to be triangle sides. >
24.         if (I = J) and (J = K) and (K = I) then
25.           --<I = J = K means triangle is equilateral.  >
26.         print ('EQUILATERAL TRIANGLE')
27.           --<Not equilateral, so check further for type.  >
28.           else
29.           if (I = J) or (J = K) or (K = I) then
30.             --<Any two values equal means isosceles.  >
31.             print ('ISOSCELES TRIANGLE')
32.             --<All three values unequal means scalene.  >
33.             else
34.               print ('SCALENE TRIANGLE')
35.           end
36.         end
37.       --<No triangle if sum of two not greater than third.>
38.       else
39.         print ('NOT A TRIANGLE')
40.       ends
41.       --<Input next data triple or EOF from system file. >
42.       read I,J,K
43.       read DONE
44.   end
45. end
```

Figure 6.2 Process Design Language (PDL) Description of Triangle Solver Program

pass the test on line 21. Therefore, it would be infeasible for a test of the path through the branch on line 24.

For this reason, numerous structural testing approaches have been defined that attempt to provide some reasonable coverage of execution paths in a piece of software and to obtain a compromise position between the extremes of minimal statement and branch testing and of full path testing. This list of approaches includes structured path testing [4], boundary-interior path testing [4], linear code sequence and jump (LCSAJ) testing [5], and a variety of methods based on data flow analysis [6].

The first two techniques, structured path and boundary-interior path, are restrictive approaches to path testing, in which there is an attempt to identify like paths (i.e., similar logic but different looping) and to use limited input samples for the path testing. For structured path testing, the input sample restricts any looping to a small number of iterations on the assumption that it is generally simpler and sufficient to check only the minimal looping cases. The suggestion for the triangle solver problem to have six or nine data values in the input file for loop testing would be a structured path consideration which would allow two or three executions of the loop. For boundary-interior testing, an input sample of only two looping cases, executing the loop code without iteration (the boundary case), and executing the loop code with at least one iteration (the interior case) would be required. The above suggestion for two input cases in loop testing would illustrate the boundary-interior approach, since the first set of input forced the execution around the loop and the second set, two or three executions of the loop.

For the LCSAJ and data flow techniques, the software is broken down into sequentially executed statement sequences which are bounded by breaks in the control flow. The LCSAJ technique uses the resulting mapping of the software to systematically step through statement and branch testing. The data flow techniques use the mapping to isolate relationships between the definition of data variables (i.e., wherever data values are assigned) and their subsequent reference or use, in order to identify detailed software functions. A number of different testing variants [7,8] have been defined which address differing levels of complexity in the relationships. In the triangle solver case, while there is a small number of variables, they get set/reset and referenced quite frequently. For the simple case of the variable DONE, it is initialized at definition (line 5), reset via input file reads (lines 12 and 43), but referenced only in the loop statement (line 15). Tracing the relationships with the few number of variables in this small program is itself difficult and points up the problems associated with path-testing programs of any significant size or complexity.

Through the use of a combination of structural testing techniques, it is not possible to check every execution path but it is possible to make reasonable conclusions about the thoroughness of testing. Generally, it is possible to exercise all housekeeping codes in the software, many special-case situations, and a reasonable number of combination cases. The combined-technique approach seems to provide acceptable levels of structural testing to satisfy the objectives of that testing in the development life cycle.

6.1.2 Software Functional Testing

Functional testing is focused on validating the correct implementation of the specified software requirements. Exhaustive functional testing for software of any reasonable complexity is also recognized as being impractical, so that sampling strategies must be introduced to prioritize and optimize the requirements validation. Functional testing is generally performed with a formal (systematic) process of identifying the requirements to be validated, preparing the necessary test materials, and executing the software with the selected test materials. A functional test is conducted to validate that the requirements addressed by a particular software specification document were correctly implemented. These are the same software specifications that developers use to design and implement the software.

A four-step process is used that covers test planning, preparation, execution, and reporting and which is performed for as many specifications as created to define a software product or the embedded software in a total system. A separate test plan is created for each software specification and identifies the method selected for validating each requirement covered in the specification. The number and hierarchy of software specifications for a given project depends on the size and complexity of the development. The test plans also address schedules, resources, tools, and support requirements. Four validation methods are typically used that include the two nonexecution techniques of inspection and analysis and the two execution techniques of demonstration and test.

The preparation step covers the detailing of a particular test plan and defines the test procedures or test cases which are executed in requirements validation. These procedures define the detailed steps to be followed, the discrete input values to be used, the expected output values which should result from the software execution, and the pass-fail criteria to be used in deciding whether the software execution was correct. The execution step covers the actual running and monitoring of the test procedure executions against the software in some predefined environment. The reporting step covers the recording and summarizing of the results from the procedure executions and the certification of the completeness or thoroughness of the requirements validation.

In general, functional testing methodology treats the software as a black box and is concerned with software externals (i.e., checking the correct mapping of software inputs to expected outputs). The internal structure of the software is not addressed since this should have been the focus of the developer-conducted structural tests. The requirements that are addressed are those defining functional capability in the software but also include performance, reliability, installability, and other considerations. Essentially any requirement identified in the specifications and of interest to the customer is considered a candidate to be addressed in the functional test process.

6.1.2.1 *Coverage versus Cost Dilemma* For the validation of a particular software specification's requirements, the test process starts with identifying the requirements to be tested and creating the steps and inputs required in the

TABLE 6.1 Software Requirements Explosion Leading to Validation Complexity

	Medium-Sized (50 Ksloc)	Large-Sized (100s Ksloc)
Per statement of work	55	420
At high-level design	510	1,930
At low-level design	2,670	7,058

NOTE: With two to five variations per three validation considerations
Medium-sized case requires 16 to 40 K test cases.
Large-sized case requires 42 to 106 K test cases.

test procedure. This latter item involves sorting out the software inputs by their source (operators, hardware, other software) and then defining the domains of data values for each input. Examining domains requires differentiating the legal and illegal data values, identifying subsets of frequently occurring values, and injecting considerations of data concurrency, interrelationships, dependencies, and so on. The objective of all of these considerations is to characterize the levels of variation in the input data which will be attempted to ensure adequate coverage of the requirements and confidence in the thoroughness of the validation for any given requirement. General rules of thumb call for software execution against nominal values of the input data, boundary values associated with the input data, and stressing values for the input data.

For software of any complexity, ensuring full coverage of requirements is a difficult task because of the number of requirements with which the tester must deal and because of the time involved in the preparation, execution, and analysis of each test case, which time is generally measured in hours. This situation is further aggravated by the fact that it is essentially impractical to attempt exhaustive testing of all input data values for all but the most trivial software. For typical software, the size of the input data domains and the underlying relationships between different inputs introduce combinatorial complexities in the selection of input values for test cases. The data in Table 6.1 illustrate the problems that arise when organizing the functional testing for typical-sized software products and demonstrate the need for working with samples of the requirements and input data rather than attempting to achieve full coverage. Various approaches to sampling have been introduced which attempt to prioritize the requirements in order to optimize coverage and to limit the number of input variations while maximizing requirements validation.

6.1.2.2 Comparison of Sampling Strategies The reported techniques for creating test samples which can be used for functional testing are few and tend to rely on an oracle or arbitrator to decide on the correctness of the execution output and whether a particular requirement was satisfied. They recognize that exhaustive testing is impossible and create subsets of the possible inputs for test execution. The approach to selecting which inputs to include in a subset distinguishes one method from another.

The *equivalence partitioning method* [9] attempts to subdivide the input domain into classes that define equivalent results from function execution and from which a few input values can be selected to represent the class execution. This approach to subsetting breaks the total domain into a finite number of sets and then relies on sampling from these sets to further restrict the test input. The *boundary value analysis method* [9] is a variant of partitioning which selects values from the edges or boundaries of the classes, since these are traditionally viewed as the more error-prone areas of the input partition. The *category partition method* [10] is another variant that defines a procedure for formal specification analysis and uses automated tools to identify full specification coverage with the minimum number of tests.

Input combinations are not addressed by the previous methods but are the focus of the *cause-effect graphing method* [11] which, as the name implies, traces the relationships between software inputs to identify the minimum combinations that provide the maximum requirements coverage. *The error-guessing method* [9] relies on test experience to isolate areas with more potential for causing software failures. Development similarities, function complexity, and first-time function implementation are clues used with this method. *Statistical sampling methods* [11] rely on the use of probability distributions to control the selection of input values from the data domains and introduce a mathematical basis (statistics) for realizing objectivity in the test samples.

For the six nonstatistical methods, the testing concerns are with the lack of rigor in prioritizing requirements and the subjectivity that enters into the input domain analysis. Since the costs for complete requirements coverage are unacceptable, sampling is necessary but, for want of a theoretical underpinning, tends to be informal, subjective, inferred, and experienced-based. Similar concerns also carry over to the identification of input suites for the selected requirements and are further aggravated by data value selection being driven more by ease of tester manipulation than usage realism (e.g., using only powers of 10). The quality of the test personnel plays a dominant role in this sampling process to achieve acceptable validation of the specifications within the schedule and staffing limits of the project.

The testing concerns with the statistical methods come from the inherent technical complexity of the statistical analyses and an apprehension about the effectiveness of coverage. The complex aspects of the methods are the upfront definition of probability distributions for both requirements and data and the ongoing need for computing expected results for randomly generated but representative test cases. The coverage concern stems from the misapprehension that statistical implies haphazard, large, and costly and that critical software requirements which may be statistically insignificant are overlooked or untested. The front-end work, if viewed as a continuation of the loading and sizing analysis performed for solution definition, should add resource but not complexity requirements, while the analysis for expected results is the penalty paid for having realism in testing. Coverage is directly related to the robustness of the probability distributions which control the selection process and has not proven to be a problem in the current application of the methods.

In looking at the productivity effects of the statistical and nonstatistical methods, there is more front-end test planning in the statistical case in developing the distributional data but this is effectively offset by less test preparation, since test cases can be generated automatically. Computing expected outputs is a problem with all methods, though possibly larger in the statistical case because of the test case realism. Long-term, as experience and confidence grow, the application of statistical sampling techniques should realize a net reduction in the numbers of test cases. From a quality perspective, the statistical methods offer more potential since they have a formal basis (statistics) which provides objectivity and realism to the test process.

6.2 WHY TESTING WITH VERIFICATION?

In the Cleanroom method, software structural testing is replaced by correctness verification of the software design but functional testing is still retained for validating the correct implementation of the software specification and for creating the inputs to be used in software reliability estimation.

The rationale behind eliminating the structural testing performed by developers prior to releasing their software to independent testers is that all the objectives of structural testing are satisfied through verification. As seen in Table 6.2, the correctness proofs defined in the functional correctness model address the same potential sources for software errors which are considered in structural tests. The major difference is that these potential sources of error can be considered as the design is formulated and never introduced into the design. Structural testing must wait until design and coding are completed before getting the opportunity to discover the error sources. The earlier detection significantly reduces the costs associated with error repair and minimizes the possibility of additional errors being introduced during repair. Published literature indicates [12] that there can be anywhere between a 10 to 1 and 100 to 1 difference in the repair costs for the same error depending on how close to its introduction it is discovered.

In Table 6.2, the testing points of interest, as discussed in the structural testing literature [13], are itemized. These represent the technical criteria that are used to decide the successful completion of the testing by the software developer. How these same points are addressed by the functional correctness model is indicated to demonstrate the similarity in capability with testing. Concurrent execution is only partially addressed in verification and requires the use of some asynchronous design model as indicated. Testing of concurrent execution is generally left to subsequent functional testing.

In addition to having equivalent capability in terms of meeting structural testing

TABLE 6.2   Comparison of Software Structural Test and Functional Correctness Model Capabilities

	Points of Testing Interest	Verification Equivalents
UNIT TEST	Each coded statement	Design verified to full detail
	Each coded branch	Loop termination and predicate checks
	All steps in math algorithms	Repeat of full detail argument
	Interfaces between programs	Parameters required for all programs
	Data domains and ranges	Domain and range in data definition
	Error conditions	All logic alternatives specified
MODULE TEST	Subfunction logic steps	Covered by module specification
	Module interfaces	Covered by parameter specification
	Data domains and ranges	Domain and range in data definition
	Error conditions	All logic alternatives in specification
	Operational mode switching	All logic alternatives in specification
	Concurrent logic execution	Covered by asynchronous design model [14]

objectives, correctness verification tends to have greater payoffs in terms of software quality and developer productivity than realizable with structural testing techniques. The results from the COBOL S/F product [15] development, where no structural testing was performed by the developers, show a significant drop in the number of defects found during functional testing and a near- zero-defect record in the field. Software developments, where structural testing was replaced by verification and/or rigorous inspection, generally report a small to significant increase in productivity, sometimes as much as a 100% improvement.

These field results triggered a further examination [16] of the productivity question, since there seemed to be gains rather than the originally assumed no impact from replacing structural testing by verification. To study this question, a randomly selected set of 100 software design segments was examined. These segments comprised some 6,500 design statements and came from a variety of applications (e.g., language processing, avionics, and manufacturing). To determine the structural test requirements, the segments were analyzed for design structures that would require testing of the resultant code. Specifically, the design structures that were extracted from the segments were sequences of statements, program and function invocations, branch statements, and loops. A sample of the results from this analysis is summarized in Figure 6.3, together with the number of steps which would be required in the correctness proofs for the same segments.

To make a productivity comparison, a working hypothesis was established which stated that the effort involved in creating and executing structural tests was equivalent to the effort involved in working through a step in a correctness proof. This may be too liberal an assumption but was adopted as a starting point. In reality, the time spent in organizing and subsequently confirming a correctness

	Stmt Count	Proof Steps	Count Of				
			Loops	Branches	Calls	Sequences	Total
1	55	9		5	2	3	10
2	51	5	1	3			4
3	127	23	1	2	15		17
4	54	4	2	2		4	8
5	52	7	1	2	1	1	7
6	55	8	2	2	1	2	8
7	57	11	1	6		2	9
8	56	9		4	2	2	8
9	55	21		7	10	1	18
10	50	11		1	7	2	10
11	54	16		4	8	1	13
12	59	5		3		4	7
13	56	8	1	4		2	7
14	54	23	1	7	8		16
15	55	10	1	4	3	1	9
16	57	9	2	3	2	3	10
17	57	14	1	4	5	4	14
18	54	5	1	2	1		4
19	54	7	2	3		1	6
20	55	7		5	1	1	7
21	54	8	2	1	4		7
22	56	16	1	5	6	1	13
23	54	8	1	3	2	1	7
24	54	10	1	3	2	2	8
25	54	4		4	1		5

Figure 6.3   Sample of Design Segment Data

proof can usually be measured in minutes, whereas the time spent in creating and executing a test is usually measured in tens of minutes or hours. A second assumption introduced into the comparison attempted to determine the minimal number of tests required for a particular design segment. For this estimate, one discrete test was defined for each statement sequence and program or function invocation but two discrete tests were defined for each branch statement and loop. The two tests to check loop execution define an execution with and without iteration which is the bare minimum consideration for loop testing.

Based on the 100-segment sample, an average of 15.4 structural tests would be required to achieve a minimal level of testing. By contrast, an average of 11.2 steps would be required in the correctness proofs based on the functional correctness model. Though the absolute numbers are not crucial, the trends are. Specifically, correctness proofs tend to be compact and require a small number of steps. Additionally, the proofs come close to confirming absolute correctness, whereas the preferred structural test method (path testing) is recognized as infeasible for typical software. These results tend to substantiate the claim that the time and effort invested in more careful design are more than offset by the savings realized through eliminating structural testing.

6.3   CLEANROOM STATISTICAL APPROACH

The major innovation of the Cleanroom method is in the area of functional testing with its definition of a statistical approach. The testing goal in the Cleanroom method is to validate software requirements through software execution in representative usage environments. This has the two benefits of validating the specified requirements and of accomplishing this in a testing environment that mirrors the planned use of the software in the field. By using probability distributions to define the use of software functions with their likely inputs and by randomly selecting which functions are tested with which inputs, the test environment is statistically representative of the real operating environment. This allows the Cleanroom practitioner to bring the full power of statistics into play for inferring the operational effectiveness of the software from its test environment. It also affords the tester the opportunity to apply statistical sampling theory in defining the sample size of test cases from the total population of all conceivable functions and inputs, which is needed to accomplish software testing to a defined level of confidence in the testing thoroughness.

   Statistical testing within the Cleanroom method requires an investment in front-end analysis and planning for software functional test. It requires a different understanding and characterization of software inputs based on their usage probabilities and not just the data typing parameters routinely provided in their programming language definitions. The probabilities drive the random selection of test data and, since the selection reflects the operational use of the software, provide a mathematical foundation (statistics) for the functional testing. This foundation creates a formal process for a functional test that introduces objectivity and completeness into test selection and quantification (with confidence levels) into thoroughness estimates.

   The upfront analysis is aimed at identifying the software functions, the software inputs and data domains, and the probabilities that would be associated with each of these. These descriptions must be organized into a data base from which test samples are selected. The samples are used to conduct the actual testing, which follows conventional practice. The tester makes the decision whether a particular test passes or fails (i.e., the required function executes correctly or incorrectly) and records the test results in a test report. The real change to functional testing is that the test sample is generated automatically with data representative of the operating environment and not data handcrafted by the tester.

6.3.1 Upfront Data Analysis

The required analysis starts with the identification of the software functions to be tested and associated inputs that trigger the execution of those functions. The software specification defines the software functions and to a lesser degree (details generally deferred to design) the inputs associated with each function. For a complete understanding of these data, additional analysis is required which examines the modes of software execution, the impacts of the software build plans, and packaging strategy. The analysis is all considered part of the planning for software functional testing.

The software specification generally provides the starting data for conducting an analysis of software operating modes, though in many cases, operational and user documentation must also be examined. The data covers the hardware and software configurations in which the software operates, the growth plans for the software, and, in the case of software embedded in hardware designs, any different forms (partial, degraded, and so on) of the functional capability that might be required. The operating environments dictate how and when software functions are executed, which functions are mutually exclusive or inclusive, and whether execution with partial forms of capability is required. These constraints scope the operational modes in which the software executes.

For most software, a single hardware and software configuration is defined and any degradation in that configuration terminates execution. In the case of distributed systems where resources are dynamically allocated, the software specification must identify all allowable resource configurations, requirements for parallel and/or partial function execution, and the reallocation rules for moving functions across configuration boundaries. Anticipated growth requirements is another analysis consideration for potential impacts on software execution. The planned introduction of additional software function or the potential for movement of function within the hardware and software configuration must be factored into the analysis.

Software design material is another source for data on software operating considerations resulting from design decisions. In general, new operating modes should not be seen in the design material but rather further definition of specified modes, whose details were left to the design. Initialization, restart, and termination are examples of typical functions which effect software operation and whose definitions are left for the software designer.

In addition to software functions, the analysis must examine the software inputs and the probabilities associated with their data values. The software specification gives an initial source for data on inputs (e.g., hardware and software interfaces), but the details come from the software design documentation. The key to successful statistical test planning is the early identification of the total set of software inputs, together with any design or operating constraints (e.g., boundary conditions, legal input combinations, and so on). To handle the validation of performance and other nonfunctional requirements, data relationships, such as concurrency, in the software inputs must also be considered, since these define the interaction and interplay between competing inputs and the operating conditions under which the interaction occurs.

The software build plans and packaging strategies, which should reflect a top-down development with incremental releases of the software, affect this analysis and need to be examined. The contents of each release identify and bound the included software function with the particular subset of software inputs needed to execute those functions. The number and timing of the incremental releases has a direct bearing on the software functional test planning, which must accept the schedules, resources, and constraints that are imposed.

6.3.2 Generators for Statistical Testing

Because of the amount of data to be considered when organizing the functions, inputs, and associated probabilities for software of any reasonable complexity, support software is needed for building data bases and generating test material from the stored data. The objective of a generator is to organize the descriptions of the software functions, inputs, and distributions into a structured data base from which test procedures for conducting the functional tests can be generated. The approach taken in the current generator [17] used in the IBM Cleanroom work is predicted on a standalone test case for each software input for which appropriate input values and corresponding initial software conditions are generated. Software initialization is included to provide known starting conditions from which the success or failure of the input processing can be decided after test-case execution. Determining processing validity when the starting point is not precisely known would not be possible with software of any reasonable complexity. In this context, standalone should not be misinterpreted as batch but rather understood as meaning self-contained since the generator has been used to address real-time and concurrent software applications.

In the current generator, which provides a menu-driven editor for entering data into the data base, a test-case skeleton is defined for each software input in an application. The skeleton identifies the domain of data values for the input and the legal software states in which that input can be received by the software. The state data identifies the initial states, which can be generated for a particular test case, from which the execution results can be evaluated. The skeletons are composed of command sequences which are formatted to correspond to the input formats of a particular application and pseudocommands which define internal generator functions. The grammar used with the current generator is shown in Table 6.3.

The command sequences are encoded as text strings for the data base and are composed of macro and terminal commands. The macro commands are references to other command sequences which allow nested and extended command sequences. The terminal commands define the actual steps generated in a test procedure and identify the operations and data variables (with specific values) which are specific to an application. Terminal commands are text strings with constant and variable data fields that represent the format of the application-specific software inputs. Command sequences for support tools for the application testing (e.g., data

TABLE 6.3   Grammar Used with Current IBM Statistical Test Case Generator

test skeleton	:: =	group*sequence
group	:: =	skel_no prob seq_count
sequence	:: =	seq_id prob cmd_count
		(pseudo | macro | terminal)
		*(macro | terminal | NOP)
skel_no	:: =	value
seq_count	:: =	value
cmd_count	:: =	value
seq_id	:: =	(1 to 16 contiguous characters)
prob	:: =	(.000) ... (.999)
pseudo	:: =	CHOICE DEL DO
macro	:: =	seq_id
terminal	:: =	''/''*(literal reference)
literal	:: =	(input text)
reference	:: =	''(''var_id '')''
var_id	:: =	(1 to 16 contiguous characters)
variable	:: =	var_id type length
type	:: =	character | decimal | hexidecimal
length	:: =	1 ... 16
range	:: =	value'':''value
value	:: =	char data | decimal data | hex data

Note: * = one or more iterations

recording, timing synchronization, and so on) can and have been defined as additional application operations.

A small number of pseudocommands has been defined for the current generator to support generic string operations. The CHOICE pseudocommand defines the selection of any one (randomly selected) entry from a list of command sequences. The SEL pseudocommand defines the random selection without duplication of a number of entries (randomly selected) from a list of command sequences. The DO pseudocommand defines the selection in listed order of a number of entries (randomly selected) from a list of command sequences. The NOP pseudocommand defines a space holder or no operation function.

When a terminal command is selected for inclusion in a particular test case, its variable fields are filled with representative application data. Data values are randomly selected for a variable field based on the domain of data values and probability distribution defined for that specific variable field. Value domains can cover both legal and illegal values for a variable field depending on the focus of the application testing.

6.3.3   Statistical Testing of a COBOL Language Processor

To illustrate the application of statistical testing, the approach to the functional testing of the COBOL S/F program product [15] is discussed. The upfront analysis for this application started with the COBOL language reference manual which served as the requirements specification. The manual identified the language syntax and semantics, which had to be recognized, and described the operating constraints which had to be observed, such as the supported computer platforms, capacities affecting COBOL program size and/or complexity, processing rates in terms of COBOL statements per minute, reliability in terms of syntax error processing, and so forth. Figure 6.4 identifies likely excerpts from a language reference manual, which define the syntax for two COBOL statements (GOTO and PERFORM) and identify the allowable formats for each statement. Specifically in this case, there are four variations on the GOTO statement and nine variations on the PERFORM statement that must be recognized by the program product and, therefore, must be considered in the functional testing.

To this point in the upfront analysis, there is not much difference between the analysis and the source information (the language reference manual) used by a statistical or a nonstatistical method. However, the next step in the upfront analysis is unique to the statistical testing method, where the probabilities must be defined for the typical COBOL statement usage and, within each statement type, the probabilities for using the different statement formats. At this point, a decision must be made on the focus of the particular functional tests, since this decision impacts the definition of probabilities. The general Cleanroom focus is on the usage of software, in order to compute software reliabilities but, in particular instances, the focus might shift to safety-critical aspects of the software, the performance drivers for the software, the handling of critical customer functions, or any number of other perspectives. In many applications, more than one focus might be used during functional testing requiring different families of probability distributions to be constructed.

In the COBOL processor case, the functional test focus was on statement usage by the typical COBOL programmer. This dictated a sampling strategy whose goal was to generate test cases which, in fact, would be actual and representative COBOL programs. The types of information needed to develop probability distributions is generally not found in the software specification and must be gathered from other sources that deal with the planned use of the software in customer or user environments. This was the case with the COBOL processor, where neither the language reference manual nor the accompanying language user guide provided the necessary information on statement usage.

Fortunately, the appropriate information was found in a published article [18] which described a study of statement usage for a large body of COBOL programs. An excerpt of the information from this article is shown in Figure 6.5, which provides tabular data on the percentage of times that a particular COBOL statement was used in the sample of COBOL programs which were studied. The article included data on the use of the different formats for each statement, as well and generally contained all the usage statistics which would be needed for the functional testing of the COBOL S/F program product. In this instance if this article had not been found, a study similar to the one reported in the article would have been performed on some body of representative COBOL programs to develop the ditributional data. The availability of the particular article saved time and effort in this case.

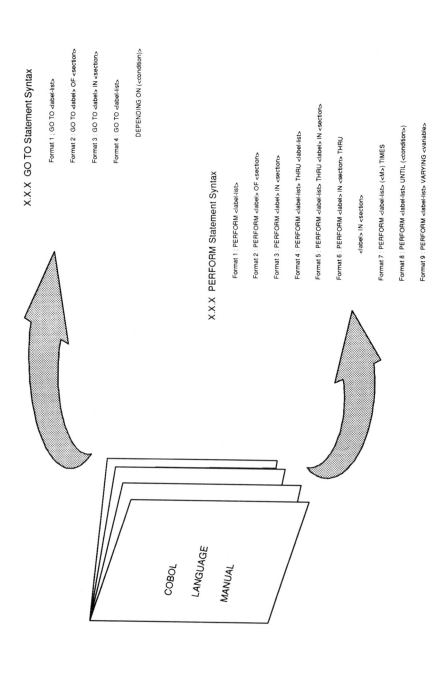

X.X.X GO TO Statement Syntax

Format 1 : GO TO <label-list>

Format 2 : GO TO <label> OF <section>

Format 3 : GO TO <label> IN <section>

Format 4 : GO TO <label-list>

DEPENDING ON (<condition)>

X.X.X PERFORM Statement Syntax

Format 1 : PERFORM <label-list>

Format 2 : PERFORM <label> OF <section>

Format 3 : PERFORM <label> IN <section>

Format 4 : PERFORM <label-list> THRU <label-list>

Format 5 : PERFORM <label-list> THRU <label> IN <section>

Format 6 : PERFORM <label> IN <section> THRU

<label> IN <section>

Format 7 : PERFORM <label-list> (<M>) TIMES

Format 8 : PERFORM <label-list> UNTIL (<condition>)

Format 9 : PERFORM <label-list> VARYING <variable>

FROM <variable> TO <variable> UNTIL (<condition>)

COBOL
LANGUAGE
MANUAL

Figure 6.4   Requirements for the COBOL Processor Case

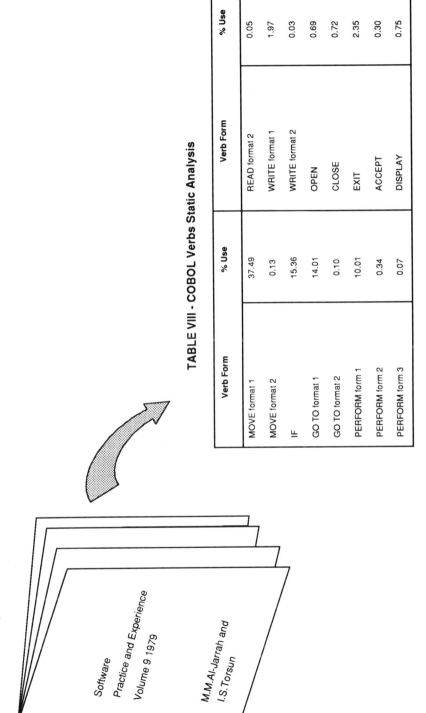

TABLE VIII - COBOL Verbs Static Analysis

Verb Form	% Use	Verb Form	% Use
MOVE format 1	37.49	READ format 2	0.05
MOVE format 2	0.13	WRITE format 1	1.97
IF	15.36	WRITE format 2	0.03
GO TO format 1	14.01	OPEN	0.69
GO TO format 2	0.10	CLOSE	0.72
PERFORM form 1	10.01	EXIT	2.35
PERFORM form 2	0.34	ACCEPT	0.30
PERFORM form 3	0.07	DISPLAY	0.75

Figure 6.5 An Empirical Analysis of COBOL Programs

Software
Practice and Experience
Volume 9 1979

M.M.Al-Jarrah and
I.S.Torsun

129

Once the information has been gathered from the software specifications and the software usage sources, the next step is to encode this information into the formats defined by a particular test case generator. For the current generator [17], this means the use of a list notation with a suitable assortment of terminal, macro, and pseudo commands. Each terminal command for the COBOL processor case uses the syntax of particular COBOL statement formats with parenthesized syntax elements used to indicate variable fields. The initial slash (/) notation identifies a terminal command. The entry labeled **GOTO-format-1** in Figure 6.6 illustrates a terminal command for this case. The field labeled **label-list** is a variable field in the syntax for which randomly selected data values have to be inserted during generation. The entry labeled **stmt-sel** in the figure illustrates the use of the **CHOICE** pseudocommand and its encoded command sequence contains many instances of macros, such as **GOTO-stmt**. The macros are effectively pointers to other entries in the data base.

Probability data is either encoded as a separate field for each data base entry or reflected through the make-up of the command sequence by the inclusion of multiple macro references to the same entry. Both forms of probability definition for the COBOL processor case are shown in Figure 6.6. The entry labeled **stmt-sel** has a .5 value in its usage field which indicates to the generator that this particular data base entry should be selected half of the time. In this particular application, the generator would spend the other half of its time generating labels, procedure statements, declarations, and the like. The other method for defining probabilities is shown in the structure of the **stmt-sel** entry. The command sequence in this entry defines five occurrences of **MOVE-stmt** telling the generator to select a **MOVE** statement 50% of the time during statement selection. The two occurrences of **GOTO**s and **IF**s indicate that each would be selected 20% of the time. The single occurrence of the **PERFORM** indicates that it would be selected 10% of the time.

The test case generator automatically creates the test sample by sequencing through the data base, creating a specified number of test cases, and filling in the contents of each test case with randomly selected data. From the data base encoded in Figure 6.6, the generator would access the **stmt-sel** entry 50% of the time and then via a random number generator decide to insert a **MOVE, GOTO, IF,** or **PERFORM** statement in the COBOL program which was being created as a test case. The particular format that would be used for a selected statement would also be randomly selected based on the encoding of an entry such as the **GOTO-stmt** entry in Figure 6.6. In this case, the generator output would be a COBOL program segment, as shown in Figure 6.7, which could be run as a functional test of the COBOL S/F program product. As shown in Figure 6.7, variable fields in a COBOL statement would be given randomly selected symbol names for labels, constants, data items, and so on (e.g., lab001, con001, and var001).

6.3.4 Statistical Testing of an Avionics Application

To further illustrate the application of the statistical testing approach, a second and quite different application is discussed. This application is the flight software in an aircraft system, for which statistical testing was used for functional testing. The

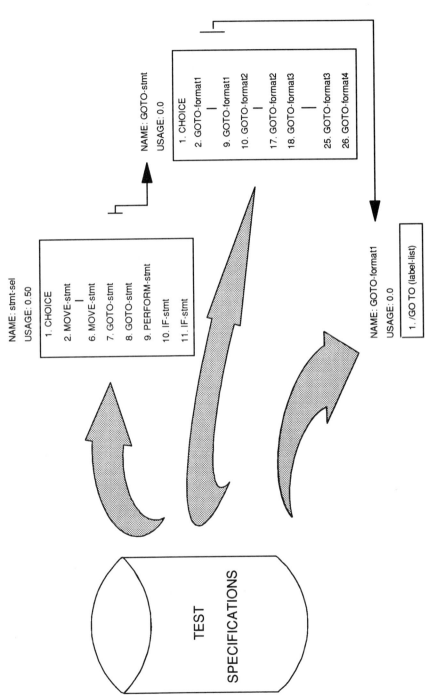

NAME: stmt-sel
USAGE: 0.50

1. CHOICE
2. MOVE-stmt
   |
6. MOVE-stmt
7. GOTO-stmt
8. GOTO-stmt
9. PERFORM-stmt
10. IF-stmt
11. IF-stmt

NAME: GOTO-stmt
USAGE: 0.0

1. CHOICE
2. GOTO-format1
   |
9. GOTO-format1
10. GOTO-format2
   |
17. GOTO-format2
18. GOTO-format3
   |
25. GOTO-format3
26. GOTO-format4

NAME: GOTO-format1
USAGE: 0.0

1. /GO TO (label-list)

TEST
SPECIFICATIONS

Figure 6.6 Data Base Excerpt for COBOL Processor Application

131

PROCEDURE DIVISION

MOVE con001 TO var001

MOVE con002 TO var002

IF var001 < var002

GO TO lab001

MOVE var001 TO var003

GO TO lab002

lab001   MOVE var002 TO var003

lab002 STOP

Figure 6.7   Randomly Generated COBOL Program Segment

starting point for the upfront analysis was the software requirements specification for the flight software component, which identified the need for a mission management function that collected all the requirements for actually controlling the aircraft's flight. Included in this function were the requirements for the periodic selection of navigational aids to assist the aircraft's personnel in tracking flight plans. A typical specification of such a requirement is shown in Figure 6.8, which provides details on which aids are selectable and what data is required with different selections. Further details on data formats and value domains for specific fields generally would be identified in an appendix to the software specification, an excerpt from which is shown in Figure 6.9. The combination of the requirements paragraph and the additional appendix details would scope the particulars for validating the implementation of the navigational aid support.

For this case, probability information was not available from the software specification nor was a report from a previous study available. Test personnel supported by system and operational personnel conducted their own study, based on an analysis of the aircraft's planned missions and of the type and number of flight-software-related functions which were performed during those missions. Since data entry to this software was via display panels, the usage and probability data for flight-software functions was developed in terms of button-pushes on panels to navigate through the functions. Figure 6.10 shows an excerpt from the analysis that identifies the key selections for the panel supporting navigational aid selection and defines, in terms of uses per mission, the usage of each key. From this data it is seen

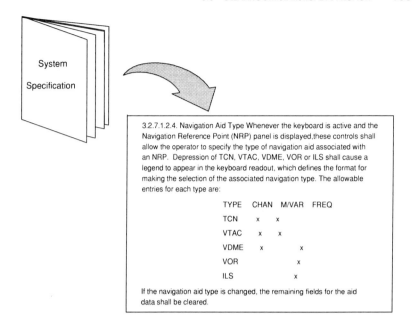

Figure 6.8 Identifying the Requirement

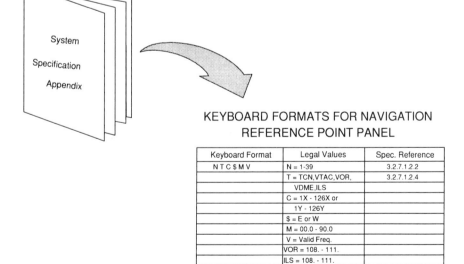

Figure 6.9 Identifying Data Value Domains

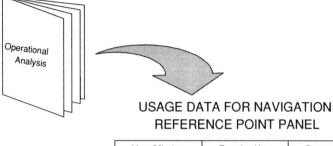

USAGE DATA FOR NAVIGATION
REFERENCE POINT PANEL

Uses/Mission	Function Key	Processing
80	L1	Next NRP
80	L2	Previous NRP
16	L3	TCN Selection
16	L4	VTAC Selection
16	L5	VDME Selection
16	L6	VOR Selection
16	L7	ILS Selection
80	L8	Control Exit

Figure 6.10   Identifying the Probabilities

that the indicated navigational aids are used with about equal frequency and that other keys on the particular panel are used five times more often.

Test cases in this application were scripts which allowed the tester to simulate the actions of the aircraft personnel in using the display panel to select and deselect flight-software functions. In addition to the function to be tested, the scripts contain all necessary keyboard actions to initialize the software to a legal known state. As can be seen in Figure 6.11, the terminal commands in this case are text strings which indicate function-key actions and the data to be inserted through the data entry keyboard. The data base entry for the **TCN selection** shows that the L3 function key is used and the **DATUM** entry identifies the value to be inserted through the keyboard. Otherwise the data base entries for this case look like those for the COBOL processor case and would be processed by the generator in the same fashion.

Figure 6.12 illustrates a typical test case for the avionics application (i.e., a hardcopy script that the tester would use to simulate aircraft personnel actions). In the illustrated case, the first three steps define initialization actions which get the software in the correct state to accept selections for navigational aids. In the particular system there was a steady-state condition where panels are in a known position, which is what step 1 accomplishes. From that state, a sequence of panel actions is then performed to call up the navigational reference panel from which an aid can be selected, which is accomplished by steps 2 and 3. After initialization is completed, steps 4 and 5 can be performed to validate that a TACAN navigational aid can be used and specific channel and tuning options can be included in the

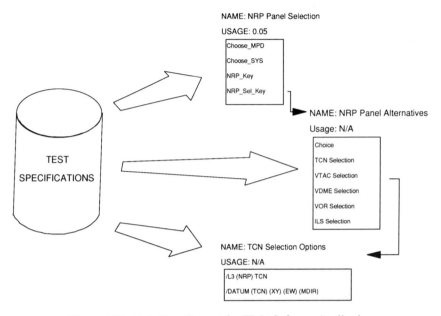

Figure 6.11   Data Base Content for Flight Software Application

selection. These latter two steps are the meat of the test case where the requirements for selecting navigaitonal aides are validated.

Note that the initialization for this step (i.e., sequencing through panels) may have been the focus of an earlier test case which was attempting to validate that the aircraft personnel could navigate through the panel hierarchy. In general, the generator capitalizes on the incremental release strategy and builds-up complicated

Case	Selected Actions	PF Key	Expected Result	Comments
1	1. Copilot Display			Start with Copilot
				Display
	2. Hit IR Key	T1	Get Initial Panel	Callup IR Menu to
				Get to NRP Function
	3. Hit NRP Key	R5	NRP Panel Selected	Select NRP
	4. Hit TCN Key	L3	TCN Selected	Select TACAN AID
	5. Enter 086 X		Channel Selected	Supply Channel Data
			and Tuned	

Figure 6.12   Randomly Generated Input Sequence for TACAN Channel Selection

test cases through the reuse of previously verified function which can now be used for process initialization.

6.3.5 Application Experience

This statistical sampling approach [19] has been used in the testing of a variety of applications, of which language processors were among the easier cases. Embedded software for avionic, surveillance, and space applications present more challenge because of the required functional capabilities, the application environment constraints, and the human operator interactions. The statistical ideas can be successfully used for these applications and provide early software exposure to realistic usage during development with resulting benefits to the quality of the delivered software and system.

To date, this approach [19] and its generator tool [17] have been used for some dozen different applications including the functional testing of the generator itself. In each case, the test personnel were able to define the requirements to be validated, the software inputs, the data domains, and the associated probability distributions, and to objectively generate realistic test cases to drive the functional testing.

6.3.6 Requirements Coverage with Statistical Testing

From the perspective of the traditional tester who methodically selects tests to match requirements, there tends to be skepticism about the requirements coverage which would be achieved with the random selection used in the statistical approach of functional testing. Experience with the statistical method indicates that this is not the case and that coverage is very satisfactory. This is not unexpected since the sampling is driven from distributions which capture all the requirements for the software and since, for the initial release of an increment, the testing is focused primarily on the functions delivered in that increment. To remove any skepticism, the requirements coverage for the flight software case was analyzed, since this represented a typical application for Cleanroom development.

The SRS was the source for requirements (''shall'' statements) information for the flight software. The analysis tallied the numbers of ''shall'' statements that defined the functions for the flight software components and then tallied the numbers of requirements for the subfunctions within each of these components. The total number of statistical test cases was then analyzed to identify which functions and subfunctions were addressed by those test cases. The coverage ratios were then computed and studied on a component and subfunction basis.

For the flight software, some 500 functions and subfunctions were identified at the component level and an additional 2,200 subfunctions were identified in the elaboration of the component subfunctions, each of which could be viewed as a requirement to be tested. The primary focus of software functional testing should be at the component level (500 requirements), since these identify the visible capability of the software in its operating environment. The secondary focus should be on the additional subfunctions (2,200 requirements), which reflect the variations and special-case situations for the visible capability.

TABLE 6.4 **Requirements Coverage in Functional Test for Flight Software Application**

Components	Functions		Functions/1st Level Subs		All Functions/ Subfunctions		Percent Tested
	Tested	Total	Tested	Total	Tested	Total	
1	6	6	23	26	31	36	86
2	6	6	23	29	33	42	79
3	6	6	39	40	74	81	91
4	3	3	15	18	78	88	89
5	2	2	10	11	21	25	84
6	2	2	7	9	19	24	80
7	3	3	26	27	61	67	91
8	2	2	2	2	2	2	100
9	4	4	12	14	25	37	73
10	3	3	12	15	25	30	83
11	6	6	13	13	13	13	100
12	5	5	14	14	25	25	100
13	6	6	13	13	35	39	90
Totals	54	54	209	231	442	509	

In this case, statistical testing exercised (i.e., one or more test cases) some 88% of the requirements for the component-level functions and subfunctions, which equals or betters the coverage achieved with traditional approaches to software functional testing. Table 6.4 provides a breakout of the requirements for each component by the specified functions and subfunctions (i.e., details on specified capabilities). The coverage of these requirements is also shown, which demonstrates that 100% of the component-level functions were tested and that 90% of the component-level functions and their first level of subfunctions were tested. The effectiveness of the statistical testing for the combined focuses (i.e., the 2,700 requirements for functions and all levels of subfunctions) was slightly under 80%, which is again a very acceptable number for a software functional testing method.

6.3.7 Test Process Impacts

When considering the impact of the statistical methods on the functional testing process, each of the four steps in that process were examined but only the first two steps (test planning and test preparation) seemed to be impacted. The latter two steps (test execution and test reporting) were not effected, since they are essentially oblivious to the source of the test cases and operate in an identical manner regardless of the source. Current experience confirms this observation.

By definition, the statistical methods extends planning to accommodate the analyses of probability distributions and the encoding of that information into a data base. Since the data base must be available to build test cases during the test preparation step, this effort must rightfully be counted against test planning. Depending on the application complexity and the availability of planned usage data, this work might add one-third to one-half more effort to test planning than would be budgeted in current test practice.

Test preparation takes on a different look with the statistical approach, since test-case generation is an automated process under the control of a generator. The effort performed with nonstatistical methods of prioritizing requirements and selecting appropriate data samples is no longer required but rather was accomplished as part of test planning. Realism in the statistically generated cases might require the expenditure of more effort in determining expected results and detract somewhat from the potential savings in the total test preparation effort. The net seems to be a one-half to two-thirds reduction in the effort which would be budgeted for test preparation in current test practice.

6.3.8 Impacts on Test Personnel

The principal tester impacts are a forced change in perspective on functional testing and the need for an appreciation of statistics and its many uses within the testing process. Current test practice calls for little involvement of the functional tester during the early phases of the development life cycle and limits that involvement to the preparation of test management plans. These provide the macro perspective on testing strategies, the planned testing levels, their schedule, test resource requirements, and planned tool usage. Statistical sampling demands early involvement to perform the distributional analyses and extended involvement to organize and encode the data bases for test-case-generation. The net increase in project costs for this extended involvement tends to be insignificant (in the 10% range) because of the savings realized during test preparation.

The change in tester perspective is difficult since it requires training and confidence in statistics and an acceptance of the functional-test role as primarily validating requirements. Current testing practice exhibits an overattention to error discovery (i.e., breaking the software), sometimes to the detriment of systematic requirements validation. Confidence must be gained in the value of the probability distributions to direct testing to the important aspects of software validation. This should lead to an appreciation that statistical sampling selects the test inputs which are most likely to force software failures while systematically directing the software requirements validation.

References

1. H.D. Mills, "The New Math of Computer Programming," *CACM*, Vol. 18, No. 1, 1975.
2. S.C. Ntafos, "A Comparison of Some Structural Testing Strategies," *IEEE TSE*, Vol. 14, No. 6, 1988.
3. W.E. Howden, "A Functional Approach to Program Testing," *IEEE TSE*, Vol. 12, No. 10, 1986.
4. W.E. Howden, "Methodology for Generation of Program Test Data," IEEE Transactions, Vol. C-24, No. 5, 1975.

5. M.R. Woodward, D. Hedley and M.A. Hennell, "Experience with Path Analysis," *IEEE TSE*, Vol. 6, 1980.

6. P.M. Herman, "A Data Flow Analysis Approach to Program Testing," *Australian Computer Journal*, Vol. 8, 1976.

7. S.C. Ntafos, "On Required Element Testing," *IEEE TSE*, Vol. 10, No. 6, 1984.

8. S. Rapps and E.J. Weyuker, "Selecting Software Test Data," *IEEE TSE*, Vol. 11, No. 4, 1985.

9. G.J. Myers, *The Art of Software Testing*, Wiley, 1979.

10. T.J. Ostrand and M.J. Balcer, "The Category-Partition Method for Functional Test," *CACM*, Vol. 31, No. 6, 1988.

11. W.R. Elmendorf, "Cause-Effect Graphics in Functional Testing," IBM TR 00.2487, 1973.

12. B.W. Boehm, *Software Engineering Economics*, Prentice Hall, 1980.

13. B. Beizer, *Software Testing Techniques*, Van Nostrand Reinhold, 1983.

14. B.I. Witt, "Communicating Modules: A Software Design Model," IEEE Computer, January 1985.

15. R.C. Linger and H.D. Mills, "Case Study in Cleanroom Software Engineering," COMPSAC '88 Proceedings, 1988.

16. M. Dyer and A. Koughakdjian, "Correctness Verification: Alternative to Software Testing," *Information and Software Technology*, Vol. 32, No. 1, 1990.

17. J.J. Gerber, "Cleanroom Test Case Generator," IBM TR 86.0008, 1986.

18. M.M. Al-Jarrah and I.S. Torsun "An Empirical Analysis of COBOL Programs," *Software Practice and Experience*, Vol. 9, 1979.

19. M. Dyer, "An Approach to Software Reliability Measurement," *Information and Software Technology*, Vol. 29, 1987.

CHAPTER 7

Software Reliability

Reliability is a product measure which, in the case of software, should describe how a software product will perform when put to use. Software reliability is estimated by observing execution behavior and, specifically, failure characteristics in the software's intended operating environment. A simulation of that environment during software testing allows the reliability estimation to be performed in parallel with the software development.

Software reliability should not be confused with measures of the software development process, such as defect counts (i.e., errors per klocs), which describe the efficiency with which development is performed. Although a correlation exists between a measure of software reliability and a count of defects, the relationship between the two statistics is not straightforward. Using defect counts and experience from similar software developments to predict defects remaining in the software at delivery should not be viewed as a reliability estimate. First, there is not a one-to-one correspondence between defects and software failures which are the basis for reliability estimation. Second, the similarity between a given development and other completed developments stemming from similarities in the conduct of inspections and project testing is open to question and the subject of ongoing research.

Since an estimate of software reliability is a statement of the future behavior of the software, some model or hypothesis is needed of the software failure process. If software failure is treated as a random process, then the model is probabilistic and randomness has to be introduced into the seemingly deterministic software execution. This is accomplished in the development process by using test samples which are statistically representative of the software inputs that are encountered in the operating environment.

141

7.1 INDUSTRY FOCUS ON PRODUCT QUALITY AND RELIABILITY

Software has become a household necessity in today's world but little has been done to measure its reliability for the consumer. During the past two decades, computers and software have moved from the scientific, industrial, and university environments where they received their first prominence into every facet of society. Homes, offices, autos, planes, whatever are operated and controlled by software, to an ever-growing degree. So much so that the complexity with which we are trying to deal is definitely overtaxing and maybe outstripping the software industry's ability to develop and deliver software that works for every consumer in every instance.

Software failures previously impacted small numbers of highly skilled technical people and could be accepted by that community, which was willing and able to adapt to workarounds, temporary fixes, and other expediencies. With the expanding consumer community, such tolerance to software failures is no longer feasible nor acceptable. The new consumer is using software as a tool to support the operation of a business, household, machine, or whatever. There is no interest or sympathy with the logical complexity, development difficulty, or technical challenge associated with the software. Like any other tool, the consumer will use software if it supports and simplifies his work, but will just as quickly discard the tool when it complicates his task or does not provide the support which was anticipated.

Based on published reports [1], the severity and frequency of software failures tends to be increasing or at least attracting more and more attention in the news media. Failures in automatic teller machines when dispensing money, collapses in large segments of public communication systems, privacy intrusions in the use and misuse of personal information, and similar dramatic examples of software failures frequent our news with alarming regularity. On a more personal level, software failures also seem to be intruding into our lives at an increasing rate as computers and their software take over more and more functions in our automobiles, household appliances, entertainment, and educational systems.

The frequency and pervasiveness of these failures has heightened the consumer's awareness and insistence on more reliable products and, where software is involved, more reliable software as well. This consumer push for reliability is forcing software providers to re-examine their positions on development processes and methods, their understanding of quality and reliability metrics, and their attention to software usage after delivery. Unfortunately, until driven by the consumer, quality and reliability were not generally key motivators for the software provider who was more focused on delivering the most function, on the shortest schedule, at the most competitive price. Since there was an unending demand for more and better function, the software provider considered that there was ample opportunity to clear up quality, usability, reliability, and other issues as the software moved from one release to the next. The consumer, however, seems to be at the end of his tolerance for this attitude and approach to product development. Quality and reliability are becoming key discriminators in the consumer's selection process and with the growing numbers of products advertising the same functionality, consumers' options are broadening.

7.1.1 Application of Existing Reliability Theory

Software is a relatively new commodity for which accepted development methods that can provide a product with adequate reliability for any given application do not exist. Except for standard commercial software packages which deal with well-understood processes (e.g., accounting), software problems always tend to require new solutions which provide limitless opportunities for the software developer to introduce new logical errors. The developer is rarely in a position to refer to a standard design, like a building architect, and since failures are logical and not physical, there is no continuity of cause and effect (i.e., small logical mistakes can lead to catastrophic consequences during execution). This underlying difference in software and hardware failure makes the direct application of existing reliability theory impractical and requires the definition of a new software-unique theory.

From a reliability perspective, a hardware product is viewed as constructed with a set of components that are taken from a population of identical devices. The reliability of these components can be estimated from the proportion of devices that fail during test to the total number of the devices in a sample. Estimating the hardware product's reliability comes down to combining the reliabilities of the individual components based on the physical use of those components within the product (i.e., their number, parallel or serial hook-up, and so on). As an illustration of the procedure, consider a product with three components, all of which must work correctly for the product to work correctly (i.e., components operate independently and in series, as shown in Figure 7.1A). The product reliability (R) would be computed as the product of the component reliabilities (r_is) or

$$R = r_1 * r_2 * r_3.$$

If the reliabilities of the individual components had been estimated at 0.99 based on some testing process, then the product reliability would be computed as

$$R = (0.99)^3 = 0.97.$$

As a design alternative, consider another product with two components, either one of which must work correctly for the product to work correctly (i.e., components operate independently and in parallel, as shown in Figure 7.1B). The product probability in this case is

$$R = 1 - [(1 - r_1)(1 - r_2)].$$

If in this case, the reliabilities of the individual components had been estimated at 0.95 based on some testing process, then the product reliability would be computed as

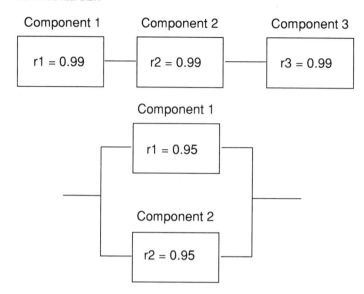

Figure 7.1   A: Model of Series Product and B: Model of Parallel Product

$R = 1 - (0.05)^2 = 0.09975.$

Another design alternative would be to introduce the parallel design for a component of a serial design. If the Figure 7.1B configuration is substituted for the first component in the Figure 7.1A configuration, such that the reliability r_1 was 0.9975 rather than 0.99, then the product reliability would be computed as

$R = 0.9975 * (0.99)^2 = 0.978.$

This latter alternative demonstrates that product reliability can be improved by using lower reliability components in a redundant configuration in place of higher reliability components. By replacing Component 1 which had a 0.99 reliability by a redundant configuration whose components had only a 0.95 reliability, product reliability was increased from 0.97 to 0.978.

Where hardware products can be decomposed into serial and parallel combinations of components, reliability computations can be made in a straightforward way. As hardware complexity grows with the introduction of integrated circuits, this is no longer the case and the problems associated with estimating software reliability are also being seen in hardware reliability work.

Software can not be viewed as just another component and have its reliability simply factored into the hardware reliability. The principal reason for this is that software failures are due to design flaws that are encountered during the software execution and not to any aging of the coded instructions after some period of software execution. Reliability of hardware components is based exclusively on device wear out and computed for a device based on failure analysis during extended life testing of an appropriate sample of the device. The reliability estimate excludes failures due to design flaws that are encountered during the testing, which are attributed to attempted operations outside of the execution limits or capabilities, defined for the device.

7.2 WHAT IS SOFTWARE RELIABILITY?

Software practitioners can not seem to reach agreement on a definition for the term ''software reliability.'' In its most basic sense, reliability is the probability that no failures will occur during a given time interval of a product's operation [2]. This definition underlies hardware reliability theory, which has been applied to mechanical, civil, electrical, electronic, and other engineering disciplines. In the hardware theory, failures are attributed to physical characteristics, primarily the aging or wear out of the hardware components. To support the theory, a rich set of mathematical models has been developed and measures, such as MTTF, have been defined. With the theory and practice, reliability predictions are routinely made for hardware systems, which establish the basis for their warranties, logistical support, maintenance, and replacement strategies.

The early work in software reliability attempted a straightforward adoption of the hardware reliability concepts and methods. Where software was embedded in a hardware system, software was treated like a hardware component and routinely assigned a reliability value of one, since, by definition, software neither ages nor wears out. With the movement of more and more function into software and out of hardware in most new system designs, this essential discounting of software from the reliability calculations is no longer realistic nor appropriate. As software content grows, system reliability should become synonymous with software reliability, but this is far from the case. System reliability predictions are still based on hardware theory with an underlying assumption that the embedded software does not fail.

Because of this unworkable situation (assuming that software does not fail), the software community attempted to establish a different definition. Instead of organizing a separate mathematical theory for software reliability, the software practitioners have defined software product reliability as somehow being generally synonymous with the quality measures for the software development process. Software reliability is routinely discussed in terms such as design complexity or defect rate (errors discovered through inspection and testing of software). The rationale for this approach to software reliability is the perceived relationship between the reliability of a software product and the process used to develop that software. Reliable software confirms a successful development process, while unreliable software gives a lesson for process improvement. The currently used measurements consider different product and process factors, which might impact reliability but which rarely afford any opportunity for assessment of product operational potential.

Reliability is viewed as just one of the many user quality objectives, which should be factored into the software design and which should be included as a criterion for the software's acceptance. Reliability is considered in the same light as objectives, such as ease of use, security, safety, and robustness. The published literature on software reliability [3,4] typically focuses on software design and testing methods, where quality objectives are stated in terms such as complexity, traceability, modularity, coverage, defect rates, and similar factors. These measures are rarely of direct interest or concern to the software user but the evolving new theories on software reliability [5,6] are treated by practitioners as theory and not practice. They tend to be relegated to the special-topics bin with other innovative but little-used techniques, such as formal specification and correctness verification.

7.2.1   Is the Current Focus Correct?

There are two obvious flaws with the current practice (assigning a reliability value of one and substituting quality measures from the process). First, system reliability predictions (MTTF, etc.) can become overly optimistic since embedded software can, in fact, fail. The extent of prediction inaccuracy depends on the pervasiveness or role of embedded software in the system operation and on the goodness of that software. With the growing demand for function in systems and the preference for introducing function through software, there is a growing need for a software reliability definition which is based on failure probability.

A widely held misconception is that, since software execution is deterministic, a reliability statistic, such as MTTF, cannot be defined [4], because there is no way of introducing failure probability. It is true that, for given input and initial conditions, software always produces the same results (correct answers or failures), no matter how often repeated. This defines deterministic execution, where any apparent erratic behavior in the software during asynchronous execution must be caused by a change in the input or initialization sequence and not a deterioration in the executed statements. From this position, current reliance on design and test methods for achieving reliable software can be appreciated and the attempted extrapolation of quality measures on the software process to make inference about software reliability can be rationalized.

In principle, the basic definition of reliability (probability that no failures will occur during a given time interval of a product's operation) should also hold for software, with a different interpretation of failure (i.e., aging does not apply). The recent studies of software reliability generally recognize that software failures must have a logical rather than physical basis, where software failures result from faults in the software design rather than from a physical property of the software. They tend to agree that software failures are triggered by the chance introduction into the processing of input values which cannot be accommodated by the software design. The consensus opinion is that software failure probability should be defined in terms of the likelihood of different software inputs being introduced into the processing (i.e., as a function of the software use).

While reliability cannot be tested into software, software testing plays a critical role in estimating software reliability. A statistically based approach to software testing is what makes the software reliability theories work. If testing is organized to use input samples which are randomly selected but based on the probabilities of the inputs occurring in the software's operating environment, then the test environment simulates execution in representative operating environments. Failure data recorded in the test environment can, in fact, be extrapolated to the operating environment and form the basis for software reliability estimation.

The second flaw in the current practice relates to the quality measures which are used as a substitute for a software reliability measure based on failure probability. These substitute measures tend to more accurately track the quality of the software development process. They focus on the potential causes of software errors within the development life cycle and the elimination of these error sources with the thought that quality process equates to reliable product.

These substitute measures attempt to address the full range of the development life cycle and include complexity measures from design, inspection data from design and implementation, and testing results from all levels of software testing. Their primary audience is the software developers and their management, though they advertise benefit (more indirect than direct) for the software users. Some measures monitor the accuracy and completeness of development and test activities (e.g., requirements traces). Others monitor the efficiency of these activities (e.g., test coverage). The bias toward the interests of the software developer results in their missing the key objective of software reliability (i.e., user satisfaction).

The consumers or users of software are primarily concerned with failures in the software execution, which have a direct impact on their work activities. They are unsympathetic to the complexity of the software unless it adds complexity to their use. They rightfully presume that there are no defects in the software delivered for their use. While the software developer knows that design complexity generally has a negative impact on reliability and that defect counts are a gauge of the goodness of development, the software user has no appreciation nor interest in such questions. Software that fails infrequently is, by definition, more reliable to the user regardless of the design complexity or the numbers of defects found during development. The user, who includes the owner and the operator as well, is interested in measures that relate to software availability or failure-free operation, such as the software's MTTF.

7.3 CLEANROOM DEFINITION OF RELIABILITY

To study and use software reliability, a new theoretical approach is required which is grounded in the concept of logical rather than physical failure. A reasonable starting position might be to assume that software errors would have similar failure rates and to suppose that software errors and the times between software failures were closely correlated. This position could then be used to support an assumption such as: If there were half the number of errors in a software product, the times between software failures might double or change by some other factor, such as 10

TABLE 7.1   Fitted Percentages of Errors: Mean Time to Error Occurrence by Failure Rate Class Defined in Thousands of Months

	60	19	6	1.9	.6	.19	.06	.019
Product 1	34.2	28.8	17.8	10.3	5.0	2.1	1.2	0.7
Product 2	34.2	28.0	18.2	9.7	4.5	3.2	1.5	0.7
Product 3	33.7	28.5	18.0	8.7	6.5	2.8	1.4	0.4
Product 4	34.2	28.5	18.7	11.9	4.4	2.0	0.3	0.1
Product 5	34.2	28.5	18.4	9.4	4.4	2.9	1.4	0.7
Product 6	32.0	28.2	20.1	11.5	5.0	2.1	0.8	0.3
Product 7	34.0	28.5	18.5	9.9	4.5	2.7	1.4	0.6
Product 8	31.9	27.1	18.4	11.1	6.5	2.7	1.4	1.1
Product 9	31.2	27.6	20.4	12.8	5.6	1.9	0.5	0.0
Average	33.3	28.2	18.7	10.6	5.2	2.5	1.0	0.5

or 20. This would allow treating the software errors in a product as reasonably equivalent and simplify the reliability computation.

However, an empirical study [7] of major IBM software products has shown this not to be the case and that contrary relationships exist. To perform the particular analysis, a set of failure rate classes was defined into which all the reported failures in the various software products were collected, based on the frequency with which the individual failures were reported. The first unexpected result from the study was the realization that there was very significant variation between the rates at which failures occurred; not the supposed factor of two or 10 or 20, but more like several orders of magnitude. This reinforced the belief that there are significant differences between software errors and their impacts on software execution. It strengthened the strategy that error correction should be driven, primarily, by the error's impact on software execution and not by side considerations, such as the ease of repair, availability of knowledgeable personnel, and the like.

The second and equally startling finding from the study was that there were equally significant differences in the number of failures in each rate class. The good news was that the majority of the failures fell into the low rate classes (i.e., occurred infrequently) and that a very small number of failures fell into the high rate classes (i.e., occurred frequently). These two results shed new light on strategies for repairing software errors (the study's original objective) and, more to the point, for developing a definition of software reliability.

Using an interpretation of the published results shown in Table 7.1, fixing errors which cause low rate failures has little or no impact on improving the reliability of the software product. Because of the real possibility of introducing new errors with a fix, an error which causes high rate failures could be introduced and significantly degrade the product reliability. For the software products considered in the study, removal of the wrong 60% of the errors (the two lowest rate classes) would have an imperceptible effect on product failures, while removal of the right 2 to 5% of the errors (the two or three highest rate classes) could make the products exhibit near zero defect performance during their useful lifetime.

These results might not be as dramatic for other software products, but the same trends should hold (i.e., a small subset of the total errors cause the bulk of the failures). This might be another instance of the 80 to 20 rule but a more plausible explanation is that the errors causing the high rate failures had to be found and corrected during development to make any progress toward product delivery. The errors remaining in the software after delivery are most likely triggered by input conditions which are less likely to occur and, therefore, cause only low rate failures. The key to ensuring delivery of software with high reliability is to organize a development process which focuses on finding the errors which are more likely to occur and cause frequent failures. This is exactly the focus of the Cleanroom method and the rationale behind the Cleanroom definition of software reliability.

7.3.1 Cleanroom Reliability Model Derivation

If there are errors in delivered software, users may experience intermittent failures as the software is executed. Unlike hardware, the software intermittent failures are repeatable. When the software is executed a second or any number of times, with the same initial and input conditions, the software fails at exactly the same point in its execution. The explanation for the software executing correctly with one set of initial and input conditions but failing with another set lies with the sequencing and interaction designed into the software logic. It has nothing to do with the operation of the machine instructions that implement the design (i.e., the reason from hardware reliability theory).

For hardware, the basis for a statistical model to compute reliability is the physical behavior of the hardware (i.e., component aging). For software, the basis for a statistical model is the use of the software in its operating environment(s). Each discrete use is an execution of the software with a particular set of initial and input conditions, which requires some number of machine cycles and results. Each execution results in either correct results from the software or the encountering of one or more software failures. For a given user, an execution lifetime could be viewed as the sequence of executions which are needed to perform the user's work. If these sequences are assembled into a collection of execution sequences, one per user, the collection identifies a stochastic process (i.e., a random assortment of possible execution sequences).

The collection of execution sequences is the basis for structuring statistical models to compute software reliability and for defining statistical measures to characterize software usage (e.g., software MTTF and variance around the MTTF). This modeling approach satisfies the Cleanroom objective for computing operational reliability for software as it is developed and for confirming a reliability estimate to a defined level of confidence. It is consistent with most other software reliability work [8,9], which identifies the need for growth models to track reliability changes throughout development and to focus on failure-free execution metrics from software testing (not defect counts).

Two underlying assumptions in constructing the model for software reliability [10] for the Cleanroom method were that the total set of possible execution sequences for the software can be defined and that probability distributions can be defined on the likelihood of each sequence's execution in the software's operating environment. As a minimum, a model definition should allow for structure in the software (i.e., modules, programs, and so on), for a categorization of software failures, and for an error repair strategy (e.g., correcting errors as failures are detected). An initial minimum capability of a software reliability model can always be expanded to support more realistic application and project situations. Modular structure in the software product, multiple categories of failures (i.e., based on severity considerations), and different error correction strategies are desirable model inclusions. The key considerations in constructing a software reliability model are that the software MTTF should be estimated relative to a given probability environment and that input samples of execution sequences should be randomly generated for that environment.

Estimating reliability during development is not straightforward and requires the use of reliability growth models that can account for error discovery and repair during software testing and which can still compute a reliability estimate for the software. As repairs are made, a new version of the software is, in essence, created which is similar to its predecessor but with a new (hopefully improved) reliability. The certification model, defined for estimating software reliability with the Cleanroom method [10], is an example of a reliability growth model. In the Cleanroom method, the functional testing of software is statistically based with randomly generated samples of representative software inputs used for the testing. The input sampling is controlled by probability distributions that describe the expected use of the software in its operating environment. The particular functional-test approach also assumes the software is developed incrementally with the delivered releases containing a defined functional capability against which testing with the randomly selected input sample is conducted.

The certification model focuses on estimating statistical measures about software, in particular the software's MTTF, rather than the number of latent software errors. It is a growth model by definition and factors into its computation the repair of the errors which were the cause of software failures. Since the errors causing the failures are removed as part of the development process, increasing MTTF values (i.e., reliability growth) should be realized. The certification model assumes a repair strategy in which errors are diagnosed and repaired whenever failures are encountered during the software testing—a fix-when-found strategy. The computational effect of this strategy is that additional instances of the same failure during test are not separately counted but ignored. The rationale is that, in a perfect development situation, the underlying error causing the failure would be fixed immediately. While that intent might not be satisfied in the real project environment, the logical consequence of the strategy (i.e., no additional occurrences of the same failure) can be and is reflected in the model's calculations.

To account for the differences in failure significance [7], the certification model also assumes a repair strategy in which errors are fixed based on the severity of their impact on software execution. This second repair strategy fits with the statistical testing objective of forcing the detection of the high-failure-rate errors. In terms of testing effectiveness, this is the appropriate strategy since the high-failure-rate errors generally affect every test execution and can quickly force curtailment of test activities.

7.3.2 Cleanroom Reliability Model Operation

The estimation of software MTTF in the certification model is of the form

$$MTTF_i = MTTF_0 * R^i$$

where the parameter R reflects the contribution to the improvement of the software MTTF which is realized from each software error repair. The value of the parameter R^i is recomputed at each MTTF computation and takes into account the impact of a particular error, as judged by the size of the interfail time (i.e., the length of failure-free execution), by the effectiveness of the error repair strategy, and by the consequences of imperfect repair on the software. The parameters $MTTF_0$ and R are estimated through the use of a corrected logarithmic least squares technique which is discussed in detail in reference **10**.

In the normal process of the software functional testing, the execution times for individual test cases are recorded using a timing unit appropriate and convenient to the particular test environment. This time unit can run from wall clock time to computer instruction execution time with the consistent use of the same unit more important than the unit itself. Interfail times which serve as the input unit for the statistical models are computed by summing the test execution times between successive occurrences of test case execution failures. For an input interfail time, the certification model computes an estimate which gives the model's projection of the software MTTF, based on the value of the current interfail time and the stored history of previous interfail times for that software. When the estimate is made, the current interfail time is added to the history of interfail times. For a subsequent input interfail time, a new projection is made, based on the new value and the stored history. In general, the ith MTTF prediction would be based on a history of $(i-1)$ interfail times, as shown in Figure 7.2.

For the case illustrated in Figure 7.2, a series of tests were executed and nine software failures were encountered. The accumulated time of software execution from the start of the first test until the first failure in a test execution was encountered is the value of the first interfail time (i.e., 27.7 seconds). The second through ninth interfail times (i.e., 50.3, 69.4, 62, 405, 306.4, 52.2, 179.7, and 232.9 seconds) are the accumulation of the failure-free execution intervals between the subsequent execution failures. The value of the tenth interfail time is arbitrarily set at twice the accumulated time from the ninth failure until the particular test sample is depleted (i.e., 189.9 seconds recorded and 379.8 seconds used). When testing is

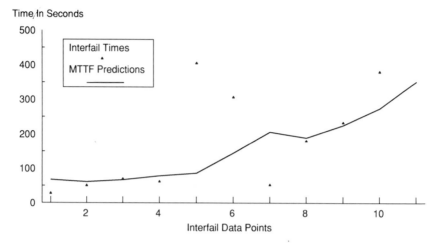

Figure 7.2 MTTF Predictions for Sample Software Increment

completed but does not end with a test-case failure, some accommodation must be made for all the successful test executions since the last failure. In the current use of the statistical models with Cleanroom development, an arbitrary doubling of the accumulated time was used to reflect the anticipation that the software should continue to run, at least, for as long as it has run since the last failure.

Based on the particular history of the ten interfail time values as shown in Figure 7.2, the certification model would estimate the software MTTF at 352 seconds. As additional functional testing of the software is performed, additional failures might be encountered but their number should generally drop off. If that is the case, the size of the interfail intervals should grow and, when input to the certification model, should result in estimates of increasing software MTTF. This growth in software reliability is subsequently discussed with an example in section 7.4.1.

To extrapolate an estimate of software MTTF which is based on execution times recorded in a testing environment into an equivalent estimate which reflects software execution in its real-life operating environment, an additional reliability calculation must be performed, as discussed in the next section.

7.4 CLEANROOM RELIABILITY MODEL EXPERIENCE

In the Cleanroom method, software is developed as a set of increments to permit an orderly development regardless of size, complexity, schedule, interfacing, and staffing considerations for a particular project. Each increment supplies some sub-set of the total function of a software product and increments build on previously delivered increments to evolve the total product function.

To optimize the functional-testing effort both for the product and each increment, the testing at each incremental release primarily addresses the function(s) in

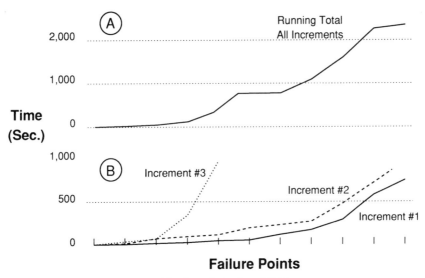

Figure 7.3 Cumulative Interfail Times

the newly delivered increment. The testing rationale is to focus the testing on the software function(s) when initially released to test, which allows the test group to plan its effort by release, to validate the requirements for the major software functions, at one time, and to build up the final product with well-tested functional building blocks. Randomly generated input samples are similarly structured for the testing of each release. To guard against regression in the delivered functions, the generated input sample for a given release also contains tests for functional increments which were delivered in previous releases. As a rule, the randomly generated samples do not contain tests for functions that are not contained in either the current or previously delivered increments. The grouping of the randomly generated inputs by functional increments is justified by the stratified sampling theorem from statistical theory and still supports the validation of software requirements with representative usage samples.

With the testing concentrated on the new function(s) in each release, an initial rash of software failures is generally encountered because of software errors which, for the first time, are being exposed in execution. The Cleanroom experience is that most errors in a function are found with the first handful of tests and that the number of errors subsequently found diminishes dramatically. These initially found errors tend to account for most of the errors in the function and to be high-failure-rate errors which affect any attempt at function execution. The reason for this initial spurt of failures in the typical Cleanroom development is that Cleanroom software is released to testing with very few errors to start with and the distribution-driven statistical testing tends to drive out any high-failure-rate errors first.

Our initial approach to software reliability measurement attempted to accumulate failures and interfail times for the total software. However, it became apparent that a plot of the cumulative interfail times with this approach, as shown in Figure 7.3A, would define an unusable distribution and would not conform to an underlying model assumption that a plot of cumulative interfail times inputs have a generally exponential shape. As can be seen, spikes in the cumulative interfail time plot occur with each new release, as the testing uncovers a rash of initial errors in the newly delivered function. When the statistical models attempt to use this data with spikes corresponding to the release points, the MTTF predictions become unstable and unusable.

However, if the failure data is collected by functional increments and the interfail times are separately computed by the functions within the increments, then the plot of interfail times has a more regular shape and essentially takes an exponential form. If the same failure data are collected by the functions within each increment, the interfail times exhibit fairly regular growth, as shown in Figure 7.3B, approximating an exponential distribution.

For the test situation illustrated in Figure 7.3, the test executions were separately collected for the different functions within each of the three increments. For the Increment 1 functions, the first 18 failures were discovered during the testing of the initial release of Increment 1. Regression testing of the functions in Increment 1 during the testing of the initial release of Increment 2 uncovered an additional failure. Similarly, regression testing of these same Increment 1 functions during the testing of the initial release of Increment 3 uncovered another additional failure. The plot of the cumulative interfail times for the functions in Increment 1 is shown separately in Figure 7.3B. The execution data for the functions in Increments 2 and 3 is also separated and the plots of their cumulative interfail times are also given in Figure 7.3B. This is exactly the kind of input distribution which is assumed by the certification model defined for the Cleanroom method.

As a result, the certification model is used only to make the MTTF predictions for the software increments and not to make the MTTF predictions for the total software product. The total software MTTF is a separate calculation that uses the certification model predictions for the software increments in a weighted sum calculation. More exactly, the failure rates for increments are used which are additive and can be approximated as the reciprocal of an MTTF value. If the model input is exponential, there is an exact reciprocal relationship between failure rate and MTTF and if the model input takes some other distribution, the use of reciprocals is still a reasonable approximation.

The form of the MTTF calculation for the total software is

$$MTFF = \frac{1}{R_i} \text{ and}$$

$$R_1 = C_{11}R_{11} \qquad \text{after Increment 1}$$

$$R_2 = C_{12}R_{12} + C_{22}R_{22} \qquad \text{after Increment 2}$$

$$\vdots$$

$$R_n = C_{1n}R_{1n} + C_{2n}R_{2n} \ldots + C_{nn}R_{nn} \qquad \text{after Increment } n$$

where a set of each increment's coefficients are introduced to account for the relative contributions of each increment's functions to the total software capability and to extrapolate testing results to operating environments. The contribution to total software capability refers to what percentage of time is a particular function exercised during software operation. As the software is developed and its function is added incrementally to the evolving baseline, the contribution from a given function and/or increment will change over time (up or down), depending on what other functions are included in the baseline and what the expected contributions of these other functions to the total capability are.

The computed product reliability can be used in two ways. First, as development proceeds, it represents the current product reliability at any point in time. Second, for process feedback and control against a target MTTF, the computed reliability gives the contribution from the released increments to making the target MTTF. The MTTF budgets for the remaining increments could be appropriately adjusted to ensure achievement of the target reliability.

7.4.1 An Example of Cleanroom Reliability Model Use

To demonstrate the procedure that is followed in estimating software MTTF, the flight software application which was discussed in the statistical approach to functional testing (Chapter 6) is used. The flight software was developed as a set of functional increments, and to demonstrate the modeling procedure the test results from the first three releases of the software are considered.

The testing approach which was followed was to focus on the functions in Increment 1 during the testing of the initial release. At the second release of the software, the approach was to concentrate on the functions in Increment 2 but to also execute a small number of regression tests against the functions in Increment 1. At the third release, the approach was to concentrate on the functions in Increment 3 but also execute a small number of regression tests against the functions in both Increment 1 and Increment 2. The software in these first three releases was tested with slightly less than 450 discrete test cases, of which 30% were used for the testing of the functions in Increment 1, 40% for the functions in Increment 2, and the remaining 30% for the functions in Increment 3. In the testing of the first three releases of the flight software, some 40 failures were encountered from which interfail times were computed which were then input to the certification model.

The interfail times associated with the Increment 1 software are given in Table 7.2 and separated according to each of the three releases in which tests were executed against that software. The table shows the history of interfail data which would be used by the model after the completion of testing for a given release. The model uses all of the times from the testing of the previous release, with the possible exception of the last value, and the times recorded in the testing of the current release.

When the testing of a given release completes without a failure, the accumulated successful execution time is arbitrarily doubled and processed as a pseudo-

TABLE 7.2   Interfail Times for First Functional Increment

At Release 1	At Release 2	At Release 3
1	1	1
1	1	1
5	5	5
10	10	10
5	5	5
4	4	4
11	11	11
9	9	9
3	3	3
4	4	4
2	2	2
61	61	61
31	31	31
23	23	23
61	61	61
61	61	61
10	10	10
282	282	282
14	150	150
	35	20
		53

interfail time. In the Increment 1 case, pseudointerfail times had to be computed for each release, since testing never stopped on a failure. The pseudo times are the last entries in each column (i.e., 14, 35, and 53 seconds, respectively). When testing is resumed for an increment in a subsequent release, the residual time (i.e., half of the pseudointerfail time) from the testing of the earlier release is used as the base for accumulating the test execution times that will go into the next interfail time for the increment. In this example, another failure in the Increment 1 function was discovered by the regression tests run during the testing of the second release. The actual interfail value for the nineteenth failure is 150 seconds rather than the pseudointerfail value (14 seconds) which had been used for the model calculations at the completion of testing for the first release. Note that, when further regression testing of the Increment 1 functions was performed during the testing of the third release, the actual interfail value for the twentieth failure point is 20 seconds and is smaller than the pseudovalue (35 seconds) which had been used for the model calculations at the completion of the testing for the second release. This anomaly results from the arbitrary doubling rule which is applied at the completion of testing for a release, which does not end with a failure, in order to create a pseudointerfail input for the model calculation.

When the testing for a given release is completed, the interfail times are computed for the certification model. The interfail times are separately collected by the

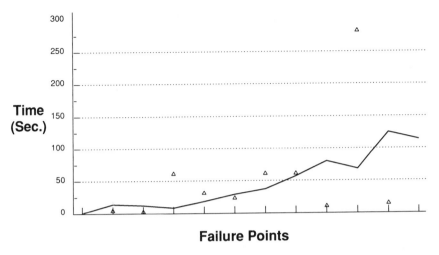

Figure 7.4 Model Estimate of MTTF for First Functional Increment After First-Release Testing

increments in which the software was packaged. This means that only the test execution times for the software in a particular increment are subtotaled in comput- ing interfail time, even though those test execution times may be interspersed between execution times for the software in other increments. Each test execution time recorded during the testing of a given release is used only once, in the interfail time calculation for the particular increment in which the software is packaged.

In this example, at the completion of the testing of the first release, all test execution times and interfail times are associated with Increment 1 which contains all of the tested software. Only one execution of the model is required using the single set of interfail times for Increment 1 and the MTTF estimates based on those interfail times are plotted in Figure 7.4. Only the MTTF estimates corresponding to the tenth through nineteenth interfail data points in the first column of Table 7.2 are shown in the Figure 7.4 plot to simplify the graphics. The reliability of the total software product (i.e., the flight software) would be easy to compute at this point, since only one functional increment has been released, and would use the follow- ing equations:

$$MTTF = \frac{1}{R_1} \text{ and}$$

$$R_1 = C_{11}\left(\frac{1}{114}\right)$$

where 114 seconds is the certification model's estimate of the *MTTF* for the first functional increment at the completion of the testing of the first release.

With the completion of testing for the second release, two separate sets of input must be collected for the model. One set would collect any additional interfail

TABLE 7.3   Interfail Times for Second Functional Increment

At Release 2	At Release 3
11	11
58	58
35	35
9	9
80	80
11	11
23	23
37	37
3	3
25	25
10	10
28	28
25	25
27	27
690	375
	97

times from the regression testing of the Increment 1 software and the second set would be the interfail times for the newly released software in Increment 2. An additional failure was encountered in the Increment 1 software from the regression testing, as shown in the second column of Table 7.2, so that 20 interfail times would be used in the certification model's estimation. The interfail times for the newly released Increment 2 software are shown in Table 7.3, and would be used as the input for a second execution of the certification model to provide an MTTF estimate for the Increment 2 software. For this second model execution, only the data in column one of Table 7.3 is used.

The reliability of the total software product (i.e., the flight software), after the testing of the second release, is slightly more complicated to compute, since there are now two MTTF estimates (Increment 1 and Increment 2 software) to consider, and would use the following equations:

$$MTTF = \frac{1}{R_2} \text{ and}$$

$$R_2 = C_{12}\left(\frac{1}{189}\right) + C_{22}\left(\frac{1}{122}\right)$$

where 189 seconds and 122 seconds are the certification model's estimates of the MTTF for the software in Increments 1 and 2, respectively, based on the testing of the second release.

TABLE 7.4 Interfail Times for Third Functional Increment

At Release 3
11
24
2
27
35
232

With the completion of the testing for the third release, three separate sets of interfail times must be collected. Two of these sets would be any additional inter-fail times from the regression testing of the Increment 1 and Increment 2 software. The third set would be the interfail data for the newly released Increment 3 software. For the Increment 1 software, another failure was discovered by a regres-sion test and, as shown in the third column of Table 7.2, 21 interfail times would be used for one execution of the certification model. An additional failure was also discovered by a regression test in the Increment 2 software and, as shown in the second column of Table 7.3, 16 interfail times would be used for a second execu-tion of the certification model. The interfail times for the newly released Increment 3 software are shown in Table 7.4, and would be used as the input for a third execution of the certification model.

The reliability of the total software product (i.e., the flight software), after the testing of the third release, is slightly more complicated, since there are now three MTTF estimates (Increment 1 software, Increment 2 software, and Increment 3 software) to consider, and would use the following equations:

$$MTTF = \frac{1}{R_3} \text{ and}$$

$$R_3 = C_{13}\left(\frac{1}{183}\right) + C_{23}\left(\frac{1}{127}\right) + C_{33}\left(\frac{1}{233}\right)$$

where 183 seconds, 127 seconds, and 233 seconds are the certification model's estimates of the MTTF for Increments 1, 2, and 3 software, respectively, based on the testing of the third release.

This process would continue until all releases of the software were tested. The MTTF for the total software product (i.e., the flight software) would be computed as the weighted sum of the MTTF contributions from the software in each of the functional increments. The coefficients in the weighted sum computation would be computed at each step. Their values would depend on the number of functional increments being considered, the contribution (at a given step) of each increment to the total software function, and the ratio (at a given step) of test environment time to operating environment time.

Time In Seconds

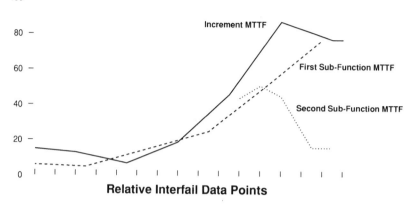

Figure 7.5 Analysis of Subfunction MTTF Predictions for a Sample Software Increment

7.4.2 Examples of Quality Analyses Using Software MTTF Data

The obvious use of the timing data from statistical testing and the Cleanroom's certification model is to track the reliability of software, as it is being developed. MTTF for delivered software which will not change can be computed, in a straightforward way by recording the number of failures during some period of operation. The software MTTF can be approximated by simply dividing the period of operation by the number of recorded failures. Estimating software MTTF during development uses the same approach but is more complicated because the software is not in a delivered form but rather takes different forms as it evolves through development. Corrections must be applied as failures are encountered, changing the form of the software. The software's operating environment must be simulated, since the actual environment requires the delivered software. Statistical modeling is the technique for making reliability predictions as software is developed.

Once the testing and modeling procedures have been established, other analyses can be performed on the quality of the software under development, using the variants of the MTTF calculations. Examining the MTTF characteristics of the component parts of the software is one such analysis, which is useful in localizing unreliable parts of the software and identifying the added controls to be placed on the development process. Examining the changes in software MTTF based on the consideration of failure severity is another useful analysis, since it provides alternatives for deciding the readiness of the software for delivery.

7.4.2.1 MTTF Analysis of Software Subfunctions
In the flight software application, two different situations were uncovered by a component-level examination of the MTTF data. The first situation involved the software in a functional increment that addressed two major subfunctions within the flight software. After seeing a steady growth in MTTF for the increment during its testing in several releases, a dramatic drop in the increment's MTTF occurred during the

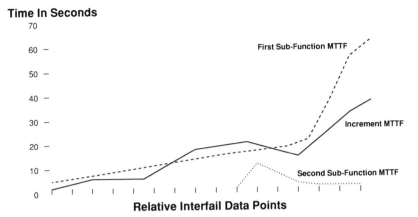

Figure 7.6 Analysis of Subfunction MTTF Predictions for a Second Sample Software Increment

testing of a subsequent release, as seen in Figure 7.5. To uncover the reason for this drop, the MTTFs for each of the two subfunctions within the increment were separately plotted, as also shown in Figure 7.5. This immediately showed that the first subfunction was still experiencing MTTF growth but that the second subfunction was indicating a significant loss in MTTF. Further examination of the testing data on the second subfunction indicated that a basic interface error existed in the software for the second subfunction. This error had gone undetected in the initial testing because the interface was simulated, but surfaced in the subsequent testing when additional hardware was connected to the test environment, which triggered the first-time testing of the erroneous interface. The detailed MTTF analysis in this situation helped to explain the cause of an MTTF drop for the functional increment and forced a change in testing procedure, which required actual (not simulated) hardware to be used in all subsequent testing.

The second situation involved the software in a different functional increment of the flight software, which addressed two different discrete subfunctions and which was exhibiting some but limited reliability growth, as shown in Figure 7.6. A closer examination of the discrete MTTF's for each of the subfunctions, as also shown in Figure 7.6, indicated that one of the subfunctions was exhibiting no growth and, in effect, dragging down the strong reliability growth in the other subfunctions. The MTTF plots for the troublesome subfunction were either flat or declining, which indicated continued testing found more and more errors in the software for this subfunction. Further investigation indicated a combination of instability in the subfunction requirements and incompleteness in the verification of the design correctness were the likely causes of the stagnant MTTF in this subfunction.

7.4.2.2 *MTTF Analysis of Software Failures* A different perspective from which to consider software MTTF is in terms of the seriousness or significance of the failures which are encountered during functional testing. A fairly

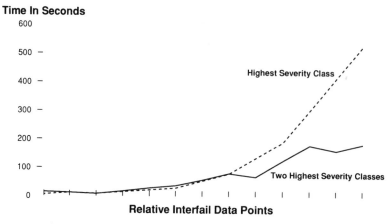

Figure 7.7   Analysis of Failure Severity for a Sample Software Increment

common software practice is to assign severity levels to the failures and errors encountered during development and to use a small number of levels to coincide with development interests. When a failure makes software basically inoperable, it is given the highest severity classification. When a failure indicates that the software is operable but a major subfunction is completely inoperable, it is given the second highest severity level. Other failures that indicate some malfunction in the software are considered less serious and classified at lower levels of severity Typically one or two levels are used to separate hard errors from nits.

User and developer interest is focused more on the two highest levels of failure severity since they really impact the software use, whereas the other levels of severity present a nuisance but something that can be worked around. For the flight software application, the failures in the software within a particular functional increment were sorted by the severity level, which had been assigned by the project personnel. The interfail times associated with failures for the highest and top two highest severity levels were computed and the certification model was rerun with those interfail times to get revised software MTTFs. The two different MTTF plots are shown in Figure 7.7 which points out that there is a more substantial MTTF when only the most severe failures are considered.

7.5   RELIABILITY MODEL CONSIDERATIONS

While a discrete statistical model was defined for the Cleanroom method [10], in practice, a set of four models (the certification and three others) was used for the software MTTF calculations. The models all assumed that software failures

TABLE 7.5 Statistical Model Characteristics

	Certification Model	Shanthikumar Model	Littlewood Model	Littlewood-Verrall Model
Distribution of inputs	Exponential	Exponential	Gamma	Pareto
Form of prediction	Means	Means	Means	Medians
Error counts	Not used	Used	Used	Used
Test times	Input	Input	Input	Input
Repair strategy	Included	Included	Included	Included
Method of inference	Log least squares	Least squares	Maximum likelihood	Maximum likelihood

resulted from design errors and that timing data from software test executions could be the basis for the software MTTF calculations. Like the certification model, the formulations for the other three models are predicated on reliability growth in the software as the functional increments proceed through test. Reliability growth is realized as the software errors which trigger the software failures are found and repaired, which results in the number and frequency of subsequent software failures to drop off. With software functional testing conducted with statistically representative samples of the software's input, the growth should be seen in the total software and not just localized to the heavily tested sections of the code.

The models used in the Cleanroom method differ in the formulation of their computational algorithms and in their assumptions on the characteristics of the interfail times used for input. Table 7.5 summarizes the similarities and differences between the four models.

In practice, as the testing of software releases is completed, reliability estimates for the appropriate set of functional increments are independently computed by each of the four models using the same set of interfail times. The use of several distinct models recognizes that different statistical models tend to react differently to specific interfail data and that no one model can be expected to handle every conceivable set of software failure data perfectly. To determine how well each model performs against a particular set of interfail data, two statistical tests, using the Quantile-Quantile plotting technique [11], are performed on the MTTF outputs from each of the models. These tests provide a statistical check on how well each of the models is tracking the reality exhibited in the recorded test execution data. For a given set of data, a model will generate MTTF estimates that are realistic, optimistic, or pessimistic as judged from the recorded test execution data and the reliability growth (or nongrowth) exhibited by the recorded data. When these tests indicate that a particular model(s) is handling a particular set of interfail data better than the other models, that model(s) tends to be used exclusively for all subsequent MTTF calculations.

7.5.1 Shanthikumar Model [12]

This model has many similarities with classical hardware reliability growth models and is a generalization of an earlier developed model [13]. Both models use a nonhomogeneous Poisson process and model the growth in reliability as a continuous process. The model focuses on estimating a mean value function which approximates the expected number of errors at some future time and takes the form of

$$M_t = A * (1 - e^{-Bt})$$

where parameter A is an estimate of the number of errors to eventually be encountered and parameter B is a proportionality constant relating failure rate to the undetected errors at any time. The model assumes a direct proportionality between failure rate and remaining errors and, unlike the other models used with the Cleanroom method, models this proportionality continuously rather than by discrete error-removal steps. The improvement introduced by the Shanthikumar model over its predecessor was the definition of a parameter which can account for imperfect repair and for the insertion of additional errors during repair.

7.5.2 Littlewood Model [5]

This model does not assume that the software failure rate is some constant multiple of the number of latent errors remaining in the code. Rather, it assumes that different errors have different effects on the software failure rate and gives more weight to errors which are detected earlier in the testing. Other assumptions made in this model are that interfail times are independently and exponentially distributed, that errors are repaired when found, and that the failure rate, at any point, is a function of the occurrence probabilities for the remaining errors. Errors are assumed to be independent and occur at rates which approximate a gamma distribution. The combined randomness in failure times and error rates tends to support the model's assumption on gamma distributions which were selected for reasons of flexibility and mathematical tractability.

7.5.3 Littlewood-Verrall Model [14]

This model considers software failures to result from uncertainties in the software inputs and the software states. It assumes that there is a set of input that will cause software failure and that this set is encountered randomly. Interfail times are therefore assumed to be independent and exponentially distributed. Uncertainty in error repair is also assumed and represented through a probabilistic process. The growth in reliability is seen as probabilistic rather than deterministic with the software failure rate being treated as a random variable. Bayesian techniques are used to combine the sources of randomness, which give a decrease in failure rate between failures and an increase in the confidence for a low failure rate as the number of failures diminish over time.

7.5.4   Deciding Model Effectiveness

Since the MTTF predictions made by the models are statistical, they must be checked to determine how closely they agree with the real-life situation defined by the recorded test execution times. If the model predictions were in perfect agreement with reality, then a normalized plot of predicted model times against actual recorded times should give a line of unit slope (45 degree angle from the origin). The generalized Quantile-Quantile plotting technique [11] uses the line of unit slope idea to measure goodness of fit and to gauge confidence in the model predictions. Goodness of fit is measured with the Kolmogorov-Smirnov statistic which tracks the maximum perpendicular distance from the line of unit slope and normalizes results in the range 0 to 1, where zero would correspond to perfect correlation.

The Quantile-Quantile plotting technique plays two roles within the Cleanroom process, evaluating the predictive accuracy of a statistical model and evaluating a model's ability to capture the trends in the failure data (increases and decreases in interfail times). Since a model predicts a MTTF value, based on a particular history of interfail times, predictive accuracy would refer to the closeness of the correspondence between a predicted MTTF value and the actual interfail time which records when the next failure is encountered. The analysis of predictive accuracy is used to examine bias (optimism or pessimism) in a model's predictions, based on plots of quantile values computed as follows:

$$\text{Quantile Value} = 1 - e^{(t\text{-}MTTF)}$$

The plotting procedure is to compute quantile values for a set of interfail times and corresponding MTTF predictions, to sort the quantile values by ascending order and to plot the sorted values against the reciprocal of the number of values. An example of such a plot is shown in Figure 7.8.

A similar procedure is followed to examine how well a model's predictions are tracking the trends seen in the failure data. In this case, logarithms of the quantile values are computed and plotted. An example of such a plot is shown in Figure 7.9.

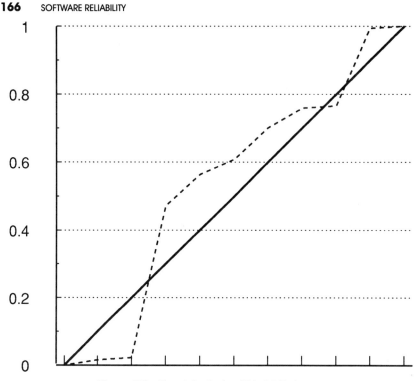

Figure 7.8   Trend Analysis of Model Estimates

7.6   MERGING SOFTWARE RELIABILITY WITH TRADITIONAL THEORY

While knowledge of software MTTF and other statistical measures may be of interest in their own right, their real contribution will come when they can be used to enhance and sharpen the total reliability prediction for systems which use software. A procedure for merging the software reliability estimates with the traditional system reliability estimates, prepared for systems with hardware and software components, must be an area of continuing study. In the traditional hardware reliability theory, three characteristic types of failure are considered: early failures from poor manufacturing control, expected component aging failures, and chance failures when design limits are exceeded. The concentration of effort has been in developing a rich theory and practice that focuses on the aging problem as the source of hardware failures.

The treatment of early failures can be adequately addressed by a "burn-in" testing procedure at the factory, which can generally catch the problems caused by the use of defective or marginal parts and which can minimize or eliminate poor manufacturing control as a failure source. Currently, chance failures are generally discounted from reliability calculations by disallowing operation of the hardware outside of the hardware's specified design limits. Software failures are essentially

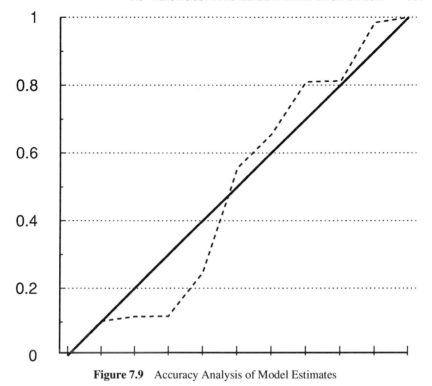

Figure 7.9 Accuracy Analysis of Model Estimates

equivalent to the hardware's chance failures and the reconsideration of chance failures in the hardware reliability calculation seems needed to merge the software and hardware reliability concepts. With the introduction of ''firmware'' control in current hardware, the problems of software failure and reliability considerations should take on a new focus and perhaps expand the horizons of system reliability theory. The subject of design failures presents a challenge to the statistician and reliability engineer, as well as the software engineer, which needs solving.

References

1. ''I Can't Work This Thing,'' *Business Week,* April 29, 1991.
2. I. Bazovsky, *Reliability Theory and Practice,* Prentice Hall, 1961.
3. G.J. Myers, *Software Reliability: Principles & Practices*, Wiley, 1976.
4. ''Standard Dictionary of Measures to Produce Reliable Software,'' IEEE 982.1, 1988.
5. B. Littlewood, ''Stochastic Reliability Growth,'' IEEE Transaction on Reliability, Vol. R30, October 1981.
6. C.V. Ramamoorthy and F.B. Bastani, ''Software Reliability: Status and Perspectives,'' *IEEE TSE,* Vol. SE-8, July 1982.
7. E.N. Adams, ''Optimizing Preventive Service of Software Products,'' *IBM Journal of Research and Development,* Vol. 28, January 1984.

8. J.D. Musa, A. Iannino, and K. Okumoto, *Software Reliability: Measurement, Prediction, Application,* McGraw-Hill, 1987.

9. M. Dyer, "An Approach to Software Reliability Measurement," *Information and Software Technology,* Vol. 29, October 1987.

10. P.A. Currit, M. Dyer, and H.D. Mills, "Certifying the Reliability of Software," *IEEE TSE,* Vol. SE-12, No. 1, 1986.

11. D.R. Cox and P.A.W. Lewis, *Statistical Analysis of Series of Events,* Methuen, London, 1966.

12. J.G. Shanthikumar, "A Statistical Time Dependent Software Reliability Model," Proceedings of the National Computer Conference, 1981.

13. A.L. Goel and K. Okumoto, "A Time Dependent Error Detection Rate Model," IEEE Transactions on Reliability, 1979.

14. B. Littlewood and J.L. Verrall, "A Bayesian Reliability Growth Model," *Applied Statistics,* 1973.

CHAPTER 8

Where Can Cleanroom Lead?

The Cleanroom idea has been around since 1980 and examples of its effectiveness have been demonstrated throughout that decade, but the method is not universally accepted in the software industry. The two major reasons for this lack of ready acceptance are Cleanroom's focus on developing quality software with certified reliability and Cleanroom's inclusion of many seemingly difficult and alien development practices.

While product quality gets media play and discussion on the loss of industrial capabilities, the reality is that new development methodologies whose primary focus is product quality do not get ready acceptance. This is especially true in the software industry, where the primary attention is paid to more function, faster turnaround, and competitive prices and where new development initiatives are sold on the basis of their productivity improvement features. Tools for automating (but not necessarily improving) human processes are in demand, as is the practice of reusing previously developed software designs and code whose availability rather than quality is the key to selection. Though not its principal thrust, Cleanroom has demonstrated that software quality can be achieved with no penalty to software productivity and after some experience with the expectation for substantial improvement in productivity. However, before Cleanroom and other methods which are focused on software quality can gain acceptance, the costs of poor quality have to be driven home to the software community. The lack of supposedly dramatic increases in near-term development productivity must be weighed against the product-life costs of required error detection and maintenance to provide the user with expected capability. Hopefully the 1990s will usher in this higher demand for software quality and bring a resurgence of interest from software management in Cleanroom and similar approaches to quality in software.

Within the software development community, practicing correctness verifica-

169

tion, dropping developer testing, introducing randomized testing, and defining an MTTF statistic for software are viewed with skepticism and disbelief. While the ideas may seem counterintuitive, bold, or outlandish, their roles within a Cleanroom development have been demonstrated to be practical and effective. Correctness verification does require education and the commitment to use a mathematics-based design method, which can be integrated with the verification practice embodied in the functional correctness model for software. The underlying concepts are not that difficult but their application to real-life problems requires learning and experience. When verification is routinely practiced, the need for developer testing quickly disappears. Surprisingly, the elimination of developer testing is the one common characteristic of all Cleanroom experience to date.

Randomized testing plays a critical role in the Cleanroom method since it is the necessary ingredient for creating a statistical environment in which inference on the MTTF of software can be realistically made. Random test selection can not be just applied uniformly but must be controlled through the definition of meaningful probability distributions in order to accurately describe the software use in its operating environment. The concept of software MTTF has real meaning, when based on logical (design) failures rather than physical (aging) failure. The concept requires extended use and interpretation within the software community before it can gain the stature and acceptance given to its hardware counterpart.

The purpose of this book is, in part, to address the inhibitors to the introduction of new software development methods particularly when they are directed at improving software quality. Possibly a lack of understanding about the Cleanroom method has been the principal obstacle to its widespread acceptance and use, which can be overcome by an understanding of this book's contents.

8.1 QUALITY SOFTWARE WITH NO PRODUCTIVITY IMPACT

An initial reaction to the Cleanroom method is that it entails more work on the part of the software developer, with a resultant decrease in the developer's productivity with its use. This would not be an entirely unexpected position, since better specifications, designs with proven correctness, more intense configuration management, statistical definition of testing, and tracking of software MTTF tend to imply more training, more work, more schedule, and more cost. *To the contrary, Cleanroom experience indicates that, while there is additional training and different types of activities, Cleanroom software is developed with less work, cost, and schedule than would be used for the same software using conventional development practice.* This higher productivity is achieved for software whose quality is also demonstrably better than what would be achievable with conventional development methods.

8.1.1 Requirements Specification Productivity

The Cleanroom direction for software specification and design demands rigor and formality generally not found in conventional practice. This would infer more effort in generating specifications, which is the case, but effort which is more than offset by the reduction in subsequent consultation on and clarification of the specifications as they are used in design and test. In conventional practice, specifications are prepared with natural language and without a formal or rigorous method, something like writing down whatever seems relevant about a requirement. The accuracy and completeness of specified information is generally not challenged until the software designer and/or software tester attempt to interpret the specification to perform their work. As these challenges are raised, the specifier is forced to reconstruct the original thought process, in order to come up with the rationale or detailed data needed to either clarify or rewrite the specification. This follow-up effort by the specifier can be considerable, depending on the elapsed time between the specification development and a particular challenge and on the depth or pervasiveness of the specification problem.

With the Cleanroom process, the software designer must verify design correctness and will be challenging functional and performance aspects of the specification from the outset of design. Similarly, the tester must identify the software inputs and organize their probability distributions, as the software design is being formulated, and will be challenging the operational aspects of the specification during the same period. The Cleanroom experience has dealt mostly with natural language specifications and has seen a concentrated but early resolution of specification problems, which has resulted in better quality specifications and higher specifier productivity. Since the designers and testers can not do much of their work without clarifications of the specification, they force early resolution.

The preferred solution would be the development of specifications which needed little clarification, which is why the Cleanroom process defines the use of formal methods for specification development. The current badgering of specifiers by designers intent on correctness verification and by testers intent on statistical completeness should hurry that movement to more rigorous and formal methods.

8.1.2 Software Design and Development Productivity

The prospect of formal design methods with stepwise correctness verification and independent confirmation is generally seen as doubling or tripling the software development effort. As shown in Chapter 2, this is not the case and development productivities higher than previously experienced by a development organization are typically reported with Cleanroom use. The reasons for this productivity gain are twofold; namely, correctness-driven refinement of a software design results in a systematic approach to software development and the introduction of correctness verification allows the elimination of developer testing. On the first point, conventional software design tends to be done in an ad hoc manner, detailing what is known about the mainline processing and retrofitting the rest as time and effort permit. Depending on the designer's knowledge and experience, this appending of design afterthoughts can be expensive and lead to mazes which defy testing and maintenance. The correctness-driven approach insists on the systematic decomposition of requirements in a stepwise fashion and on the verification of correctness at each step of the design refinement, with a continuous assurance of the requirements integrity during decomposition (i.e., nothing added, nothing dropped). With the correctness roadmap, the Cleanroom designer is more productive at creating designs whose correctness can be verified. Research directed at building designs directly from the specification of the decomposed requirements holds the promise for even more dramatic increases in software productivity but this work is probably a decade away from being turned into routine development practice.

As shown in Chapter 5, the functional correctness model for software verification satisfies all the objectives of the developer (structural) testing performed in current software processes. Because verification is performed at each step in the design, the structural considerations about a design can be considered more completely than is currently possible with the after-the-fact testing of the implementation of sizable pieces of that design. Aside from the quality improvement, the difference in human effort between performing the proof for a single verification as compared with executing a test with comparable capability, is itself an order of magnitude, which further speaks to the productivity gain in development. Cleanroom experience universally shows that significant software can be routinely developed without recourse to any testing by the developer. While the dropping of developer testing may have been initially adopted by developers through persuasion, the developers quickly accepted the approach through preference. While no attempt was made to also replace functional testing by correctness verification, this would be a future direction as confidence in the superiority of verification over test is solidified. This step may need the specification to code automation mentioned above and may itself be a decade away from routine development practice.

8.1.3 Software Test Productivity

Software test is an expensive and labor-intensive activity within current software development. The need to perform some form of input sampling to conduct software functional test is a recognized fact and statistically based sampling seems to provide the only objective and quantifiable approach for satisfying this need. The immediate benefit is the generation of realistic test cases of any number and complexity that provide identifiable and sufficient coverage for the testing of software requirements. Realism in testing relates directly to software acceptance in the postdelivery user environment and is difficult to achieve with current practice and its ad hoc sampling procedures. Cleanroom experience has shown that the added effort for defining the statistical structure for representative sampling is more than offset by the elimination of the time-consuming effort involved in formulating test cases.

The direction in which statistical testing should be pushed is the expanded automation of other steps in the test process (system, acceptance, operational, and so on) and the further minimization of that testing through the application of statistical sampling theory. In the near term, existing generators for statistical test samples should be extended to address the test documentation requirements, normally imposed by customers on the formally conducted tests for software requirements validation. The preparation of complete test documentation, the analysis of requirements coverage, and the definition of special-case tests for untested requirements are all achievable extensions to current test sample generators.

Long term, the principle benefit of statistical testing is in providing an objective basis for selecting the necessary sample size and quantifying the associated risks, in order to make the business decision on how much testing is enough for a given software product. In current practice, the stopping of software test is a subjective decision based primarily on schedule and cost considerations with little guidance on the thoroughness and applicability of the completed testing. Statistical techniques should be used in software testing, just as they are used in other real-life problems where the uncertainties of how much effort to expend need to be quantified (e.g., political polling, product marketing, and so on). There are strong similarities between the testing required to build confidence in the safety of products for public consumption and in the correctness of software for user consumption. Extending the role of statistics into the business decisions on when software has been sufficiently tested is a definite direction for future work, particularly when considering that testing accounts for an estimated 50 to 70% share of current software development costs.

8.2   STATISTICAL PROCESS CONTROL

In the Cleanroom definition, software development under statistical quality control should exhibit three properties:

1. The release of software from development prior to any execution.
2. The testing of software under randomized conditions which correspond to expected usage.
3. The certification of software reliability estimates at software delivery.

Software reliability measurement should be the underpinning for placing software development under statistical quality control in order to reap the same benefits as realized in the hardware manufacturing area. Reliability measurement should play two major roles in the development process. The first would be for maturity assessment of the software product (i.e., the certification of product readiness for operation). The second would be for quality assessment of the development process itself (i.e., an ongoing evaluation of the process to produce products of sufficient quality for user needs). Process assessment should encompass product maturity assessment with the measurement focus on repairing the process when diagnosed as needing correction.

The reliability measurement, as defined in the Cleanroom method, provides an ideal structure for statistical control of the development process. The software MTTF estimation and the tracking of the rate of change in software MTTF at each step in the test process can be used to adjust the development process and, in essence, put the development process under statistical control. The significance of a development process under statistical quality control is well illustrated by modern manufacturing techniques, where the sampling of output is directly fed back into the development process to control the quality of process output. Once the discipline of statistical quality control is in place, software management would have visibility into the software development process and into the controls by which the process can be changed to achieve software quality objectives.

Management experience indicates that introducing measurement into any development process does impact the quality of the work being measured and usually for the better. In the Cleanroom method, eliminating testing by the software developers and randomizing the test selection should increase the attention and thoroughness of the software designers in considering all situations which need to be addressed in the design. This focus on the total design reduces by an order of magnitude the number of software errors introduced into a product through omission, ambiguity, and incompleteness in the design. The Cleanroom requirement for defining a statistical environment for software functional testing introduces rigor and structure into test planning and conduct. There is a shift in testing attitude from software error discovery to the more positive demonstration of error-free execution, where software quality relies on successful software execution to realize large MTTF and not assertions about ''no known errors'' in the software.

Development process control is driven by the comparison of measured software MTTF against the software's MTTF goals, which comparison should signal the need for further analysis of the steps in the development process. Either the steps in the development process need re-examination and redefinition or their application to the particular software increment(s) needs reinforcement and more stringent monitoring. The incremental approach to software development provides sufficient opportunities for diagnosis of reliability achievement and for the application of appropriate process corrections when measured reliability is falling short.

8.2.1   Why the Cleanroom Method
Allows Statistical Process Control

The Cleanroom method incorporates error prevention into the software process, which is a departure from current development practice which assumes that software errors are always present and relies on error detection mechanisms for their removal. It recognizes as impractical any attempt at placing software under statistical control, which was developed through a trial-and-error process. Meaningful statistics can not be obtained from the attempted execution of software developed in that manner, because of its high error content and unpredictable execution characteristics.

To apply statistical process control, a statistical basis for evaluating the software product is required. Unlike the manufacturing world, this basis can not be found in the large numbers of similar products which are produced, since software is a logical, one-of-a-kind product. Rather the basis has to be found in the testing of the software product, which must be a statistical rather than a selective process and performed on the total product rather than its parts. With hardware, physical dimensions and statistical tolerances on the physical parts are additive components and can be combined for considering the statistical quality of the product. In software, the combination of the parts is a more complicated question, with no practical rules for collecting part failures into product failures because of the deep and complex interactions between parts.

In contrast to current development practice, the Cleanroom method embeds the software development and testing within a formal statistical design. Software engineering methods support the creation of designs with sufficient quality to forgo developer testing, so that testing is used to make statistical inference on reliability. The systematic process of assessing and controlling software quality during development permits the certification of product reliability at delivery. Certification in this sense attests to a public (visible) record of error discovery and repair and to a measured level of operating reliability.

As the executable increments of a software product are delivered and tested, the product reliability can be projected from the testing experience with the software functions delivered in each increment. While the initial projections will depend on the functions in the earlier increments, the functions in later increments can be expected to behave and mature in the same way, since all the software is developed under a uniform process. The projections at each incremental release permit the assessment of product reliability and its growth, which in turn should trigger any corrective action to the process. Subsequent projections will verify whether those corrective actions had the intended effect or whether further process correction is required to ensure that development is carried out under strict control.

Cleanroom demonstrates that software can be produced under statistical quality control and delivered to the user community with certified reliability statistics. Statistical quality control forces subjective assessments on software development to be replaced with objective evaluations on the process and the resultant product. Requiring statistical quality control in the procurement of software may force the automatic transfer of the state-of-the-art technology in the Cleanroom method (formal specifications, functional correctness model, verification-based inspections, statistical testing, and software MTTF).

8.3 PRODUCT CERTIFICATION WITH RELIABILITY WARRANTY

The basis for the certification of software products is, first, to develop a standard measure of software reliability and, second, to define a process which supports reliability measurement. For the Cleanroom method, the standard measure that has been defined is the software's projected MTTF when operating in a representative user environment.

Traditional development practice relies on defect removal counts as a measure of software quality. However, these counts are inconclusive for establishing a software reliability measure and are only of academic interest to software users. The user is more interested in knowing how long the software can be expected to run before failing and what the operational costs to the user are (e.g., downtime) when the software fails.

The times between successive software failures, as measured with user representative testing, are numbers of direct user interest. The higher these interfail times are, the more user satisfaction can be expected. In fact, increasing interfail times represent progress toward a reliable software product, whereas increasing defect discovery may be a symptom of an unreliable software product.

Software can be certified from a public record of failure detection, the measurement of interfail times, and the calculation of an MTTF based on this execution record. Thus certification can be a guarantee that all failure data has been correctly recorded and used to calculate the software product's MTTF in a prescribed way.

Certification for a software product should be viewed in the same sense as a certified public accountant's report on the state of any commercial corporation. In the accountant's case, certification implies that all the assets and the liabilities are recorded and then combined into a net worth by a prescribed accounting procedure. Other aspects of the company's operation, such as the amount of goodwill it has among customers, are not measured. In the case of software, the certification procedure vouches that all detected failures are reported and used in a standard MTTF computation. There will be other software properties, such as its modifiability or portability, which are not considered.

8.3.1 What Are the Future Prospects?

Reliability should become a product measure for software as it is for systems. As software plays a larger role in systems that are essential for society's use, there will be a growing demand for a certified measure of the software's reliability. The current set of quality measures used by software practitioners (defects per line of code, design complexity measures, and so on) will be unacceptable to the nontechnical user and usage-oriented measures, such as MTTF, MTTR, and the like will be demanded. The reliability measurements for systems will need to be augmented with appropriate data on the reliability of embedded software, since factoring software into hardware estimates as a constant will also be unacceptable. If software reliability certification is the goal, the current software development processes must be extended to explicitly include a measurement and evaluation subprocess for monitoring software reliability during development.

Since a reasonable technical basis can be defined to defend the business risks, software warranties based on reliability estimation should become a viable business option. As the technical feasibility for certifying software reliability in user-relevant terms (i.e., MTTF) becomes an accepted part of software development, the associated theory and practice provides the technical basis for making sound business decisions on software risks and warranties. Software warranty could be defined in terms of a guaranteed MTTF for a software product's operation in its planned operating environment and could represent the software industry's first real commitment to software quality. Until a systematic development process focused on reliability certification is established, the software industry has no sound technical (i.e., mathematical) framework for basing the business decisions on which to define warranties.

8.3.2 The Cleanroom Role in Software Warranties

Software products that are selected as candidates for warranty offering must be developed under the strictest interpretation of the Cleanroom method. This would ensure a systematic process for developing software with sufficient quality to risk a warranty and a structured process from which software reliability can be estimated with sufficient confidence to make the business decision on a warranty.

The Cleanroom method is based on a structured software specification that spells out the functional and performance requirements for the software but adds two new elements: statistics on product usage and plans for the incremental software release. This new data provides the foundations for statistical testing and reliability estimation. The specification would also be the basis for a warranty agreement and for the resolution of warranty claims if any arose. The Cleanroom method strives for a complete and stable software specification to minimize risks in product completion and in product quality.

Cleanroom development insists on the use of mathematics-based design methods and on the verification of the correctness of the software design to its full detail. This is viewed as the only approach to achieving high-quality software against which MTTF estimates can be made and for which warranties could be issued. The functional correctness model is the only available software verification procedure that can be applied to industrial-size software.

In the Cleanroom method, software reliability is certified as part of the software development through a formalized process that (1) attests to a public (i.e., visible) record of all software execution and failure discovery and (2) establishes a scientific basis for statistical inference about the software's operating capabilities. All testing is performed with statistical methods by a test organization independent of the development organization. Traditional development testing is replaced by correctness verification, and total visibility into the test process is guaranteed by placing the software under formal configuration control prior to any software execution.

Software reliability is estimated in terms of the software's MTTF from the recorded test executions against statistically representative samples of the operational inputs to be seen in the field. The software warranty could be defined as an MTTF or a failure rate (i.e., MTTF reciprocal). Warranty compliance would be based on software operation within the user's operating environment for some defined period of time. At the end of that period, the actual failures, if any, would be used to compute the realized MTTF, which would be compared to the projected value to determine compliance. As necessary, the appropriate remedies, specified in the contract, could be applied as part of the compliance process.

The Cleanroom method provides the technical foundation for making the business decision of offering a warranty on software. Without the mathematical and statistical rigor imposed by Cleanroom on software development, the warranty decision must be made on qualitative and not quantitative information.

Cleanroom Test Case Generator

A prototype test case generator (CRT) was developed in 1984 and used for the Cleanroom projects within IBM. The generator is a menu-driven editor that supports the entering of definitions and probability data for application inputs into a data base of test specifications. A test specification contains all the data on a particular application that would be required to produce test samples that are used in the statistical testing process. The generated samples are representative of a software's operating environment, since they are based on the probability distributions of input usage. Standardized formats are used within the data base for data representation so that the generator can be used for a variety of applications. The generator is designed as a table-driven processor that can be modified to accommodate the specific processing requirements of a given application.

USING THE TEST CASE GENERATOR

The two functions performed by the prototype generator are the interactive construction of test specification data bases and the generation of test samples from these data bases. The processing flow for the execution of the generator functions is shown in Figure A.1. At entry to the generator, the user is responsible for identifying the physical storage files that will be used for the test specification data base. When a new test specification data base is identified the bounds for the data base extents are requested from the user.

The data (input descriptions and probabilities) for a single application are organized into a separate test specification. The basic unit of logical storage within the test specification data base is defined as the command, where commands are

179

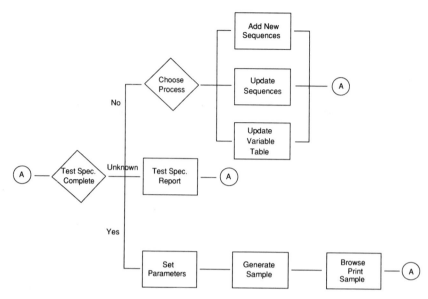

Figure A.1   Test Case Generator Flow

organized into hierarchies of lists which are called command sequences. These sequences generically define the steps for an application test and are used to achieve efficiencies in data base creation and retrieval. Three types of commands which are fixed format are defined: pseudo, macro, and terminal. The pseudo commands control prototype functions (i.e., choosing from a list), the macro commands are application-defined pointers to other command sequences, and the terminal commands describe the exact syntax for application inputs. For each test specification data base, a separate variable table is also created that contains the definitions of any variable fields within terminal commands defined for an application. During test sample generation, application-specific data values are randomly selected and inserted in the variable fields within application inputs.

The prototype offers three primary editing processes to the user in organizing a test specification data base:

1. Add new command sequences: enter name, probability, and commands.
2. Update an existing command sequence: either field modification or sequence deletion.
3. Update a variable table: the variable fields within an application input can be defined, modified, or deleted.

All test specification or variable table changes are saved within the physical files upon return from any of these editing operations.

The second capability offered to the user is a report function. When a data base listing is needed to determine the changes, additions, and deletions required in the

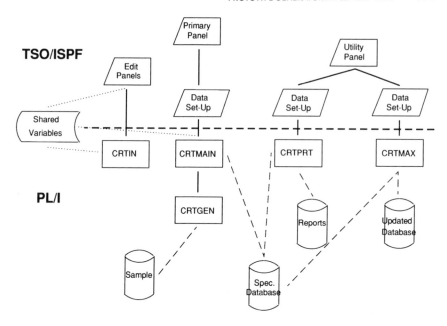

Figure A.2   Test Generator Structure

test specification, the report function is used to produce an output file for on-line browsing and/or hardcopy printing.

When a test specification or a closed subset of a specification is completed (i.e., self-contained with no dangling references), requests for test-sample generation can be handled. The generation process allows the user to specify run-time options or temporary overrides on the sample size, headings for hardcopy outputs, the designation of a random generator seed for repeatability, and the definition of a group schedule. The group schedule defines for the generator a roadmap for selecting the command sequences that will be organized into application tests. Additionally, the user can override the probabilities associated with command sequences to temporarily define a different probability distribution than stored in the test specification data base or to temporarily inhibit the selection of a command sequence by assigning it a zero probability. These overrides are in effect for one sample generation. When the user-specified or default values for these options are set, the generator creates a test sample for application testing in an output file for on-line browsing, hardcopy printing, or postprocessing.

PROTOTYPE GENERATOR IMPLEMENTATION

The prototype generator, as shown in Figure A.2, is an interactive application that runs on IBM platforms which can execute the Interactive System Productivity Facility (ISPF) program product. The prototype is composed of a set of PL/I language procedures, of Time Shared Option (TSO) command procedures (called "clists"), of ISPF panels (menus), and of an internally managed data base and various output files. The prototype generator executes under the IBM MVS operating system with the TSO extended option, version 2 of the ISPF program product, and the PL/I optimizer compiler. Less than five cylinders of IBM 3380 disk space, exclusive of the requirements for test specification data bases, are required for the operation of the prototype generator.

The prototype PL/I language procedures are packaged into three separate PL/I programs, which total some 2,500 PL/I statements. In addition, there are a set of utility routines for report preparation, various data conversions, and random number generation, which account for an additional 1,000 PL/I statements. There are also three command procedures (i.e., the TSO "clists") for allocating the input and output files or datasets which are appropriately formatted for the generator's use. Finally, the prototype has 45 ISPF panels which are divided into 25 for an in-line tutorial and 20 for the user dialog control and input editing.

Data Base Organization

The contents of the test specification data base are mapped into two PL/I arrays of data structures for processing by the prototype: one for the variable tables and the other for the command sequences. The data base is moved between storage and memory with PL/I stream I/O file operations. The test specification data base is processed as both an input and output file by the generator and the generated test sample is organized in a fixed tabular format.

The two main data structures, as shown in Figure A.3, for the test specifications are CNTRL for the command sequences and VARMAP for the variable table. The bounds on the two structures (MXGRPS and MXVARS), the substructures, and the arrays within these two PL/I structures can be set by the user to define the extent of a particular test specification. These parameters are solicited via a set of ISPF dialogues with the user at the start of an editing session.

Each instance of the command sequence structure (CNTRL) allocates storage for groups of command sequences where the probability of selecting a sequence from the group is indicated by the field GRPFREQS. As mentioned earlier, groups were defined within the prototype as a method for forming collections of related command sequences within an application (e.g., separating the inputs for navigation from the inputs for display processing from other functions within an avionics application). The group does not have to be used but provides the user a method for defining some structure for the application inputs. The number of command sequences collected within each group is indicated by the field SEQCOUNT.

Each command sequence is a named set of some number, specified by the field DWCOUNT, of discrete commands (macro, pseudo, or terminal) which are stored in the array (DATA). A relative probability, specified by the field SEQFREQS, is included which allows the user to specify the probability for selecting each named sequence within a group once the group is selected. It is a relative probability since it is dependent on the group first being selected. Each command sequence allows

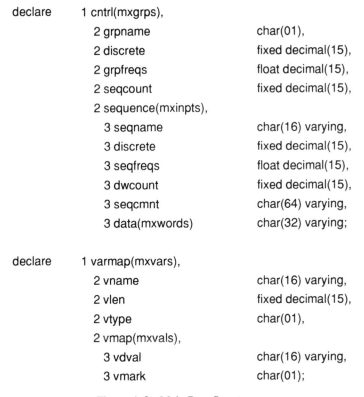

declare	1 cntrl(mxgrps),	
	2 grpname	char(01),
	2 discrete	fixed decimal(15),
	2 grpfreqs	float decimal(15),
	2 seqcount	fixed decimal(15),
	2 sequence(mxinpts),	
	3 seqname	char(16) varying,
	3 discrete	fixed decimal(15),
	3 seqfreqs	float decimal(15),
	3 dwcount	fixed decimal(15),
	3 seqcmnt	char(64) varying,
	3 data(mxwords)	char(32) varying;
declare	1 varmap(mxvars),	
	2 vname	char(16) varying,
	2 vlen	fixed decimal(15),
	2 vtype	char(01),
	2 vmap(mxvals),	
	3 vdval	char(16) varying,
	3 vmark	char(01);

Figure A.3   Main Data Structures

for the inclusion of commentary in field SEQCMNT, which allows the user to include explanatory text in the generated test sample.

During test-sample generation, the different probabilities at the group (GRPFREQS) and command sequence (SEQFREQS) levels are converted to counts based on the selected sample size. These values, which are stored in the DISCRETE fields, indicate the maximum number of entries from a particular group and the maximum number of a particular command sequence that can be included in the particular sample. At least in the prototype design, it was considered more efficient to work with these computed counts rather than the underlying probabilities when deciding on the composition of a particular sample.

Each instance of the variable table structure (VARMAP) allocates storage for the definition of the data to be inserted in variable fields defined within terminal commands. Each entry in the structure is used for a named variable field and defines the type of data (e.g., character, decimal, and so on) that goes in the variable field, the length of the variable field in bytes, and the domain of possible data values. The domain of data values is stored in the array (VMAP), which can have MXVALS entries. Data values are stored either as discrete values or as the endpoints of a value range, which is flagged by the encoding of the VMARK field. When the generator must include a data value for a variable field within a selected

Test Case Number	Test Case Type	Test Steps	Commentary
case #1	base command		
	first command	first step values	first comment
	---	---	---
	nth command	nth step values	nth comment
case #2	base command		
	first command	first step values	first comment
	---	---	---
	nth command	nth step values	nth comment
---	---	---	---

Figure A.4   Test Generator Sample Output

terminal command, a value is randomly selected from the indicated domain for the variable stored in this structure.

Output Data Structures

The test case sample is formatted in a tabular form, as shown in Figure A.4, where the fields are defined as follows:

The number of the test case within the sample.

The sequence names are the labels for the starting and selected command sequence.

The test steps are the terminal commands with filled-in data fields.

The commentary is optional text included with the command sequence.

PROTOTYPE PROGRAM ORGANIZATION

The CRTMAIN PL/I program initializes the PL/I run-time environment, allocates memory for the data structures associated with the specified test specification, and establishes the shared global variables for ISPF dialog processing. This program performs the reading and writing of the test specification data bases between the PL/I data structures and the physical storage files. When a new data base must be built for a test specification, CRTMAIN obtains the user-specified parameters defining the extents of the PL/I data structures (CNTRL and VAR-MAP), or the default system parameters when none are specified. The storage for these data structures is dynamically allocated based on the PL/I dynamic storage technique.

The CRTMAIN program controls the generator processing based on the user selection of editing functions or of the test sample generation function. For test sample generation, CRTMAIN obtains user-specified or default run-time options to structure the particular sample (i.e., the sample size, the starting value for the random generator seed, and so on) and performs any user-specified overrides of stored probability distributions.

The PL/I program CRTIN is called by CRTMAIN to process the inputs for the editing functions against a test specification data base—new command sequences, updates to command sequences, and updates to variable tables. When the editing is completed, CRTIN returns control to the CRTMAIN program, which writes the new or updated data bases to the physical storage files.

In the CRTIN processing, new command sequences can be added to user-specified groups and any parts of existing command sequences can be modified. When reference is made to an undefined variable field in a terminal command, the user is immediately prompted to define a variable-table entry and value domain for that variable. In the processing, existing command sequences can be deleted as can entries in the variable table.

The PL/I program CRTGEN is called by CRTMAIN but returns to the primary selection panel rather than CRTMAIN to ensure against storing temporary overrides to existing data bases. The CRTGEN program does not have any interaction with the user through ISPF variables or panels since all the initialization for the test-sample generation has been handled by CRTMAIN. In the prototype, the CRTGEN processing is divided into four main sections, primarily to support the introduction of any special-purpose logic that might be required for a particular application.

The first section declares the global variables and output buffers and computes the DISCRETE counts for each group and each sequence based on the probabilities and requested sample size. As discussed earlier, these counts are used to limit the number of entries from a particular group and the number of times that a particular command sequence within a group is selected for a test sample. The actual selection of a particular command sequence is then performed based on a random selection of group and command sequence within group. When a particular command sequence is selected, the second section of CRTGEN is called to build an entry for the test sample which is written to the output file upon return.

The second section of CRTGEN does the organizing of an entry for the test sample by processing the command sequence selected by the first section. This processing involves examining the commands within the command sequence and performing whatever actions these commands request. If a command is a pseudo-command, then some form of command selection within the command sequence is usually required (e.g., select some random number of members, randomly, from the command sequence, select a specific member from the command sequence, and so on). Otherwise, the commands within a command sequence are processed in order, with recursive processing of another command sequence required when a macro command is encountered. When a terminal command is encountered the third section is called.

The third section of CRTGEN processes terminal commands by (1) scanning the terminal command for variable fields, (2) calling the fourth section of CRTGEN for value substitution when a variable field is encountered, and (3) concatenating the terminal-command text and the selected values for variable fields into a test-sample entry which gets built in an output buffer. The data values are randomly chosen from the domain specified in the variable table, where each value, whether specified discretely or as a range receives equal weighting. Values within ranges are computed from the endpoints.

The PL/I program CRTPRT is a report-generation utility that produces various reports on a test specification that can be either browsed on-line or printed as hardcopy. The reports available in the prototype include:

Listing of the parameters defining the bounds on a test specification data base.

Listing of command sequences in the stored order, by group and command sequence, for a specified test specification data base. Each entry includes a formatted listing of the data in the CNTRL data structure.

Alphabetic cross-reference of commands by group and command sequence.

Alphabetic listing of variables. Each entry includes a formatted listing of the data in the VARMAP data structure.

Cross-reference of variables to the sequences in which they are referenced.

The PL/I program CRTMAX is a utility routine which allows a user to make a copy of a test specification data base and then increase the parameters that control the bounds on the data base extents. This function is offered in the prototype because the command sequences and variables are stored in arrays of data structures and processed with the PL/I ''put data stream'' I/O functions. When these test specifications are edited, the data structures are allocated in PL/I static storage (i.e., the bounds can not be changed). CRTMAX dynamically allocates additional arrays of data structures, with the user-specified bounds, copies the data from the existing to the new structures from the initial array, and outputs the data in the new test specification data base to a physical storage file.

Cleanroom Reliability Analysis Package

A prototype reliability analysis package (CRA) was developed in 1985 and used for the Cleanroom projects within IBM. The analysis package is a menu-driven set of software that supports the analysis of recorded test data, the prediction of software MTTF for both software functional increments and software products, and the validation of MTTF predictions. The MTTF predictions are performed by a set of statistical models which were defined to track reliability growth within software and which base their predictions on the history of times between successive software failures recorded during software test. The analysis package provides an interface for users to enter and manipulate test data, to compute times between failure from the recorded data, to run one or more of the statistical models supported by the package, and to generate reports and graphs of any analysis results.

USING THE RELIABILITY ANALYSIS PACKAGE

The three functions performed by the interactive analysis package are the construction of formatted data bases of test execution data; the selection, initialization, and running of reliability growth models; and the support of analyses of the generated predictions. The processing flow for the execution of the analysis functions is shown in Figure B.1. At entry to the generator, the user is responsible for identifying the physical storage files which contain recorded test data or will be used to store the prediction and analysis results.

The test execution data can be entered interactively by the user or loaded from a physical storage file. The data is assumed to be organized into discrete records, where a record contains the data on the execution of a single test case. The records are assumed to be in execution order, though the analysis package allows for reor-

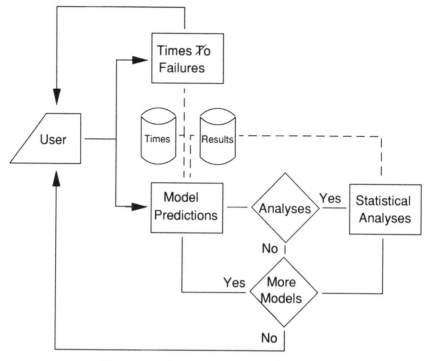

Figure B.1   Reliability Analysis Package Flow

dering the test records for MTTF predictions and failure analyses. In addition to test case identifiers, the test record contains the identification of which functional increment and the application function which was tested, the recorded execution time for the test case, the indication of successful or failed test case execution, and, in the case of test case failure, the severity code assigned to the failure. Since PL/I stream I/O functions are used for accessing these test records, the prototype package is reasonably flexible in the encoding of the test record data (e.g., the size and format of timing data).

When performing model predictions, if earlier predictions exist, then the new predictions are appended to the stored data on the existing predictions. The previous last prediction is recomputed since the time between successive failures generally changes with the introduction of additional test execution data. The user can request charts or reports to be generated for the results of any analysis (i.e., MTT and median predictions, accuracy, and trend analyses). In the prototype package, charts can only be displayed on-line and not printed.

PROTOTYPE IMPLEMENTATION

The prototype reliability analysis package is an interactive application that runs on IBM platforms which can execute the ISPF program product. The prototype is composed of a set of PL/I language procedures, a set of Statistical Analysis System (SAS) language procedures, of TSO command procedures (called "clists"), of ISPF panels (menus), and of an internally managed data base and various output files. The prototype analysis package executes under the IBM MVS operating system with the TSO extended option, version 2 of the ISPF program product, the SAS program library version 5, and the PL/I optimizer compiler. Less than 50 tracks of IBM 3380 disk space, exclusive of the requirements for test execution data bases, are required for the operation of the prototype analysis package.

The prototype PL/I language procedures, exclusive of the statistical model software, total some 2,000 PL/I statements, 1,000 assembly lines for the command procedures (i.e., the TSO "clists"), and 750 lines of SAS commands. In addition, there are a set of four statistical models in the prototype package, which require an additional 2,000 PL/I statements, 500 assembly lines for "clists," and 250 lines of SAS commands. Finally, the prototype analysis package has 25 ISPF panels, which are divided into 15 for an in-line tutorial and ten for the user-dialog control.

A standard interface has been defined between the processing environment for the analysis package and the different statistical packages (i.e., models and analysis routines). This interface should facilitate the introduction of different statistical models or analysis methods within the existing environment defined for the prototype. The existing prototype environment can support up to six statistical models and a variety of analysis and plotting routines.

Data Base Organization

Two datasets are required for the execution of the prototype analysis package. These can be allocated by the user via the ISPF interactive dialog or they can be preallocated using the parameters discussed below.

The test execution dataset contains the timing data for the executed test cases. It is a fixed-block sequential dataset with 80-byte records. If this dataset is to be preallocated, the space requirements for physical storage files must be estimated from the planned number of test cases. If the allocation is to be handled through user interaction, then space is allocated in increments of 200 records up to a maximum of 3,200 records.

The analysis library contains the results from the various analysis options. The library has members for the computed times between successive failures (the IFD member), for status information (the STATUS member), and for the predictions from each of the statistical models (the PDxx members). The encoding of the member name (PDxx) for the model outputs uses two-character model codes to distinguish the different models. For the prototype, the codes are CE for the Cleanroom-defined certification model, LI for the Littlewood model, LV for the Littlewood-Verrall model, and SH for the Shanthikumar model. The analysis library is a fixed-block partitioned dataset within the IBM MVS file definition and also uses 80-byte records. This dataset can also be allocated interactively by the user or preallocated; in either case a primary and secondary allocation of one 3380 cylinder with five directory blocks is made.

The records in the IFD member give the time between two successive failures and the identification of the two failing test cases. When computing these times, either an entire test execution dataset is used or subsets of the text execution data based on the selection of specific software functions, functional increments, or failure severities. The records in the STATUS member identify the source of the test execution data, the dates and times when statistical model and analysis runs were made, and the goodness-of-fit measures on the model predictions. There is one status record for each model and one record for the times-between-successive-failures computations. The records in the PDxx members provide the outputs for a single-model prediction and are ordered sequentially. The data stored in each record are the prediction number, the predicted MTTF and median values, and the values for the Quantile-Quantile plots for this prediction (accuracy and trend).

APPENDIX C

Cleanroom Verification-Based Inspection Syntax Analyzer

A prototype syntax analysis program to support verification-based inspections was developed in 1988 and used for the study of Cleanroom designs developed within IBM projects. The analyzer is a menu-driven program which scans PDL descriptions of software designs to determine the refinement structure exhibited by the design and the use which was made of the structured programming constructs in the design refinement. The analysis is performed in order to generate a hardcopy script that can be used for the verification of design correctness, based on the functional correctness model. The generated script is a roadmap of the sequence in which the questions for a specific correctness proof should be asked, as well as providing the actual questions to be asked in the proof. The analysis program provides an interface for users to perform correctness proofs as designs are constructed and to confirm design correctness during a verification-based inspection of the software.

USING THE SYNTAX ANALYSIS PROTOTYPE

The function performed by the analysis program is the construction of formatted script that reflects the application of an informal correctness proof to a design based on the functional correctness model's definition of correctness proofs. These proofs are discussed in the Linger, Mills, and Witt book, *Structured Programming: Theory and Practice.* The informal method makes verification possible without a knowledge of predicate logic and allows a developer to formulate his correctness arguments in English, without losing the rigor of the formal methods.

The prototype analyzer is interactively accessed by the user to analyze any user-specified number of design descriptions. At entry, the user is responsible for identifying the physical storage file which contains the design language descriptions to be analyzed. Each description is stored in a separate dataset within the storage file and, for each analysis, the user must identify the dataset to be processed. For each analysis, four separate print files are created, which include a formatted (indented) listing of the design description, a script with the structured correctness proof for the design description, a summary of the design language constructs (keywords) used in the design description, and a listing of missing or redundant specifications within the design description.

The program scans the design language descriptions, parses the source statements to identify the design constructs and flow, and organizes the structure of the correctness proof for the particular design. The benefit of the tool is the structuring of a correctness proof for designs of any size, which is a nontrivial task if performed manually. Secondary benefits from the tool are the flagging of missing or redundant design specifications, the assessment of verification feasibility with missing levels of specifications, and the generation of diagnostics on the design language description.

The tool is organized to be independent of the design language used for the design description. The syntax of the design language is stored in tabular form which can be modified by a user through recompilation of the prototype software. The prototype is organized to process two design languages: the one described in the Linger, Mills, and Witt reference and a design subset of the Ada programming language.

PROTOTYPE IMPLEMENTATION

The prototype syntax analysis program is an interactive application that runs on IBM platforms which can execute the ISPF program product. The prototype executes under the IBM MVS operating system with the TSO extended option, version 2 of the ISPF program product, and the PL/I optimizer compiler. The prototype is composed of a set of six PL/I procedures (approximately 500 language statements), of assembly lines for a set of command procedures (i.e., the TSO ''clists''), and a set of ISPF panels (menus).

The PL/I procedures include a control procedure that handles initialization and the interfacing between the processing procedures, procedures to input PDL text and scan for keywords, parse procedures that interpret keywords and manage the design structure, and output procedures that format the inspection script.

INDEX

B

Baseline Capability, 8, 44

C

Certification, 2
Certified Reliability, 2
Cleanroom Component Roadmap, 8
Cleanroom Method, 1
  Background, 1
    Kerne! Idea, 2
  Design Simplicity, 62
  Elimination of Developer Testing, 120
Cleanroom Experience, 27-29
  COBOL Structuring Facility, 33
    Example of Testing Approach, 126-130
  NASA Software Engineering Laboratory,
    34
Cleanroom Introduction, 43
  Baseline Capabilities, 44
  Component Selection, 8-11, 49
  Process Tailoring, 27
  Technology Insertion, 55
Cleanroom Statistical Testing, 111

  Approach, 123
  Avionics Example, 130-136, 136-137
  Generators, 125, 179
  Impacts, 137-138
Cleanroom Component Usage Profile, 27
COBOL S/F, see COBOL Structuring
    Facility
  Defect Rates, 22
Correctness Verification, 86
  Design Construction Example, 91-94

D

Development Process Impacts, 4, 11-12,
    16-17
  On Design, 18-19
  On Development Organization, 20-21
  On Implementation, 19
  On Specifications, 17-18

E

Early Experiments, 29
  Development Method Feasibility, 32
  Statistical Test Approach, 30-32

University of Maryland Study, 32

F

Formal Software Development, 70
   Mathematics Based Design, 61
   Requirement Decomposition, 61
   Requirement Elaboration, 73
   Top Down, 71
Functional Correctness Model, 87
   Correctness Proof, 87

H

Hardware Reliability Theory, 143, 166

I

IBM Federal Sector Division, 1
IBM Federal Systems Division, 2
Incremental Development, 63, 152
Inspections, 96
   Design an Code Inspections, 98
      I0 Inspection, 97
      I1 Inspection, 97
      I2 Inspection, 97
   Fagan Inspection, 96
   Formal Inspections, 97
      Benefits, 99
      Importance to Process, 96

K

Known Mean Time To Failure, 13

L

Lessons Learned, 35-40
   Problem Closure Rates, 37

M

MTBF, *see* Mean Time Between Failure

MTTF, *see* Mean Time To Failure
   MTTF Analysis, 161

N

NASA SEL, *see* NASA Software Engineering Laboratory
   Defect Rates, 23

P

PDL, *see* Program Design Language
Probability Distributions, 119, 123
   Operational Usage, 124
   Test Role, 123
Process Models:
   Cleanroom, 3-6
   Life Cycle, 11
   Spiral, 11
   Waterfall, 11
Product Usage, 124
Project Management, 54
Project Planning, 49
   Selection, 51-53
   Measurement, 51-53
   Process Adjustment, 51-53

R

Requirements Validation, 112, 117

S

Sampling Approaches, 118
   Random, 119
   Usage Driven, 124
   Tester Defined, 119
SEI, *see* Software Engineering Institute
Software Engineering Institute, 7
Software Design Expression, 78
   Program Design Language, 78
Software Failures, 141
   Failure Rates, 148
Software Product Impacts:
   On Defect Rates, 21-23

On Design Simplicity, 24
On Development Productivity, 24-25
Software Productivity:
  Design and Implementation, 171
  Developer Testing, 172
  Specification Development, 170
Software Reliability, 145
  Analysis, 187
  Cleanroom Definition, 147, 154
  Mean Time Between Failures, 2
  Mean Time To Failure, 151
Software Quality:
  Cleanroom Experience, 15, 21
  Industry Focus, 142
    As Reliability Substitute, 146–147
Software Warranties, 175
Software Specifications, 67
  Formal, 67
    Grammars, 69
  Methods:
    Box Structures, 68
    Vienna Design Method, 68
    Z Language, 68
Statistical Analysis, 159, 165
  Quality Considerations, 160–162
  Qauntile/Quantile Plots, 165
Statistical Control, 173
Statistical Modeling:
  Interfail Times, 151
  Reliability Growth, 152
Statistical Models:
  Certification, 149
    Application, 151, 155–160
    Derivation, 149
  Littlewood, 164
  Littlewood-Verrall, 164
  Shanthikumar, 164
Statistical Testing:
  Effectiveness, 31
  Feasibility, 30
Statistical Testing Experiments, 30
Structured Data Design, 77
  Controlled Access, 77
Structured Design Example, 79-84
Structured Programming
  Stepwise Refinement, 65-67, 72-73
  Structure Theorem, 70
    Axiom of Replacement
    Constructs, 75

Correctness Theorem, 70
Expansion Theorem, 70
Top Down Corollary, 70

T

Testing Methods, 111
  Black Box, see Functional,
  Cost of Coverage, 113, 117, 136-137
  Functional, 117
    Boundary Value Analysis, 119
    Category Partitioning, 119
    Cause Effect Graphing, 119
    Error Guessing, 119
    Equivalence Partitioning, 119
    Random Testing, 119
    Statistical Testing, 119
  Role With Verification, 120
  Structural, 112
    Branch, 113
    Boundary-Interior Path, 116
    Data Flow, 116
    Linear Code Sequence and Jump, 116
    Path, 113
    Statement, 113
  White Box, see Structural
Training, 47
  Workshops, 56-60
    Specification, 57
    Statistical Testing, 58
    Verification, 58
Triangle Solver Problem:
  Illustrating Design Simplicity, 62
  Illustrating Inspection Practice, 102
  Illustrating Structural Testing, 113

U

Underlying Concerns, 40
  Too Theoretical and Radical, 40
  Too Mathematical, 41
  Need For Developer Testing, 41
  Random Testing Ineffective, 41
Usage Analysis, 124

V

Verification Based Inspection, 94, 100

Analyzer, 191
Avionics Application, 105-110
Level of Formality, 101
Practice, 101
  Proof Questions, 104
  Question Structure, 102
VDM, see Vienna Design Method

W

Warranties, 175

Z

Zero Defects, 15

About the Author

Michael Dyer, an IBM Senior Programmer, was responsible for developing the Cleanroom method in association with retired IBM Fellow, Dr. Harlan D. Mills. He defined the practice for realizing the original ideas on developing software with certified reliability, which is used as the current standard for Cleanroom developments. His specific technical contributions to the Cleanroom method were the definitions of the statistical testing approach and the verification based inspections.

Mr. Dyer has worked at IBM for the past 25 years and held numerous management and technical positions in systems and software development. During the past dozen years, he has made significant contributions to the systems and software engineering programs within IBM's Federal Sector Division. He was the recipient of an IBM outstanding technical achievement award for his work in developing software engineering standards and practices.

In addition, Mr. Dyer was on the technical staffs of RCA, General Precision, and Pratt & Whitney Aircraft prior to joining IBM. He holds a degree in Mathematics from Fordham University.

Mr. Dyer has some three dozen articles published in technical journals and conference proceedings and has contributed major sections to more than a half dozen technical books. He has delivered tutorials on the Cleanroom process and its major technical components (e.g., verification based inspections, statistical testing, etcetera) to numerous IBM and industry audiences. Included in his journal publications are the following:

"*Correctness Verification,*" co-authored with A. Kouchakdjian, *Information and Software Technology*, October 1990.

"An Approach to Software Reliability Measurement," *Information and Software Technology*, October 1987.

"Cleanroom Software Engineering," co-authored with H.D. Mills and R.C. Linger, *IEEE Software*, September 1987.

"A Formal Approach to Software Error Removal," *Journal of Systems and Software*, July 1987.

"Certifying the Reliability of Software," co-authored with H.D. Mills and P.A. Currit, *IEEE Transactions of Software Engineering*, January 1986.

"The Management of Software Engineering," co-authored with H.D. Mills, et al., *IBM Systems Journal*, July 1986.

Included in his contributions to technical book publications are the following:

"Designing Software for Provable Correctness," *The Software Life Cycle*, Butterworth Scientific, 1990.

"Inspection Data," *Software Reliability: State of the Art Report*, Pergamon Infotech, 1986.

"The Cleanroom Software Development Process," *Measurement for Software Control*, Elsevier Applied Science, 1989.